PSYCHOLOGY SORTED
BOOK 2 – APPLIED PSYCHOLOGY

Key research for students and teachers

Laura Swash & Claire Neeson

International Baccalaureate, Baccalauréat International, Bachillerato Internacional and IB are registered trademarks owned by the International Baccalaureate Organization. The material in this book has been developed independently of the IB, which was not involved with the production of this writing and in no way endorses it.

However, this textbook is primarily written for IB Diploma psychology students and their teachers. The layout is organised around the IB Diploma psychology guide, and the topics and content are specially chosen to be relevant to the curriculum. Nonetheless, other psychology students and teachers will also benefit from the breadth and depth of the clear layout, cross-topic links and detailed key studies.

Dedications
Thank you again to Uwe and to the rest of my family who are so patient and encouraging when I am always writing. And to John Crane, who has been very supportive throughout this project. Laura

To Simon, let's have a G and T to celebrate! Claire

Front cover image adapted from a Creative Commons licensed image from Pixabay, at https://pixabay.com/en/pattern-background-patterns-tiles-1245991/

Other images are creative commons licensed for commercial use, also from Pixabay.

PSYCHOLOGY SORTED: KEY RESEARCH FOR STUDENTS AND TEACHERS
BOOK 2 – APPLIED PSYCHOLOGY

CONTENTS

INTRODUCTION	1
ABNORMAL PSYCHOLOGY	
Overview	3
1. Factors influencing diagnosis	4
2. Etiology of abnormal psychology	9
3. Treatment of disorders	15
Key studies	
1. Normality versus abnormality	20
Classification systems	24
Role of clinical biases in diagnosis	28
Validity and reliability of diagnosis	31
Critical thinking points	37
2. Explanations for disorder(s)	39
Prevalence rates and disorder(s)	65
Critical thinking points	71
3. Biological treatment - MDD	73
Psychological treatment - MDD	77
Biological treatment - PTSD	81
Psychological treatment - PTSD	85
The role of culture in treatment	90
Assessing the effectiveness of treatment	94
Critical thinking points	94
DEVELOPMENT	
Overview	97
1. Developing as a learner	98
2. Influences on cognitive and social development	101
3. Developing an identity	104
Key studies	
1. Brain development	108
Cognitive development	113
Critical thinking points	121
2. Role of peers and play	123

PSYCHOLOGY SORTED: KEY RESEARCH FOR STUDENTS AND TEACHERS
BOOK 2 – APPLIED PSYCHOLOGY

Childhood trauma and resilience	127
Poverty/socio-economic status	133
Critical thinking points	135
3. Attachment	136
Gender identity and social roles	142
Development of empathy and theory of mind	150
Critical thinking points	155

HEALTH
Overview — 157
1. Determinants of health — 158
2. Health problems — 161
3. Promoting health — 163

Key studies
1. Biopsychosocial model of health and well-being — 165
   Dispositional factors and health beliefs — 170
   Risk and protective behaviour — 174
   Critical thinking points — 175

2. Explanations of health problem(s) — 177
   Prevalence of health problem(s) — 181
   Critical thinking points — 185

3. Health promotion — 187
   Effectiveness of health promotion programme(s) — 192
   Critical thinking points — 196

HUMAN RELATIONSHIPS
Overview — 199
1. Social responsibility — 200
2. Personal relationships — 205
3. Group dynamics — 210

Key studies
1. Bystanderism — 213
   Prosocial behaviour — 218
   Promoting prosocial behaviour — 232
   Critical thinking points — 236

PSYCHOLOGY SORTED: KEY RESEARCH FOR STUDENTS AND TEACHERS
BOOK 2 – APPLIED PSYCHOLOGY

2. Formation of personal relationships — 237
   Role of communication — 250
   Explanations for why relationships change or end — 254
   Critical thinking points — 258

3. Cooperation and competition — 260
   Prejudice and discrimination — 265
   Origins of conflict and conflict resolution — 270
   Critical thinking points — 274

BIBLIOGRAPHY AND INDEX — 275

PSYCHOLOGY SORTED: KEY RESEARCH FOR STUDENTS AND TEACHERS
BOOK 2 – APPLIED PSYCHOLOGY

PSYCHOLOGY SORTED: KEY RESEARCH FOR STUDENTS AND TEACHERS
BOOK 2 – APPLIED PSYCHOLOGY

INTRODUCTION

This is the second book in the *Psychology Sorted* series. Again, it is for teachers and students, and is structured to help you use examples of the wealth of psychological research that is relevant to the IB Diploma Psychology applied psychology (options) of abnormal psychology, development, health and human relationships. These are just recommendations based on the knowledge of two highly experienced IB Diploma Psychology teachers, who know how teachers and students struggle to find, understand and summarise original research so it may be used to answer questions.

This saves teachers thinking time and writing time, as the key studies are there, ready to use, with full references to the originals, should you need them. We received excellent feedback on Book 1, and know that librarians, teachers and students worldwide are finding it valuable. It allows teachers time for those fun activities that are often swamped by the need to rewrite complex original research for student understanding. Questions? See our Psychology Sorted blog at https://psychologysorted.blog/. We're here to help you.

HOW TO USE THIS BOOK

Each chapter in the book comprises a one-page overview of each option, followed by a structured layout of topics, content and author-recommended studies, in a table format, that also includes links to other areas of the psychology curriculum. Use the tables to identify relevant studies that you might like to read and use the indexed bibliography at the back to find the key study summaries. You will see that we have indicated clearly where studies may be used to meet several different content points, as well as providing links to where they are relevant in the core approaches. This allows for advance curriculum planning that exploits the overlaps between the core approaches and the options. Studies are split into *classic, critique/extension* and *recent* categories, to give a feel for how thinking is debated and has progressed on the key issues. You do not have to use all of the studies recommended; you can dip in and out as you please. Further resources that are easily accessible for reading/watching at home come after every table, with QR codes included where space allows to enable easy access by mobile devices. These are ideal for homework reading and watching.

The chapter on abnormal psychology is longer than the others, because we have included both major depressive disorder and post-traumatic stress disorder, to broaden the use of this book. Note that only one needs to be studies by students. Although our health chapter has focused mainly on stress, links have been included to research on obesity and tobacco consumption.

Use them together – all you need to structure your course

Book 1 is devoted to the core approaches – biological, cognitive and sociocultural.

Book 2 comprises the options – abnormal psychology, development, health and human relationships.

Remember, if you are an IB Diploma teacher you don't have to teach all options, just enough to allow students to answer one (SL) or two (HL) questions. Pick and choose and this book will help you.

THE OPTIONS

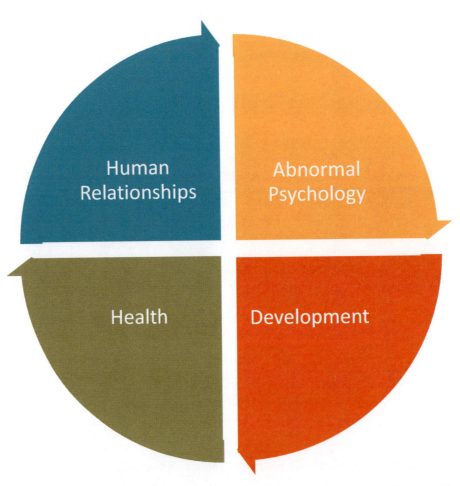

The options in the book have been colour-coded to help you find your way through the text. The bibliography at the end is combined with an index for even easier searching. We ae sure that you will find *Psychology Sorted 2* helpful at all levels of Psychology.

Abnormal Psychology

Ethics ⬇ ⬇ ⬇ **Methods**

Factors influencing diagnosis
- Normality versus abnormality
- Classification systems
- Role of clinical biases in diagnosis
- Validity and reliability of diagnosis

Etiology of abnormal psychology
- Explanations for disorder(s)
- Prevalence rates and disorder(s)

Treatment of disorders
- Biological treatment
- Psychological treatment
- The role of culture in treatment
- Assessing the effectiveness of treatment(s)

To what extent?

Contrast   Evaluate   Discuss

PSYCHOLOGY SORTED: KEY RESEARCH FOR STUDENTS AND TEACHERS
BOOK 2 – APPLIED PSYCHOLOGY

ABNORMAL PSYCHOLOGY

Topic 1: Factors influencing diagnosis
Key Idea: Identifying what is normal and abnormal behaviour is problematic

Content	Research	Use in Abnormal Psychology	Links to
Normality vs. abnormality	Classic **Jahoda (1958)**	Mental health criteria – identified 6 characteristics of mental health.	
	Critique/Extension **Wakefield (1992)**	Reviewed and critiqued earlier theories of mental disorder and proposed that mental disorder be redefined as 'harmful dysfunction'.	
	Recent **Mojtabai (2011)** can also be used for classification systems (below)	The DSM 5 should not have removed the 'bereavement exclusion' as this now means the normal process of grieving after bereavement is treated as abnormal. Retrospective longitudinal study into grieving and depression.	

Further resources

Carey, B. (4 Jan 2012). Grief Could Join List of Disorders. *New York Times.*
https://tinyurl.com/83pcfrq

Grief could join list of disorders

Kleinman, A. (2012). The art of medicine. Culture, bereavement and psychiatry. *The Lancet (379),* pp.608-609. https://tinyurl.com/y2nf74o6

Culture, bereavement and psychiatry

Maisel, E.R. (15 Nov 2011). What Do We Mean by 'Normal'? It is time to rethink 'normal' and 'abnormal'. *Psychology Today* blog. https://tinyurl.com/yac8fjey

What do we mean by 'normal'?

PSYCHOLOGY SORTED: KEY RESEARCH FOR STUDENTS AND TEACHERS
BOOK 2 – APPLIED PSYCHOLOGY

ABNORMAL PSYCHOLOGY

Topic 1: Factors influencing diagnosis
Key Idea: Identifying what is normal and abnormal behavior is problematic

Content	Research	Use in Abnormal Psychology	Links to
Classification systems	Classic **Nicholls et al. (2000)** (Also used in reliability of diagnosis, see below).	How classification systems affect inter-rater reliability - evaluated the reliability of diagnostic classification systems for eating disorders in children and young adolescents. Found variations in diagnosis between 2 raters, using either the ICD 10, DSM IV or Great Ormond St. Hospital criteria (6 raters in all). Found GOSH criteria gave highest inter-rater reliability and ICD the lowest.	
	Critique/Extension **Mojtabai (2011)**	The DSM 5 should not have removed the 'bereavement exclusion' as this now means the normal process of grieving after bereavement is treated as abnormal. Retrospective longitudinal study into grieving and depression.	**Abnormal Psychology**: Factors influencing diagnosis – normality vs. abnormality
	Recent **Haroz et al. (2017)**	Investigated cultural bias in diagnostic tools by conducting a review of qualitative studies into cultural differences in depression worldwide. Their argument is that the DSM-5 criteria and standard measuring scales and instruments based thereon are not culturally sensitive enough to identify and reflect the experiences of depression cross-culturally.	

Further resources

Frances, A.J. (2 Dec 2012). DSM-5 Is Guide Not Bible. *Psychology Today* blog. https://tinyurl.com/j9us2ch

McPherson, S. & Armstrong, D. (2006). Social determinants of diagnostic labels in depression. *Social Science & Medicine, 62,* pp. 50-58. https://tinyurl.com/y6m3vgkf

Wyatt, R.C. (2001). Interview with Thomas Szasz. https://tinyurl.com/y2vl3pp6

DSM-5 is guide not bible

PSYCHOLOGY SORTED: KEY RESEARCH FOR STUDENTS AND TEACHERS
BOOK 2 – APPLIED PSYCHOLOGY

ABNORMAL PSYCHOLOGY

Topic 1: Factors influencing diagnosis
Key Idea: Identifying what is normal and abnormal behavior is problematic

Content	Research	Use in Abnormal Psychology	Links to
The role of clinical biases in diagnosis	Classic **Jenkins-Hall and Sacco (1991)**	European American psychiatrists watched a filmed clinical interview with four women and rated an African American woman with depression in more negative terms and saw her as less socially competent than the depressed European American woman. This demonstrated ethnic bias.	**Sociocultural Approach: Stereotyping -** women from ethnic minority group seen as less capable of managing their depression.
	Critique/Extension **Bertakis et al. (2001)**	Gender bias in diagnosis: women more likely to be diagnosed with MDD than men with the same level of symptoms as measured by the Beck Depression Inventory.	
	Recent **Haroz et al. (2017)**	Investigated cultural bias in diagnostic tools by conducting a review of qualitative studies into cultural differences in depression worldwide. Their argument is that the DSM-5 criteria and standard measuring scales and instruments based thereon are not culturally sensitive enough to identify and reflect the experiences of depression cross-culturally.	**Abnormal Psychology: Validity and reliability of diagnosis –** Western-developed tools have validity and reliability for Westernised cultures only. **Classification systems:** These are mainly Western-developed, even the most recent DSM 5 (produced by the APA) and so are not culturally-sensitive tools.

Further resources

Appignanesi, L. (6 Sep 2011). The mental illness industry is medicalising normality. *The Guardian.* https://tinyurl.com/y4opvjnj

BBC article (12 Feb 2016). What is mental health? https://tinyurl.com/y4yaof5m

BBC. What is mental health?

PSYCHOLOGY SORTED: KEY RESEARCH FOR STUDENTS AND TEACHERS
BOOK 2 – APPLIED PSYCHOLOGY

ABNORMAL PSYCHOLOGY

Topic 1: Factors influencing diagnosis
Key Idea: Identifying what is normal and abnormal behavior is problematic

Content	Research	Use in Abnormal Psychology	Links to
Validity and reliability of diagnosis Validity	Classic **Rosenhan (1973)**	A field study using 8 pseudo-patients at different times in US hospitals, to test the validity of the admission diagnosis process and the subsequent confirmation bias that arose from the invalid diagnosis.	
	Critique/Extension **Langer & Abelson (1974)**	Labelling bias can lead to a lack of validity in diagnosis: when an interviewee was labelled as a 'job applicant' rather than a 'patient', his behaviour was judged as fairly normal by analytic therapists viewing the videotaped interview. When they heard him described as a 'patient' then they were far more likely to judge his behaviour as abnormal.	**Sociocultural approach: Stereotyping** – a stereotypical view of what being a patient entails.
	Recent **Haroz et al. (2017)**	Validity and reliability in diagnostic tools: investigated cultural bias in diagnostic tools by conducting a review of qualitative studies into cultural differences in depression worldwide. Their argument is that the DSM-5 criteria and standard measuring scales and instruments based thereon are not culturally sensitive enough to identify and reflect the experiences of depression cross-culturally.	**Abnormal Psychology: The role of clinical biases in diagnosis** - Cultural bias in diagnostic tools: a review of qualitative studies into cultural differences in depression worldwide.
Reliability	Classic **Nicholls et al. (2000)** (Also used in classification systems, see above).	Inter-rater reliability - evaluated the reliability of diagnostic classification systems for eating disorders in children and young adolescents. Found variations in diagnosis between 2 raters, using either the ICD 10, DSM IV or Great Ormond St. Hospital criteria (6 raters in all). Found GOSH criteria gave highest inter-rater reliability and ICD the lowest.	**Abnormal Psychology: The role of clinical biases in diagnosis** – Age bias in diagnostic tools: the same tools cannot be used for adults and children, as symptoms vary.

	Critique/Extension **Silverman et al. (2001)**	Test-retest reliability - examined the test-retest reliability of the DSM-IV anxiety symptoms and disorders in children with the Anxiety Disorders Interview Schedule for DSM-IV (ADIS). Found that it is a reliable instrument for deriving DSM-IV anxiety disorder symptoms and diagnoses in children.	
	Recent **Haroz et al. (2017)**	Reliability and validity in diagnostic tools: a review of qualitative studies into cultural differences in depression worldwide. Their argument is that the DSM-5 criteria and standard measuring scales and instruments based on this are not culturally-sensitive enough to accurately be used for diagnosis of depression cross-culturally.	

Further resources

Youtube interview with David Rosenhan regarding his 1973 research.
https://www.youtube.com/watch?v=j6bmZ8cVB4o

Interview with David Rosenhan

Szabo, L. (17 Aug 2010). Youngest in class get ADHD label. *USA Today*
https://tinyurl.com/amgwush

Youngest in class get ADHD label.

Youngest in class gets ADHD label

PSYCHOLOGY SORTED: KEY RESEARCH FOR STUDENTS AND TEACHERS
BOOK 2 – APPLIED PSYCHOLOGY

ABNORMAL PSYCHOLOGY

Topic 2: Etiology of abnormal psychology

Key Idea: There are variations in both explanations for disorders and also prevalence rates.

Content	Research	Use in Abnormal Psychology	Links to
Explanations for disorder(s) – Major depressive disorder (MDD) Biological.	Classic **Caspi et al. (2003)**	Identified gene-environment interaction in major depressive disorder: found that a functional change in the 5HTT serotonin transporter gene is linked to a higher or lower risk of depression in an individual.	**Biological approach: genes and behaviour** – genetic predisposition interacts with environment to produce behaviour.
	Critique/Extension **Risch et al. (2009)**	Meta-analysis of 14 research studies into effects on depression of the interaction between the serotonin transporter genotype and stressful life events. Found no relationship between depression and the genotype or stress and the genotype, though there was a relationship between stress and depression.	**Biological approach: genes and behaviour** – questions the explanation put forward by Caspi et al.
	Recent **Schmaal et al. (2015)**	Correlation between changes in hippocampus and amygdala and major depressive disorder. Suggests localization of MDD in limbic system, though does not rule out effects elsewhere in brain.	**Biological approach:** localization – correlation between changes in the limbic system and the behavioural symptoms of depression.
Cognitive	Classic **Beck & Haigh (2014)**	Generic cognitive model is an update of Beck's classic cognitive triad model from 1967. Can be used as an explanation for MDD and PTSD.	
	Critique/Extension **Hankin & Abramson (2001)**	Cognitive vulnerability-transactional stress model of MDD explaining females' higher rate of depression from about 13 years of age.	
	Recent **Haeffel & Hames (2014)**	Suggested cognitive vulnerability for depression was susceptible to change during major life transitions like moving to college. Found cognitive vulnerability transferred between roommates via a contagion effect.	

Sociocultural	Classic **Brown & Harris (1978)**	Investigated the psychosocial causation of depression. Proposed 4 'vulnerability factors' that interact with 'provoking agents' to increase the risk of depression.	
	Critique/Extension **Auerbach et al. (2010)**	Examined the relationship between stress, social support and depression. Suggested that a lack of parental and classmate support was played a greater role in adolescent depression than any lack of peer support outside of this.	
	Recent **Bryant et al. (2017)**	Assessed the extent to which depression after a disaster is associated with social network structures. Found that depression appears to co-occur in linked individuals, and MDD is associated with a lack of social networks.	

Further resources

The classic work on sociocultural factors and women's depression is Brown, G.W. & Harris, T. (1978). *Social Origins of Depression: A study of psychiatric disorder in women.* Oxford: Tavistock

Greenblatt, J.M. (23 Nov 2011). The brain on fire: inflammation and depression. *Psychology Today.* https://tinyurl.com/odre9rn

Inflammation and depression.

TED talk by Jill Bolte Taylor (2008). My stroke of insight.
https://tinyurl.com/q8bfz2c

Harris, T. (1 March 2001). Recent developments in understanding the psychosocial aspects of depression. *British Medical Bulletin, 57 (1),* pp. 17 – 32.
https://tinyurl.com/y5v5xnkt

An excellent article on an integrated cognitive-social approach to MDD.

TED talk. My stroke of insight.

PSYCHOLOGY SORTED: KEY RESEARCH FOR STUDENTS AND TEACHERS
BOOK 2 – APPLIED PSYCHOLOGY

ABNORMAL PSYCHOLOGY

Topic 2: Etiology of abnormal psychology
Key Idea: There are variations in both explanations for disorders and also prevalence rates.

Content	Research	Use in Abnormal Psychology	Links to
Explanations for disorder(s) – Post-traumatic stress disorder (PTSD) Biological.	Classic **Geracioti et al. (2001)**	Investigated noradrenaline levels in cerebro-spinal fluid of participants with chronic PTSD. Found that the levels were significantly higher in participants with PTSD than in a control group of those with no PTSD. There was a positive correlation between the levels and the severity of the PTSD symptoms.	**Biological approach: Neurotransmitters and their effect on behaviour –** neurotransmitters and mood and memory. (Noradrenaline mainly acts as a neurotransmitter - in the brain, between the synapses - rather than as a hormone in the blood).
	Critique/Extension **Klaassens et al. (2012)**	Conducted a meta-analysis into the relation between hypothalamic-pituitary-adrenal function and PTSD. Neither adulthood trauma exposure nor PTSD were associated with differences in HPA-axis functioning. More evidence on other dynamic tests of HPA-axis functioning in PTSD and adulthood trauma exposure is needed.	
	Recent **Nicholson et al. (2014)**	Suggested that release of cortisol (hormone) and noradrenaline (neurotransmitter) together lead to greater intrusive memories in PTSD.	
Cognitive	Classic **Beck & Haigh (2014)**	Generic cognitive model is an update of Beck's original cognitive triad model from 1967. Can be used as an explanation for MDD and PTSD.	
	Critique/Extension **El Leithy et al. (2006)**	Pre-occupation with alternative outcomes after trauma (counter-factual thinking) was positively correlated with the continuation of post-traumatic stress.	

	Recent **Wild et al. (2016)**	Conducted a study into paramedics to identify which risk factors best predicted future PTSD or MDD. Found that participants at risk of developing episodes of PTSD or depression could be identified within the first week of paramedic training, using cognitive predictors.	
Sociocultural	Classic **Silva et al. (2000)**	Investigated a stress-diathesis model of interaction between experiences and pre-existing vulnerability that contribute to the development of post-traumatic stress disorder (PTSD) in children and adolescents. Found that observation of or engagement in violence and the stress associated with that increases the probability that a child will develop PTSD symptoms.	
	Critique/Extension **Kilpatrick et al. (2003)**	Exposure to interpersonal violence (i.e. physical assault, sexual assault, or witnessed violence) increases the risk of PTSD and of comorbidity with a major depressive episode and/or substance abuse or dependence.	
	Recent **Bryant et al. (2017)**	Assessed the extent to which PTSD after a disaster is associated with social network structures. Found that PTSD is associated with fragmented social networks.	

Further resources

TED talk on using a drug to prevent MDD and PTSD, by Rebecca Brachman (2016). Could a drug prevent depression and PTSD? https://tinyurl.com/zbf9vsv

Watters, E. (2010). *Crazy like us. The globalization of the American Psyche.* USA: Free Press. Chapter 2 on 'The Wave that Brought PTSD to Sri Lanka', argues for cross-cultural differences in PTSD symptoms and prevalence.
https://tinyurl.com/y65dw3sq

Drug for MDD and PTSD

(For a summary of this, read Slanzi, C. [Oct 2011]. Culture and PTSD: Lessons from the 2004 Tsunami. *The Trauma and Mental Health Report blog,* York University).

PSYCHOLOGY SORTED: KEY RESEARCH FOR STUDENTS AND TEACHERS
BOOK 2 – APPLIED PSYCHOLOGY

ABNORMAL PSYCHOLOGY

Topic 2: Etiology of abnormal psychology

Key Idea: There are variations in both explanations for disorders and also prevalence rates.

Content	Research	Use in Abnormal Psychology	Links to
Prevalence rates and disorder(s). Major depressive disorder.	Classic **Levav et al. (1997)**	Explored the relationships between religion, gender, alcoholism, and major depression. Found that Jewish males had significantly higher rates of major depression, but lower rates of alcoholism, than Catholics, Protestants, and all non-Jews combined. This links diagnosis to prevalence.	**Abnormal Psychology: Validity and reliability of diagnosis** – cultural and gender bias in that men maybe turn to alcohol rather than the medical profession, and so are not diagnosed.
	Critique/Extension **Hankin & Abramson (2001)**	The researchers propose a cognitive vulnerability-transactional stress model of MDD to explain the emergence of the gender imbalance in depression prevalence from about 13 years of age.	
	Recent **WHO (2017)**	Global health estimates of depression and other common mental disorders: proportion of the global population with depression in 2015 is estimated to be 4.4%, with depression more common among females (5.1%) than males (3.6%). The different prevalence rates between regions is to be focused on. (See Appendices of WHO document).	**Abnormal Psychology: Validity and reliability of diagnosis** – cross-cultural issues.
2. Post-traumatic stress disorder.	Classic **Mueser et al. (1998)**	Discovered that several severe mental disorders had a comorbidity with PTSD. Their findings were that 43% of their sample had symptoms that fit a diagnosis of PTSD, though only 2% had actually been diagnosed with this. This has implications for prevalence rates of PTSD.	

	Critique/Extension **Kilpatrick et al. (2013)**	Compared the prevalence rate of PTSD in a USA national sample when diagnosed using the DSM-IV and DSM-5. Found that DSM-5 PTSD prevalence was higher among women than men, and prevalence increased with greater traumatic event exposure. DSM-5 prevalence estimates were slightly lower than their DSM-IV counterparts, because of the exclusion of non-accidental, nonviolent deaths from the DSM-5, and the new requirement of at least 1 active avoidance symptom.	**Abnormal Psychology: Factors influencing diagnosis** – changes in the diagnostic manuals criteria for any disorder have an effect on the diagnosis of, and therefore the prevalence of, that disorder.
	Recent **WHO (2017)**	Global health estimates of depression and other common mental disorders: proportion of the global population with anxiety disorders (which includes PTSD) in 2015 is estimated to be 3.6%. As with depression, anxiety disorders are more common among females than males (4.6% compared to 2.6% at the global level). The different prevalence between regions is to be focused on. (See Appendices of WHO document).	**Abnormal Psychology: Validity and reliability of diagnosis** – cross-cultural issues.

Further resources

Summary of the prevalence, course and correlates of MDD worldwide. Kessler, R.C. & Bromet, E.J. (2013). The Epidemiology of Depression Across Cultures. *Annual Review of Public Health, 13,* pp. 119-138. https://tinyurl.com/y4ab5ya8

MDD worldwide.

TEDx talk on experiencing teenage depression, by Emily Angstreich (2017). Mental illness: it's normal. https://www.youtube.com/watch?v=xfWm2SYrnmU

TED talk. Teenage depression.

PSYCHOLOGY SORTED: KEY RESEARCH FOR STUDENTS AND TEACHERS
BOOK 2 – APPLIED PSYCHOLOGY

ABNORMAL PSYCHOLOGY

Topic 3: Treatment of disorders
Key Idea: Treatments vary according to beliefs in etiology and according to culture

Content	Research	Use in Abnormal Psychology	Links to
Major depressive disorder. Biomedical treatment (Biological)	Classic **Kroenke et al. (2001)**	Compared the effectiveness of three common selective serotonin reuptake inhibitors and found that all were equally effective in treating MDD.	
	Critique/Extension **Kirsch et al. (2008)**	Drug–placebo differences in antidepressant effectiveness increase with more severe MDD, but are relatively small even for this group. The increase is attributable to decreased responsiveness to placebo among very severely depressed patients, rather than to increased responsiveness to medication.	
	Recent **Singh et al. (2016)**	Double-blind study evaluating the effectiveness of ketamine for MDD that had resisted previous treatment. Found intravenous ketamine to be equally effective at treating depression, as measured after 15 days of the trial, whether administered twice or three times weekly. In both cases it was significantly more effective than a placebo.	
Major depressive disorder. Psychological treatment (Cognitive)	Classic **Beck (2005)**	Cognitive behavioural therapy (CBT) as treatment for major depressive disorder. Review of the last 40 years of CBT.	**Cognitive approach: schema theory** – role of negative schemas. **Abnormal psychology: etiology of disorders** - cognitive explanations.

	Critique/Extension **Keller et al. (2000)**	Comparison of treatment outcomes between CBT, antidepressants or a combination of both in patients with chronic MDD.	
	Recent **Kuyken et al. (2016)**	Research into the effectiveness of mindfulness-based cognitive therapy in preventing remission in people with recurrent depression.	

Further resources

Boseley, S. (21 Feb, 2018). The drugs do work: antidepressants are effective, study shows. *The Guardian.* https://tinyurl.com/yawe2mat
[It is worthwhile doing some evaluation and critical analysis of this study and the news article.]

The drugs do work.

Burnett, D. (27 May 2013). Brain-controlling magnets: how do they work? *The Guardian.* https://tinyurl.com/y5b6hvhq

Brain-controlling magnets.

Transcranial magnetic stimulation for treating MDD.

PSYCHOLOGY SORTED: KEY RESEARCH FOR STUDENTS AND TEACHERS
BOOK 2 – APPLIED PSYCHOLOGY

ABNORMAL PSYCHOLOGY

Topic 3: Treatment of disorders
Key Idea: Treatments vary according to beliefs in etiology and according to culture.

Content	Research	Use in Abnormal Psychology	Links to
Biomedical treatment (Biological) Post-traumatic stress disorder.	Classic **Davidson et al. (2001)**	Because few large trials of treatment for PTSD have been conducted, this research tried to remedy this. Conducted a multicentre, double-blind comparison of sertraline (an SSRI) and a placebo in the treatment of PTSD.	
	Critique/Extension **Davidson et al. (2006)**	To evaluate the efficacy of venlafaxine (a serotonin norepinephrine reuptake inhibitor) in treatment of PTSD. In this study, venlafaxine was effective for patients with PTSD, with remission rates of 50.9% for venlafaxine and 37.5% for placebo.	
	Recent **Boggio et al. (2010)**	Repetitive transcranial magnetic stimulation (rTMS)—a method of noninvasive neuromodulation—has been emerging as a potentially effective technique in the treatment of PTSD. This study compares high-dose rTMS with a placebo.	
Psychological treatment (Cognitive) Post-traumatic stress disorder	Classic **Foa et al. (1986)**	Cognitive behavioural therapy (CBT) used in controlled study of female assault survivors. Found to be an effective treatment.	
	Critique/Extension **Rothbaum (1999)**	Case study of virtual reality exposure therapy (VRET) used to successfully treat a 29-year-old Iraq war veteran PTSD sufferer.	**Cognitive approach HL extension:** 1. Methods used to study the interaction between **digital technology and cognitive processes.** 2. The influence of digital technology on cognitive processes – emotion and cognition (memory).

| | Recent | Mindfulness-based Cognitive Therapy (MBCT) is effective for prevention of depression relapse but has been less studied in anxiety disorders. This study investigated the use of MBCT group intervention adapted for combat PTSD. | |
| | King et al. (2013) | | |

Further resources

TED talk on art therapy for PTSD sufferers, by Melissa Walker (2015). Art can heal PTSD's invisible wounds. https://tinyurl.com/mqk3zy5

TEDx talk on giving psychological support, by Guy Winch (2014). Why we all need to practise emotional first aid. https://tinyurl.com/lsms5kz

Art therapy for PTSD.

Art Therapy for PTSD sufferers

ABNORMAL PSYCHOLOGY

Topic 3: Treatment of disorders
Key Idea: Treatments vary according to beliefs in etiology and according to culture.

Content	Research	Use in Abnormal Psychology	Links to
The role of culture in treatment (Sociocultural)	Classic **Smith & Griner (2006)**	Meta-analysis of 76 studies evaluating culturally-adapted therapies. Concluded that therapies targeted to a specific cultural group were 4 times more effective than interventions provided to groups consisting of clients from a variety of cultures. Interventions conducted in clients' native language (if other than English) were twice as effective as interventions conducted in English.	
	Critique/Extension **Hinton et al. (2005)**	Examined the efficacy of culturally adapted CBT for Cambodian refugees with treatment-resistant PTSD.	
	Recent **Hodge & Nadir (2008)**	Four common therapeutic models are discussed in light of their level of congruence with Islamic values - psychoanalytic, group, strengths based, and cognitive. They suggest that cognitive therapy is particularly congruent with Islamic discourse, but the self-statements central to this approach need to be 'repackaged' to reflect Islamic values.	

Further resources

Monbiot, G. (8 Feb 2018). The town that's found a potent cure for illness – community. *Guardian* article on social isolation, illness and depression.
https://tinyurl.com/ycoud73u

TED talk on the loneliness of modern society for veterans with PTSD by Sebastian Junger (2015). 'Our lonely society makes it hard to come home from war.'
https://tinyurl.com/yyh4x22n

TED talk. Lonely Society.

Pollard, J. (12 August 2001). A problem shared: From its origins after the Second World War, group therapy has grown into a treatment for our times.
https://tinyurl.com/y2p2ug5y

Pollard. Group therapy.

ABNORMAL PSYCHOLOGY

TOPIC 1: FACTORS INFLUENCING DIAGNOSIS

Key Idea: Identifying what is normal and abnormal behaviour is problematic
Content 1: Normality vs. abnormality

KEY STUDY 1.1: *Jahoda (1958). Current concepts of positive mental health*

Brief Summary
Marie Jahoda developed her theory in response to the labelling and classification of mental disorders, arguing that the concept of mental health is what requires definition, and rather than focusing exclusively on mental disorders, attention should be paid to this. In some ways she was a pioneer of the positive psychology movement.

Aim
To identify the characteristics of mentally healthy people.

Theory
She identified, partly through her earlier work on unemployed people in an area of Germany, and partly through a literature review, six characteristics that, together, demonstrated ideal mental health in a person:

1. **A positive attitude towards oneself** - self-confidence, self-reliance, and initiative, along with an understanding of one's strengths and weaknesses.
2. **Growth, development, and self-actualization**
3. **Integration** – an integrated outlook on life and resistance to mental stress.
4. **Autonomy** – self-determination and independence in decision-making.
5. **Accurate perception of reality** – uses objective evidence to see the world and others as they really are. Has empathy.
6. **Environmental mastery** - appropriate function in social roles.

Evaluation of Jahoda (1958)
Strengths
- ✓ Grounded theory developed from observations of unemployed people, and from literature review, and so therefore has some reliability and validity.
- ✓ Later studies based on surveys of psychiatrists have supported the theory.

Limitations
- ✗ Mental health is culturally specific and definitions vary cross-culturally. Jahoda was Austrian, and therefore from a fairly individualistic society where self-reliance is seen as positive. Those from a more collective society may not agree.
- ✗ Psychologists have suggested that accurate perception of reality is not a good measure of mental health, with optimism being a better sign of a mentally healthy person.

Reference
Jahoda, M. (1958). *Joint commission on mental health and illness monograph series: Vol. 1. Current concepts of positive mental health.* New York, NY, US: Basic Books.

****

TOPIC 1: FACTORS INFLUENCING DIAGNOSIS

Content 1: Normality vs. abnormality

KEY STUDY 1.2: *Wakefield (1992). The Concept of Mental Disorder: on the boundary between biological facts and social values.*

Brief Summary
Wakefield discusses his belief that there is no agreed upon adequate analysis of the concept of (mental) disorder. He argues that the concept of disorder lies on the boundary between the given natural world and the constructed social world, being a 'harmful dysfunction,' wherein *harmful* is a value term based on social norms, and *dysfunction* is a scientific term referring to the failure of a mental mechanism to perform a natural function (p. 373).

Aim
To investigate the nature of the concept of mental disorder.

Theory
He uses a critique of six other accounts of disorder to provide support for his theory of disorder as harmful dysfunction:

- **Antipsychiatry view** – the anti-psychiatrists of the 1960s and 1970s (Laing, Scheff and Szasz, for example) make an error when they take the stigmatization, misdiagnosis and diagnosis as a means of social control associated with the concept of 'mental disorder' as indication that there is no such concept. Moreover, just as a physical dysfunction can indicate a physical problem, so can a dysfunction of mental processes indicate a mental problem.

- **Value approach** – this states that both mental and physical disorders are value and culture-relative with no scientific content. They are just what is seen as undesirable behaviour. Wakefield argues that to say a condition is undesirable does not mean that you are taking a value decision and labelling it as a disorder. This would imply that anything that is undesirable is being falsely labelled as a disorder, which is not the case.

- **Disorder as whatever professionals treat** – this suggests that disorders are what physicians treat, and mental disorders are what psychiatrists treat. This would mean (wrongly) that anyone suffering from a disorder who is not treated is not in fact suffering from a disorder.

- **Statistical deviance** – this suggests that anything that statistically veers from the normal must be a disorder, especially if it is in a negative direction. But there are many rare behaviours that might be criminal, immoral or repugnant but are not disorders.

- **Biological disadvantage** – this argument states that a lowered fitness (mental or physical) in an evolutionary sense in that it is lower than the optimal fitness, signifies a disorder. Wakefield counters that the failure of specific mental mechanisms to perform their assigned tasks, that shows that something has gone wrong with the organism, not a failure to perform to the optimum, else everyone with an IQ of less than 180 would be deemed to have a mental disorder.

- **Disorder as unexpectable distress or disability** – this was put forward as a theory by Spitzer et al. (1978) and formed part of the DSM III-R in 1987. However, there are many unexpectable conditions that are not disorders (such as occupational problems or disruptive behaviour) and many expectable ones that are (such as PTSD or long-lasting depression during a severe illness).

Wakefield's theory - disorder as harmful dysfunction

Wakefield points out that disorder requires a factual basis as well as a value component, and the theory of harmful dysfunction meets these criteria. Just as the heart's natural function is to pump blood around the body, so mental mechanisms, such as cognitive, linguistic and affective mechanisms have natural functions, and failure to perform these to a normal everyday (rather than an optimal) level suggests a dysfunction.

But to be considered a disorder, a dysfunction must also cause some harm to the person. For example, if having one kidney is not causing a person any problem, then it is not classified as a disorder. For a disorder to be a mental disorder, there must be some mental dysfunction that is causing mental harm, even if it is secondary to a physical dysfunction. Huntington's disease or personality changes caused by a stroke or other brain damage would be examples of this.

The harmful dysfunction framework is therefore proposed as a useful framework for analyzing the concept of mental disorder.

Evaluation of Wakefield (1992)

Strengths
✓ Wakefield's requirement that a mental disorder has to involve a dysfunction of a mental mechanism protects against the labelling of socially stigmatized conditions as disorders. It distinguishes between valid and invalid applications of the term 'mental disorder'.

Limitations
X Mental mechanisms are not obviously correlated with behavioural disorder, and so it is not clear how these 'mental mechanisms' are to be identified.
X Stating that a mental mechanism is not functioning as it should is a normative, not a factual, statement, and therefore the 'dysfunction' component of Wakefield's theory is not as objective as stated.

Reference
Wakefield, J.C. (1992). The Concept of Mental Disorder: on the boundary between biological facts and social value. *American Psychologist, 47*(3), pp.373-388.

****

TOPIC 1: FACTORS INFLUENCING DIAGNOSIS

Content 1: Normality vs. abnormality

KEY STUDY 1.3: *Mojtabai (2011). Bereavement-Related Depressive Episodes: characteristics, 3-year course, and implications for the DSM-5*

Brief Summary
Mojtabai argues that the DSM 5 should not have removed the 'bereavement exclusion' (that stated that up to two months' depressive symptoms immediately following a bereavement was normal) as this now means the normal process of grieving after bereavement is treated as abnormal. This is a retrospective longitudinal study into grieving and depression to test the hypothesis that individuals with bereavement-related depressive episodes do not have a higher risk of subsequent depressive episodes compared with individuals without a lifetime history of depression.

Aim
To compare the characteristics of participants with bereavement related, single, brief (less than 2 months) depressive episodes and other types of depressive episodes, and to compare the future risk of depression between these groups and participants without a history of depression.

Participants
The sample comprised US participants in the *National Epidemiologic Survey on Alcohol and Related Conditions* wave 1 (n=43,093) and wave 2 (n=34,653).

Procedure
The design was a longitudinal, community-based, epidemiological study conducted from 2001 to 2002 (wave 1), and from 2004 to 2005 (wave 2). Structured interviews were conducted with all participants, using the *Alcohol Use Disorder and Associated Disabilities Interview Schedule–DSM-IV version*—a structured diagnostic interview used to diagnose mood, anxiety, substance abuse, and other common mental disorders.

The researchers measured demographic characteristics, age at onset, history of depression in close relatives, trouble in carrying out roles, psychiatric co-morbidities, mental health service use during their lifetime, and new depressive episodes during the 3-year follow up period. Major depressive episodes were characterized by a period of 2 weeks or longer, during which the participant experienced 5 or more of the 9 *DSM-IV* symptoms and also met the clinical significance criteria of impairment and/or distress.

Results
1. Those with bereavement-related, single, brief depressive episodes had a later age at onset, were more likely to be black, and less likely to have had impairment of role function, comorbid anxiety disorders or a previous treatment history.
2. They were also less likely than other participants with bereavement-unrelated single, brief episodes to experience fatigue, increased sleep, feelings of worthlessness, and suicidal thoughts.
3. They also ran a much lower risk of new depressive episodes during the follow-up period.

Conclusion
Single, brief depressive episodes that are bereavement-related, are qualitatively and measurably distinct from other types of depressive episodes and are not associated with increased risk of future depression. Therefore, the DSM 5 should exclude bereavement-related depression from the list of depressive episodes requiring treatment.

Evaluation of Mojtabai (2011)
Strengths
- ✓ This was a large and well-controlled longitudinal study comparing two distinct groups over a period of time. Therefore, the results have reliability, albeit for the general US population only.
- ✓ An extensive set of measurements was taken to compare the two groups, using standardised structured interviews, again increasing reliability.

Limitations
- X The participants in the study were all from the USA and therefore population generalizability is limited.
- X The methods used were quantitative and based on self-report and therefore may lack validity, as participants may have been subject to the social desirability effect, especially in reporting, or not reporting, later episodes of depression.

Reference
Mojtabai, R. (2011). Bereavement-Related Depressive Episodes: characteristics, 3-year course, and implications for the DSM-5. *Archives General Psychiatry, 68*(9), pp. 920-928

****

TOPIC 1: FACTORS INFLUENCING DIAGNOSIS

Content 2: Classification systems

KEY STUDY 2.1: *Nicholls et al. (2000). Children into DSM Don't Go: a comparison of classification systems for eating disorders in childhood and early adolescence.*

Brief Summary
Inter-rater reliability – the researchers evaluated the reliability of diagnostic classification systems for eating disorders in children and young adolescents. Found variations in diagnosis between 2 raters, using either the ICD 10, DSM IV or Great Ormond St. Hospital criteria (6 raters in all). Found GOSH criteria gave highest inter-rater reliability and ICD the lowest. Diagnostic manuals lack reliability in the classification of child and adolescent eating disorders.

Aim
To evaluate the reliability of diagnostic classification systems for eating disorders when applied to children and young adolescents.

Participants
Eighty-one children were randomly selected from a population of 226 children aged 7-16 who presented with eating difficulties to a specialist clinic.

Procedure
Diagnoses were assigned according to three classification manuals: the ICD-10, the DSM-IV and the Great Ormond Street Hospital (GOSH) criteria. Ratings using each were performed by two clinicians blind to the diagnosis of the other. A total of 6 clinicians was used.

Results
Inter-rater reliability values for the three systems were:

- ICD 10 = 0.357
- DSM-IV = 0.636
- GOSH = 0.879

The GOSH definitions included anorexia and bulimia nervosa, and added food avoidance emotional disorder, selective eating and pervasive refusal to eat. The results showed that the GOSH criteria, which were specially developed to classify child and adolescent eating disorders, were more reliable than the others, which were of little consistency, especially the ICD-10, which had the lowest inter-rater reliability.

Conclusion
ICD-10 has 8 categories, some of which are not overlapping. For example, a patient who had lost a large amount of weight associated with a fear of (and actual) vomiting was diagnosed as having psychogenic loss of appetite (F50.8) by one clinician, and as having vomiting associated with psychological disturbance (F50.5) by the other. There are two separate categories for eating disorder (F50.8) and eating disorder unspecified (F50.9), but they are not differentiated, so the separation seems unnecessary. The diagnostic manuals' criteria for eating disorders are too preoccupied with weight and body shape to be valid for children, and therefore the traditional eating disorder categories are not suitable for the diagnosis of eating disorders in children.

Evaluation of Nicholls et al. (2000)
Strengths
- ✓ This was a carefully-controlled study, with a blind design, so the psychiatrists did not know the diagnosis given by their counterpart.
- ✓ The definitions were based on symptoms observed in children, which are different from those in adults.
- ✓ The categories were specific, rather than including categories such as 'other' (ICD) and 'unspecified' (ICD and DSM).

Limitations
- X This is a small sample of UK children presenting to the hospital with eating disorders, and does not include those treated at home, and therefore the results cannot be generalised to those presenting to general practitioners or other professionals, or children from other cultures, who may be more easily diagnosed using the other manuals. More research is needed.

Reference
Nicholls, D., Chater, R. & Lask, B. (November, 2000). Children into DSM Don't Go: a comparison of classification systems for eating disorders in childhood and early adolescence. *International Journal of Eating Disorders,28*(3), pp. 317-324.

****

TOPIC 1: FACTORS INFLUENCING DIAGNOSIS

Content 2: Classification systems

KEY STUDY 2.2: *Mojtabai (2011). Bereavement-Related Depressive Episodes: characteristics, 3-year course, and implications for the DSM-5.*

See above, under **TOPIC 1: FACTORS INFLUENCING DIAGNOSIS,** *Content 1: Normality vs. abnormality.* This study may also be used for discussing classification systems.

****

TOPIC 1: FACTORS INFLUENCING DIAGNOSIS

Content 2: Classification systems

KEY STUDY 2.3: *Haroz et al. (2017). How is depression experienced around the world? A systematic review of qualitative literature.*

Brief Summary
The researchers investigated cultural bias in diagnostic tools by conducting a review of qualitative studies into cultural differences in depression worldwide. Their argument is that the criteria and standard measuring scales and instruments based thereon are not culturally sensitive enough to identify and reflect the experiences of depression cross-culturally.

Aim
To investigate the possibility that there are features of depression in non-Western populations that are not captured in the diagnostic criteria of the DSM-5 and also criteria in this classification system are that not relevant cross-culturally.

Procedure
This was a review of qualitative studies of depression worldwide, using 9 online databases. Initial searches were conducted between August and December 2012, and an updated search was conducted in June 2015. 16,130 records were identified, with 138 studies published between 1976 and 2015 meeting the criteria for the research. These studies reported data on 170 different samples and 77 different nationalities/ethnicities. Fisher's exact test (a statistical test used with small numbers to determine if there are non-random associations between two categorical variables) was used to compare features of depression across region, gender and context. Four independent authors rated each article 1 (low) to 5 (high) on credibility, transferability,

dependability, confirmability, non-leading approach to data collection, and use of *a priori* theory in analysis. These features were compared with the DSM-5 and also with instruments for measuring depression that are based on this classification system.

Results
Researchers found that 7 out of the 15 features with the highest relative frequency form part of the DSM-5 diagnosis of Major Depressive Disorder (MDD), and so there was agreement here between the DSM and frequently reported features of depression. However, many of the other features with relatively high frequencies across the studies are associated features in the DSM but are **not** prioritized as diagnostic criteria and therefore not included in standard instruments for measuring depression. For example, the DSM-5 diagnostic criteria of problems with concentration and psychomotor agitation or slowing were infrequently mentioned

Conclusion
The DSM model and standard instruments currently based on the DSM may not adequately reflect the experience of depression at the worldwide or regional levels. Therefore, they lack validity when used for diagnosis, and demonstrate that instruments originally developed in Western populations, even if locally adapted and tested, may still retain a substantial cultural bias.

Evaluation of Haroz et al. (2017)
Strengths
- ✓ This was a careful review of 138 selected samples of published cross-cultural qualitative research from the 1970s till 2015, using a standardised set of criteria and features of depression and a recognised statistical analysis of the results. Therefore, it has reliability.
- ✓ Four independent authors rated each article 1 (low) to 5 (high) on credibility, transferability, dependability, confirmability, non-leading approach to data collection, and use of *a priori* theory in analysis.
- ✓ For inclusion in the review, qualitative studies had to be focused on depression and features of depression, be written in English, be based on data from people aged 18-65, and any records reporting data on one individual or a very small series of case studies using fewer than 8 people were excluded. Therefore, the study had high validity in measuring features of depression.

Limitations
- X Although the articles were independently rated for their credibility and other factors (see above), none was excluded on a lack of rigour alone. This may have meant that non-credible or non-transferable data was used, possibly affecting validity and reliability.
- X Limited information on how some of the original studies were conducted may also have affected the validity of the results of the original studies on which this review is based, affecting the validity of Haroz et al.'s findings.

Reference
Haroz, E.E., Ritchey, M., Bass, J.K., Kohrt, B.A., Augustinavicius, J., Michalopoulos, L., Burkey, M.D. & Bolton, P. (2017). How is depression experienced around the world? A systematic review of qualitative literature. *Social Science & Medicine, 183,* pp. 151-162.

****

PSYCHOLOGY SORTED: KEY RESEARCH FOR STUDENTS AND TEACHERS
BOOK 2 – APPLIED PSYCHOLOGY

TOPIC 1: FACTORS INFLUENCING DIAGNOSIS

Content 3: The role of clinical biases in diagnosis

KEY STUDY 3.1: *Jenkins-Hall and Sacco (1991). Effect of Client Race and Depression on Evaluations by White Therapists.*

Brief Summary
This study into clinical biases in diagnosis examined the effect of client race and depression level on global and interpersonal evaluations by European American psychiatrists who watched a filmed clinical interview with four women. They rated an African American woman with depression in more negative terms and saw her as less socially competent than the depressed European American woman.

Aim
To investigate if and how racial bias affected clinicians' judgements regarding clients with mental disorders.

Participants
A volunteer sample of 62 white USA psychotherapists (23 male, 39 female, mean age of 36 years old) with at least a Master's degree and/or 3 years of experience in individual psychotherapy.

Procedure
Participants were shown a 3 min section of a video showing interaction between a 'client' and a 'therapist'. The 'client' was either a white or black female and was acting a 'depressed' or 'non-depressed' role (4 conditions). Each therapist viewed only one of the possible 4 conditions. The videos were developed using a script of questions from a standardised depression inventory and contrived answers to those questions, showing the presence or absence of common major symptoms of depression. Participants thought they were viewing a real client/therapist interaction.

Participants were also given a brief written description of the client they viewed, as a 27-year-old seeking therapy for 'communication problems' with her husband. The depressed condition included complaints of depressed mood, difficulty sleeping, and fatigue. After viewing the video, they completed a questionnaire containing multiple rating scales of social competence, depression and psychological states, referring to the 'client' whom they had just viewed.

Results
Participants rated the depressed clients significantly higher on depression than the non-depressed clients, although the black non-depressed and the white non-depressed clients were rated similarly. However, they rated the black depressed clients significantly more negatively on global and interpersonal dimensions than the white depressed clients. A combination of being both black and depressed resulted in a more negative rating than any other condition.

Conclusion
The therapists showed a racial bias against black clients in that they evaluated depressed black clients more negatively than depressed white clients. This finding supports other research that has found that white people will discriminate against black people in situations where a failure to

respond favourably could be attributable to factors other than ethnicity. The negative evaluations could affect a diagnosis of social competency while depressed, and if maintained during therapy, could also affect the outcome of therapy.

Evaluation of Jenkins-Hall & Sacco (1991)
Strengths
- ✓ Clinicians completed several different standardised measures for each client, measuring social competence, depression and psychological states. This triangulation of data and standardisation increased reliability of findings.
- ✓ Necessary deception was employed, which reduced participant expectations.
- ✓ Because the questions asked of the 'client' were from a standardised depression inventory, this added to the ecological validity of the study, as the participants believed this was a routine client/therapist interaction.

Limitations
- X This is a very small US study, and there is no reason to believe that the results could be generalised to other populations in other locations.

Reference
Jenkins-Hall, K. & Sacco, W.P. (1991). Effect of Client Race and Depression on Evaluations by White Therapists. *Journal of Social and Clinical Psychology, 10*(3), pp. 322-333.

****

TOPIC 1: FACTORS INFLUENCING DIAGNOSIS

Content 3: The role of clinical biases in diagnosis

KEY STUDY 3.2: *Bertakis et al. (2001). Patient Gender Differences in the Diagnosis of Depression in Primary Care*

Brief Summary
Gender bias in diagnosis: women are more likely to be diagnosed with major depressive disorder (MDD) than men with the same level of symptoms, as measured by the Beck Depression Inventory.

Aim
To explore why women are more likely than men to be diagnosed by their doctor (primary care physician) as depressed.

Participants
Opportunity sample of 821 male and female English-speaking outpatients at a university health centre. The patients were randomly assigned either to the family practitioner clinic or the general medicine clinic. 313 (38%) of these patients had to be excluded from the study because they did not keep their appointment, could not be included for scheduling reasons, or had incomplete questionnaires. Thus, 508 patients (315 women – 62%, and 193 men – 38%) participated in the study, which took place between 1990 and 1993. While women and men had similar ages and

ethnicities, women had significantly lower level of education and income, and significantly more children. Fewer women than men were in the never-married category, and more women than men were separated, divorced or widowed.

Procedure
Participants were interviewed before their first appointment, for sociodemographic data and to measure self-reported depressive symptoms (using the Beck Depression Inventory) and general health. The physicians were unaware of the BDI score of each patient.

Medical care was given by second and third-year family practice and general internal medicine residents, who each saw an average of 4.8 patients.

Results

MEASUREMENT	WOMEN	MEN
Mean BDI score (BDI score $\leq$ 9 indicates moderate depression).	6.4	4.3
No. of visits to primary care physicians	4.0	3.1
No. with high BDI score diagnosed as depressed	31 (out of 94)	5 (out of 36)
No. with low BDI score diagnosed as depressed	29 (out of 221)	12 (out of 157)
Total % diagnosed as depressed	19.1% (60 out of 315)	8.8% (17 out of 193)

For both men and women, those with most visits to primary care physicians were most likely to be diagnosed as depressed. This was so for those with low and with high BDI scores. Women who were separated, divorced or widowed were almost 5 times as likely to be diagnosed as depressed as were the never-married. This pattern was not seen with men.

Conclusion
Women in this study were significantly more likely than men to be diagnosed with depression. The gender-specific analyses revealed that the diagnosis of depression for both women and men was significantly predicted by primary care use and BDI score. However, women with high BDI scores were more likely than men to be diagnosed as depressed by their primary care physicians, even with a similar number of visits. Moreover, it is suggested that physicians perceive divorced, separated or widowed women presenting with health issues as more likely to be depressed than men presenting with the same issues. This could represent a sexist tendency to characterise women's problems as psychosomatic.

Evaluation of Bertakis et al. (2001)
Strengths
- ✓ Many variables were measured to increase the reliability of the results: sociodemographic and health variables; mean BDI scores; number of primary care visits.
- ✓ Comparing the diagnosis of those with high BDI scores with the diagnosis of those with low BDI scores was a useful control that illustrated the validity of the identification of gender bias only in those with high BDI scores.

Limitations

- ✗ The primary care physicians were senior residents; community physicians may interact differently with their patients.
- ✗ Chart notation by the physician was used as an index of depression, but this may not accurately measure the physician's recognition of depression.

Reference

Bertakis, K.D., Helms, J., Callahan, E.J., Rahman, A., Leigh, P. & Robbins, J.A. (2001). Patient Gender Differences in the Diagnosis of Depression in Primary Care. *Journal of Women's Health & Gender-Based Medicine, 10*(7), pp. 689-698.

****

TOPIC 1: FACTORS INFLUENCING DIAGNOSIS

Content 3: The role of clinical biases in diagnosis

KEY STUDY 3.3: *Haroz et al. (2017). How is depression experienced around the world? A systematic review of qualitative literature.*

See above, under **TOPIC 1: FACTORS INFLUENCING DIAGNOSIS,** Content 2: Classification systems. This study may also be used for discussing the role of clinical biases.

****

TOPIC 1: FACTORS INFLUENCING DIAGNOSIS

Content 4: Validity and reliability of diagnosis.
Validity.

KEY STUDY 4.1: *Rosenhan (1973). On being sane in insane places.*

Brief Summary

A field study using 8 pseudo-patients at different times in US hospitals, to test the validity of the admission diagnosis process and the subsequent confirmation bias that arose from the invalid diagnosis.

Aim

To investigate whether or not sane confederates would be admitted to a range of mental hospitals across the USA with a diagnosis of mental illness.

Rosenhan's 'Pseudopatients'

Rosenhan recruited 8 confederates to help him carry out his research, from a variety of backgrounds (3 were psychologists, one was a psychology graduate in his 20s, one was a housewife, one was a paediatrician, one was a painter). Rosenhan also took on a pseudopatient role. The sample of pseudopatients comprised 5 males, 3 females, all of whom assumed an invented identity for the purposes of the study.

Participants
The sample consisted of the staff and patients of 12 different mental hospitals from 5 different states in the USA. The hospitals were not all of the same standard: some were old, some new, some had high staff/patient ratios, some low, some were shabby and in a state of disrepair, and some were well maintained.

Procedure
The pseudopatients were instructed to report to their assigned hospital and to report that they had been hearing voices in their head which said 'empty', 'hollow' and 'thud'. Rosenhan chose these words as they are indicative of an existential crisis in a person's life (e.g. 'What is the meaning of my life? I feel empty', etc.) The pseudopatients were instructed to behave in a completely normal way and not to say or do anything else of an 'insane' nature.

Every one of the 8 pseudopatients was admitted to a mental hospital, 7 with a diagnosis of 'schizophrenia' and one with 'bi-polar disorder'. The pseudopatients – after an initially nervous start – behaved in their usual, normal way, taking part in activities, speaking to staff and patients, assuring them that they felt fine and were now symptom-free. The job of the pseudopatients was to convince the hospital authorities that there was nothing wrong with them and that they should be released (this formed, in essence, the dependent variable of the study: number of days spent in the institution).

The pseudopatients observed the behaviour and interactions of staff and patients and took notes of what they saw and heard. Rosenhan had also instructed some of the pseudopatients to ask specific questions of the medical staff whilst they were in the hospital, concerning when they might be released and other less loaded questions concerning the daily events in the hospital.

Results
The number of days spent by the pseudopatients in hospital ranged from 7 to 52 days, with 19 days as the average number of days in hospital. None of the hospital staff realised that the pseudopatients were not real patients although some of the actual patients voiced their suspicions that the pseudopatients were in role or faking. Records kept by hospital staff revealed that behaviours exhibited by the pseudopatients whilst in hospital were viewed through the prism of their diagnosis: a pseudopatient who was observed by a staff member writing in his journal was reported as the 'patient engaging in writing behaviour'; queuing for lunch was labelled 'oral acquisitive syndrome'. Only 4% of psychiatrists and 0.5% of nursing staff ever stopped to talk to pseudopatients when invited to. Medical staff spent around 90% of the time at their stations, not engaging with patients and it was estimated that only 7 minutes per day was spent in staff-patient interaction.

Conclusion
Being admitted to a hospital with a diagnosis of mental illness becomes a 'sticky label', with all subsequent behaviours being viewed in the light of this diagnosis: this results in a system where patients feel powerless and depersonalised.

Evaluation of Rosenhan (1973)

Strengths
- ✓ This was an ambitious and unique study to plan and undertake and its use of real, unsuspecting hospital staff and patients makes it high in ecological validity and ensures that the findings are valid.
- ✓ Rosenhan's findings raised real concern about how people are initially diagnosed and then subsequently treated by medical institutions.

Limitations
- ✗ There was some risk involved in this study as the burden of proof was on the pseudopatients to have themselves released from hospital: this could have impacted on their health considerably.
- ✗ This study would be impossible to replicate due not only to ethical constraints but to the specific time, place and nature of each separate pseudopatient's experience which means that the findings are not reliable.

Reference
Rosenhan, D. L. (1973). On being sane in insane places. *Science, 179* (4070), pp. 250-258.

****

TOPIC 1: FACTORS INFLUENCING DIAGNOSIS

Content 4: Validity and reliability of diagnosis.
Validity.

KEY STUDY 4.2: *Langer & Abelson (1974). A patient by any other name... Clinician group difference in labeling bias.*

Links to
- **Sociocultural approach: stereotyping** – a stereotypical view of what being a patient implies.

Brief Summary
Labelling bias can lead to a lack of validity in diagnosis: when an interviewee was labelled as a 'job applicant' rather than a 'patient', his behaviour was judged as fairly normal by analytic therapists viewing the videotaped interview. When they heard him described as a 'patient' then they were far more likely to judge his behaviour as abnormal.

Aim
To investigate the effect of the label of mental illness on subsequent assessment of behaviour by clinicians.

Participants
The sample consisted of 40 clinicians whose professions involved them giving diagnoses of mental illness/behavioural traits as part of their working life. All of the participants were based in universities or institutions in the state of New York.

Procedure
The participants were tested separately. There were two conditions of the independent variable:

- The 'job applicant' condition: each participant received instructions which told them that they would be watching a short video of 'a man who has recently applied for a new job' being interviewed. After watching the video, the participants were asked to fill in a questionnaire giving an assessment of the job applicant.
- The 'patient' condition: each participant received instructions which told them that they would be watching a short video of 'a patient' being interviewed. After watching the video, the participants were asked to fill in a questionnaire giving an assessment of the patient.

There was no difference between the 'job applicant' video and the 'patient' video.

Results
The participants who were behaviour therapists did not view the 'patient' as being much different from the 'job applicant'. The analytic therapists, however, viewed the 'patient' as being very different from the 'job applicant', using terms such as 'passive-aggressive', 'conflicted over homosexuality', 'hostile', 'repressed'. None of these terms was used about the 'job applicant'.

Conclusion
Being given the label of 'patient' may trigger stereotyped assumptions about that person's behaviour and their mental state.

Evaluation of Langer & Abelson (1974)
Strengths
- ✓ The use of a standardised video which was the same in each condition highlights the bias in some diagnoses and could be used to help avert similar stereotyping within clinical settings.
- ✓ Using practising clinicians gives the findings of this study external validity as it can be inferred that the ways in which the participants assessed the person in the video is reflective of how they might reach a diagnosis in real life.

Limitations
- X This study reveals that labelling of people may result in different diagnoses, but it does not explain *why* it happens.
- X It is possible that some of the participants may have worked out what the aim of the study was and may have changed their behaviour accordingly which would affect the validity of the findings.

Reference
Langer, E. J., & Abelson, R. P. (1974). A patient by any other name... Clinician group difference in labeling bias. *Journal of Consulting and Clinical Psychology, 42*(1), p.4.

****

PSYCHOLOGY SORTED: KEY RESEARCH FOR STUDENTS AND TEACHERS
BOOK 2 – APPLIED PSYCHOLOGY

TOPIC 1: FACTORS INFLUENCING DIAGNOSIS

Content 4: Validity and reliability of diagnosis.
Validity

KEY STUDY 4.3: *Haroz et al. (2017). How is depression experienced around the world? A systematic review of qualitative literature.*

See above, under **TOPIC 1: FACTORS INFLUENCING DIAGNOSIS,** *Content 3: The role of clinical biases in diagnosis.* This study may also be used for discussing validity of diagnosis.

****

TOPIC 1: FACTORS INFLUENCING DIAGNOSIS

Content 4: Validity and reliability of diagnosis.
Reliability

KEY STUDY 4.4: *Nicholls et al. (2000). Children into DSM Don't Go: a comparison of classification systems for eating disorders in childhood and early adolescence.*

See above, under **TOPIC 1: FACTORS INFLUENCING DIAGNOSIS,** *Content 1: Normality vs. abnormality.* This study may also be used for discussing reliability of diagnosis

****

TOPIC 1: FACTORS INFLUENCING DIAGNOSIS

Content 4: Validity and reliability of diagnosis.
Reliability

KEY STUDY 4.5: *Silverman et al. (2001). Test-Retest Reliability of Anxiety Symptoms and Diagnoses with the Anxiety Disorders Interview Schedule for DSM-IV: Child and Parent Versions*

Brief Summary
The researchers examined the test-retest reliability of the DSM-IV anxiety symptoms and disorders in children with the Anxiety Disorders Interview Schedule for DSM-IV (ADIS). They found that it is a reliable instrument for identifying DSM-IV anxiety disorder symptoms and deriving from them diagnoses for children.

Aim
To examine the test-retest reliability of the DSM-IV anxiety symptoms and disorders in children.

Participants
62 children aged 7–16 years (mean age = 10.15 years) and their parents. The children had been referred to the Child and Family Psychological Research Center at Florida International University, by school counsellors, other mental or medical health professionals, or self-referral, because of difficulties with excessive fear and/or anxiety.

Procedure
Participants underwent two administrations of the ADIS with a test-retest interval of 7-14 years. They were interviewed by trained psychology graduates using the ADIS, with the children interviewed using the child version (ADIS-C) and the parents with the parent version (ADIS-P), providing combined data. DSM-IV symptoms were judged as being present or absent ('yes' or 'no' by children and parents) and then the participants were asked to rate the level of impairment ('messing things up') on a 0-8 scale. Upon completion of the first interview, the child interview, parent interview and combined interview were used to derive DSM diagnoses from the symptoms.

For the retest, 7 to 14 days later, the same interviewer readministered the second interview to the children and parents, in exactly the same way as before. Participants did not need to remember their answers from the first interview.

Results
The most prevalent disorder for the total sample was specific phobias (SP) for the child interview, followed by generalized anxiety disorder (GAD) and separation anxiety disorder (SAD). For the parent interview, the most prevalent disorder for the total sample was also SP, followed by GAD and SAD. For the combined diagnosis, the most prevalent disorder for the total sample was GAD, followed by SAD and SP. Correlation coefficients between the two interviews for these disorders were calculated and indicated high reliability, with values spanning from 0.78 to 1.00, with no significant age differences in the reliability of symptom scale scores between younger children (7-11 years) and adolescents (12-16 years).

Conclusion
These results suggest that the latest revision of the ADIS-C/P gives highly reliable diagnoses in children and adolescents, with excellent test-retest reliability. This study is reassuring, as it provides information showing the reliability of diagnosing DSM-IV anxiety disorders and symptoms in children, with the ADIS-C/P, a commonly-used tool.

Silverman et al. (2001)
Strengths
- ✓ This study used an outpatient sample, which meant that less prevalent anxiety disorders and symptoms, like GAD, could be examined, rather than just the most prevalent disorder, which is usually SAD.
- ✓ Outpatient sampling meant that overreporting of symptoms that is present in inpatient samples was avoided.
- ✓ The triangulation of data from parents and children and the use of a standardised questionnaire added to the study's reliability.

Limitations

X Giving yes/no answers to the presence or absence of criteria, and rating symptoms on a level of impairment scale is subject to participant expectations, especially amongst older children and parents, and therefore validity of some answers may have been decreased.

X The same interviewer was used for both interviews, which meant that interviewer variance was controlled, but this potentially could have inflated the reliability, as the feeling that one should give the same answers may have been present, despite reassurances that this was not necessary. A longer time before the retest may have solved this.

Reference

Silverman, W.K., Lissette, M., Saavedra, M.S. & Armando, A. Pina (2001). Test-Retest Reliability of Anxiety Symptoms and Diagnoses with the Anxiety Disorders Interview Schedule for DSM-IV: Child and Parent Versions. *Journal of the American Academy of Child and Adolescent Psychiatry, 40* (8), pp. 937- 944.

****

TOPIC 1: FACTORS INFLUENCING DIAGNOSIS

Content 4: Validity and reliability of diagnosis.
Reliability.

KEY STUDY 4.6: *Haroz et al. (2017). How is depression experienced around the world? A systematic review of qualitative literature.*

See above, under **TOPIC 1: FACTORS INFLUENCING DIAGNOSIS,** *Content 4: validity and reliability of diagnosis.* This study may also be used for discussing reliability of diagnosis.

****

TOPIC 1: FACTORS INFLUENCING DIAGNOSIS

Critical thinking points

Are concepts of normality and abnormality social constructs?
Most people will have a general concept of what the term 'normal' means in terms of behaviour. 'Normal', for most people, will constitute any type of behaviour which appears familiar, reasonable and which adheres to the norms of their society, their culture or their family and friendship groups. There is no absolute 'normal', no objective reality in which 'normal' behaviour could be said to be defined in absolute terms and yet diagnoses the world over are based on concepts of 'normal'. Wakefield's (1992) concept of mental disorder as a 'harmful dysfunction,' is a value term based on social norms which may well differ depending on the context e.g. in some cultures, homosexuality is still viewed as a deviant, abnormal behaviour. Wakefield argues that to say a condition is undesirable does not mean that you are taking a value decision and labelling it as a disorder. This would imply that anything that is undesirable is being falsely labelled as a disorder, for example

speaking with your mouth full of food. It is unpleasant to watch, and certainly undesirable but it cannot be termed a 'disorder' or 'abnormal' behaviour; it is simply a lack of table manners!)

Are the DSM and ICD useful diagnostic tools or could they lead to misdiagnosis?

The DSM 5 is a manual that is used world-wide, particularly in Westernised cultures to ascertain the diagnostic criteria of disorders in patients presenting symptoms. It is certainly comprehensive and far-reaching and it is reviewed on a regular basis, undergoing changes/amendments with each new version. Like any 'set in stone' guide though, it is not without its flaws and blind spots which might lead to faulty or damaging diagnoses occurring. For example, Mojtabai (2011) argues that the DSM 5 should not have removed the 'bereavement exclusion' (that stated that up to two months' depressive symptoms immediately following a bereavement was normal) as this now means the normal process of grieving after bereavement is treated as abnormal. This idea may lead to someone being labelled as 'depressed' simply because after two months of mourning they have not 'got better' or 'snapped out of it': it belies the grieving process which may take many months or even years and which is unique per person and per bereavement. Nicholls et al. (2000) found that Great Ormond Street children's hospital were far more successful using their own diagnostic criteria in identifying eating disorders in children than both the DSM IV and the ICD 10 (which was particularly unreliable). This is a problem if practitioners rely heavily on diagnostic manuals (which may be the case if the doctor is inexperienced or under-confident) and training should be in place to enable doctors to use their own medical instinct/experience to reach a diagnosis that may not agree with diagnostic manuals.

To what extent do gender and culture influence a diagnosis?

In an ideal world all medical professionals would be impartial, neutral and unbiased so that each diagnosis was judged purely on the symptoms presented rather than being viewed through the prism of extraneous factors such as gender and/or race. This, however, appears not to be the case, with the tendency over the years for doctors to fall into a particular demographic (male, white, middle-class) which can result in diagnoses based on prejudiced and misinformed ideas. Jenkins-Hall & Sacco (1991) found that the race of female patients had an effect on the global and interpersonal evaluations made by European American psychiatrists who watched a filmed clinical interview with four women. They rated an African American woman with depression in more negative terms and saw her as less socially competent than the depressed European American woman. Bertakis et al. (2001) found that women are more likely to be diagnosed with major depressive disorder than men with the same level of symptoms, as measured by the Beck Depression Inventory. Although these studies are not conclusive due to the small samples used, they do shed some light on the hidden biases that some doctors may harbour, and which may ultimately lead to misdiagnosis or to dismissing their patient as simply being typical of a particular stereotype rather than as a individual.

****

PSYCHOLOGY SORTED: KEY RESEARCH FOR STUDENTS AND TEACHERS
BOOK 2 – APPLIED PSYCHOLOGY

TOPIC 2: ETIOLOGY OF ABNORMAL PSYCHOLOGY

Key Idea: There are variations in both explanations for disorders and also prevalence rates.

Content 5: Explanations for disorder(s) – Major depressive disorder (MDD) *Biological.*

KEY STUDY 5.1: *Caspi et al. (2003) Influence of Life Stress on Depression: Moderation by a Polymorphism in the 5-HTT Gene.*

Links to
- **Biological approach: genes and behaviour** – genetic predisposition interacts with environment to produce behaviour

Aim
To investigate whether a functional change in the 5HTT gene is linked to a higher or lower risk of depression in an individual.

Participants
847 participants aged 26 years old split into three groups, depending on the length of the alleles on their 5HTT transporter gene.

Group 1 – two short alleles
Group 2 – one short and one long allele
Group 3 – two long alleles

Procedure
A number of methods were used to ascertain the link between length of allele, stressful life events and depression:

1. Stressful life events occurring after the 21st birthday and before the 26th birthday: assessed using a life-history calendar.

2. The Diagnostic Interview Schedule was used to measure the instances and frequency of depression over the past year per participant.

3. Correlational analyses were calculated between stressful life events and depression, length of alleles and depression and perceived stress and the length of alleles.

4. A further test was done to see if life events could predict an increase in depression over time among individuals with one or two short alleles.

Results
The participants with two short alleles in the 5HTT transporter gene reported more depression symptoms in response to stressful life events than either of the other two groups. Participants with two long alleles reported fewer depression symptoms. Participants with one or two short alleles who had been mistreated (e.g. abused or neglected) as children had scores that could be used to predict depression in adulthood.

Conclusion
There appears to be a correlation between having short alleles on the 5HTT gene and instances of depression linked to stressful life events. Having long 5HTT gene alleles seems to offer protection from stress-related depression.

Evaluation of Caspi et al. (2003)
Strengths
- ✓ The study used a very large cohort of males and females and the age was controlled in order to isolate the variable of number of stressful life events between the ages of 21 and 26.
- ✓ It was a natural experiment, with the naturally occurring IV being the length of the alleles so it would be impossible for demand characteristics to bias this aspect of the study.

Limitations
- X Attempting to isolate the action of one gene is a highly complex and difficult undertaking: it is unknown as to how many other genes may be involved in the experience of stress and subsequent depression.
- X The symptoms of depression were self-reported which could produce biased, unreliable results due to a deliberate attempt to mislead the researchers, memory impairment, wanting to please the researchers too much.

Reference
Caspi, A., Sugden, K., Moffitt, T. E., Taylor, A., Craig, I. W., Harrington, H., ... & Poulton, R. (2003). Influence of life stress on depression: moderation by a polymorphism in the 5-HTT gene. *Science, 301*(5631), pp. 386-389.

****

TOPIC 2: ETIOLOGY OF ABNORMAL PSYCHOLOGY

Content 5: Explanations for disorder(s) – Major depressive disorder (MDD)
Biological.

Key study 5.2: *Risch et al. (2009.) Interaction Between the Serotonin Transporter Gene (5-HTTLPR), Stressful Life Events, and Risk of Depression.*

Links to
- **Biological approach: genes and behaviour** – questions the explanation put forward by Caspi et al.

Brief Summary
Looked at the relation between inherited short alleles on the 5HTT serotonin transporter gene and incidences of stress and subsequent depression.

Aim
To investigate whether a functional change in the 5HTT gene is linked to a higher or lower risk of depression in an individual.

Participants
The researchers conducted a meta-analysis of 14 studies which investigated possible links/interaction between stressful life events, depression and the serotonin 5HTT gene. A total of 14,250 participants comprised the overall sample.

Procedure
Statistical tests were applied to the results of the studies in the meta-analysis.

Results
The researchers found that there was a significant association between stressful life events such as bereavement or job loss with depression. However, they did not find that this also had a biological root: no association was found between depression and the 5HTT gene and no interaction was found between stressful life events and the 5HTT gene.

Conclusion
The 5HTT gene alone does not appear to trigger depression, nor does it appear to be associated with stressful life events.

Evaluation of Risch et al. (2009)
Strengths
- ✓ This research used a very large sample comprising the quantitative data from a range of studies which means that the findings are robust and reliable.
- ✓ Using an objective, statistical measure to analyse the results of the studies should ensure that the study is free from researcher bias.

Limitations
- X Very little is really known about the role of neurotransmitters on behaviour so these results are only partially useful, and no firm conclusions should be drawn from them.
- X A meta-analysis is a rather 'cold', detached way of measuring human behaviour, particularly a variable so complex and unpredictable as depression.

Reference
Risch, N., Herrell, R., Lehner, T., Liang, K. Y., Eaves, L., Hoh, J., ... & Merikangas, K. R. (2009). Interaction between the serotonin transporter gene (5-HTTLPR), stressful life events, and risk of depression: a meta-analysis. *Jama, 301*(23), pp. 2462-2471.

****

TOPIC 2: ETIOLOGY OF ABNORMAL PSYCHOLOGY

Content 5: Explanations for disorder(s) – Major depressive disorder (MDD)
Biological.

Key study 5.3: *Schmaal et al. (2106). Subcortical brain alterations in major depressive disorder: findings from the ENIGMA Major Depressive Disorder working group.*

Links to
- **Biological approach: localization** – correlation between changes in the limbic system and the behavioural symptoms of depression.
- **Techniques used to study the brain:** The use of the fMRI method; localisation of brain function.
- **Abnormal Psychology**: Huge meta-analysis of MRI data showed that Major Depressive Disorder (MDD) in some cases, but not all, is correlated with a decrease in size in the hippocampus and amygdala.

Brief Summary
Suggests that MDD may be localised in the limbic system, though it does not rule out effects elsewhere in brain.

Aim
To investigate structural alterations in the brain associated with MDD.

Participants
The researchers used the existing MRI scans of a total of 8,927 participants: 1,728 of whom were suffering from MDD and 7,199 of whom were non-depressed, healthy controls.

Procedure
The researchers used statistical tests (e.g. multiple linear regression) and MRI-specific software to analyse and measure the grey matter in seven different areas of the brain including the amygdala, nucleus accumbens and hippocampus.

Results
The participants with MDD showed 1.24% reduction in their hippocampal grey matter compared to the controls. This was particularly prevalent in participants with early-onset MDD (i.e. MDD which started before the age of 21). The early-onset MDD participants also had less grey matter in the amygdala.

Conclusion
Early-onset MDD may be localised to the hippocampus and amygdala.

Evaluation of Schmaal et al. (2016)

Strengths
- ✓ This meta-analysis used a huge sample comprising a total of 8,927 individual MRI scans which means that the resulting quantitative data is robust and reliable. Using statistical analyses means that the measure is free of bias and objective which also increases reliability.
- ✓ The researchers obtained written informed consent from each participant which means that they followed ethical guidelines and did not compromise the privacy of the participants.

Limitations
- ✗ The use of a meta-analysis involves analysing secondary data over which the researchers have had no control: they have no way of ensuring that the MRI scans were carried out properly, with accurately calibrated equipment. This could mean that reliability is compromised somewhat.
- ✗ The conclusions reached by the researchers is based to some extent on correlations between brain regions and MDD: it cannot provide a cause-and-effect explanation of where MDD may be localised.

Reference
Schmaal, L., Veltman, D. J., van Erp, T. G., Sämann, P. G., Frodl, T., Jahanshad, N., ... & Vernooij, M. W. (2016). Subcortical brain alterations in major depressive disorder: findings from the ENIGMA Major Depressive Disorder working group. *Molecular psychiatry*, *21*(6), p. 806.

****

TOPIC 2: ETIOLOGY OF ABNORMAL PSYCHOLOGY

Content 5: Explanations for disorder(s) – Major depressive disorder (MDD)
Cognitive.

Key study 5.4: *Beck & Haigh (2014). Advances in Cognitive Theory and Therapy: the Generic Cognitive Model.*

Brief Summary
The generic cognitive model proposed is an update of Beck's classic cognitive triad model from 1967. It can be used as an explanation for major depressive disorder (MDD) and post-traumatic stress disorder (PTSD), as well as other psychological disorders.

Aim
The updated theoretical model provides a framework for explaining the etiology of and addressing the symptoms of regarding psychological disorders not explained in previous versions of Beck's original model.

Theory
The model (visual representation of the theory) is below. It comprises four interacting components: situation (stimulus), biased belief, focus, and maladaptive behaviour. Psychological

disorder is initiated and maintained when the schema-activated components - beliefs, focus, and maladaptive behaviour - are triggered by situational stimuli and interact.

The stimulus may reflect a broad spectrum of possible events, such as being rejected or abandoned, failing an exam, or being fired, or personal stressors like having to speak in public, travel in an elevator, or be in a crowd.

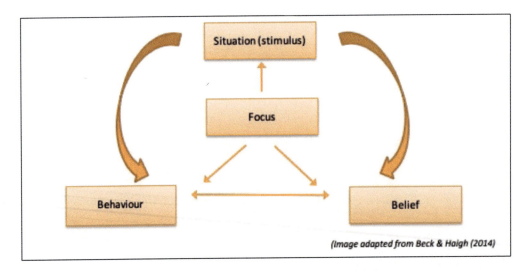

(Image adapted from Beck & Haigh (2014)

The memories, feelings and sensations (such as chest pain or sweating) associated with personal stressors may function as activating stimuli. The stimuli trigger latent schemas (which often lay dormant after repeated stressful or traumatic events) that determine the content of current cognitive processing. Once activated, these maladaptive schemas prevent normal information processing and bias the beliefs associated with the stimulus event.

Examples of how this model applies to three common psychological disorders

Disorder	Stimulus	Belief	Behaviour
MDD	Loss/rejection	'Nothing I do is right.'	Social withdrawal
PTSD	Reminder of trauma	'The world is dangerous, and I have no power to protect myself.'	Avoid triggers or reminders
OCD	Public toilets	'I am at risk of contracting a deadly disease.'	Avoid contaminated stimulus and engage in excessive compensatory behaviours

The theory explains psychological problems as the result of an exaggeration of beliefs, affect, and behaviours that are usually helpful in dealing with problems and satisfying goals. Problems occur when the beliefs are significantly distorted. Beliefs consist of schemas and the progressive activation of a schema from low to high intensity transforms normal adaptation into a psychological disorder such that beliefs, affect, and behaviours become over-significant.

Conclusion
This theory and the derived generic cognitive model can explain the etiology of many disorders, from MDD to sleep and substance disorders. It can therefore be very useful for psychologists and psychiatrists trying to diagnose and treat a wide range of psychological disorders.

Evaluation of Beck & Haigh (2014)
Strengths
- ✓ The components of the GCM (maladaptive beliefs, focus and behaviour) can all be empirically tested with patients through cognitive interview, and therefore the model has reliability.
- ✓ It answers criticisms of Beck's earlier 'cognitive triad' model that was accused of not explaining the origin of maladaptive thoughts, by positing latent schemas from earlier memories that are triggered by the environmental or physical stimulus.

Limitations
- X The model explains all psychological disorders as originating from dysfunctional thinking, expressed as beliefs and resulting in maladaptive behaviours, but it cannot therefore explain the etiology of psychological disorders about which such beliefs remain unexpressed. It lacks validity for patients who cannot articulate their feelings.
- X Literature on the GCM is currently limited.

Reference
Beck, A.T. & Haigh, E.A.P. (2014). Advances in Cognitive Theory and Therapy: The Generic Cognitive Model. *Annual Review of Clinical Psychology, 10* (1), pp.1–24.

****

TOPIC 2: ETIOLOGY OF ABNORMAL PSYCHOLOGY

Content 5: Explanations for disorder(s) – Major depressive disorder (MDD)
Cognitive.

Key study 5.5: *Hankin & Abramson (2001). Development of gender differences in depression: An elaborated cognitive vulnerability–transactional stress theory.*

Brief Summary
The researchers propose a cognitive vulnerability-transactional stress model of MDD to explain the emergence of the gender imbalance in depression prevalence from about 13 years of age. The cognitive vulnerability-transactional stress model of MDD is based on the idea that the ways in which a person thinks and processes information is actively linked to, affects and affected by different stressors and symptoms of depression.

Aim
A review of research to assess the extent to which gender plays a role in the onset of depression, with research highlighting the tendency of girls to develop depressive symptoms around the age of 13.

Main comments and findings

- Girls are far more likely than boys to develop depressive symptoms around the age of 13.
- Both girls and boys report more feelings of depression during adolescence.
- Girls tend to experience higher levels of anxiety and eating disorders than boys do. Anxiety is often a precursor to the full onset of depressive symptoms.
- The hopelessness theory of depression predicts that individuals who make more negative attributions about stable, global events have a high tendency to feel a sense of hopelessness which in turn leads to depression. This hopelessness interacts with cognitive factors to make the depressive symptoms severe.
- A 'ruminative' cognitive style (thinking about things deeply) is linked to depression, with more girls than boys using this style of information-processing, be it obsessing over their physical appearance, brooding over friendships or relationships with boys.
- The higher levels of depression experienced by girls also contribute to the triggering of negative events which means that there is a bi-directional relationship between the two i.e. a negative event may trigger depression/depression may mean that an event is viewed negatively. This then brings on the feelings of depression in a kind of vicious circle. For example, a girl may have a negative body image: if she then tries on a pair of trousers that don't fit, this event may trigger more self-loathing and depression.

Conclusion

There may be gender differences in the onset of development in adolescence with the cognitive-vulnerability transactional explanation offering an integrative method of explaining this phenomenon.

Evaluation of Hankin & Abramson (2001)

Strengths

- ✓ A good range of studies are reviewed in this research which adds to the reliability of the findings.
- ✓ This research provides a descriptive timeline of the difference in depression development between boys and girls which means that it has good application to clinical, therapeutic and educational settings.

Limitations

- X This research was carried out pre-social media so it may now be outdated: future research should focus on the prevalence of anxiety and depression in both genders linked to social media use.
- X There may be other reasons for girls reporting higher levels of depression than boys: biological factors linked to hormonal changes; social factors which make it more acceptable for girls to admit to feeling vulnerable, hopeless or anxious.

Reference

Hankin, B. L., & Abramson, L. Y. (2001). Development of gender differences in depression: An elaborated cognitive vulnerability–transactional stress theory. *Psychological bulletin, 127*(6), pp.773-796.

****

PSYCHOLOGY SORTED: KEY RESEARCH FOR STUDENTS AND TEACHERS
BOOK 2 – APPLIED PSYCHOLOGY

TOPIC 2: ETIOLOGY OF ABNORMAL PSYCHOLOGY

Content 5: Explanations for disorder(s) – Major depressive disorder (MDD)
Cognitive.

Key study 5.6: *Haeffel & Hames (2014). Cognitive vulnerability to depression can be contagious.*

Brief Summary
Suggested cognitive vulnerability for depression was susceptible to change during major life transitions like moving to college. Found that cognitive vulnerability could be transferred between roommates via a contagion effect.

Aim
To investigate the idea that vulnerability to depression can be contagious i.e. it is possible to 'catch' depression from spending time in close proximity with a depressed person.

Participants
The sample consisted of pairs of roommates from a university in the Midwest of the USA (103 pairs in total with a mean age of 18 years; 80% white; 9% Hispanic; 6% Asian; 3% black; 2% 'other'). The researchers used the directory of first-year students to obtain a random sample of participants whom they contacted via email to ask for participation in the study. The students were paid $5 per questionnaire completed over the course of the study.

Procedure
The participants filled in a series of questionnaires comprising question on the following:

- **Cognitive vulnerability:** Using a Likert scale the participants responded to questions asking about their degree of negative mood states, feelings of hopelessness, brooding on bad moods.
- **Stressful life events:** The participants were asked to assess 30 items on a list of stressful life events which had particular relevance to them as college students. The higher the score, the more stressful were the events perceived to be.
- **Depressive symptoms:** The researchers used the Beck Depression Inventory which is a questionnaire using 21 items that relate to symptoms of depression e.g. trouble sleeping, pessimistic outlook, low mood with possible scores ranging from 0-63, the higher scores being evidence of increased depression.

Participants filled in a baseline assessment questionnaire within a month of moving onto campus and then they completed the three questionnaires above 3 months and 6 months later.

Results
The researchers found that their hypothesis was supported by the results: participants who shared a room with another participant who registered high on the cognitive vulnerability to depression scale were influenced by their roommate's depression. Participants who had not registered as depressed on their initial baseline assessment were showing signs of having 'caught' depression

from their roommate, even after only 3 months of sharing a room. This was particularly true of the depressed roommate had a 'brooding' style of depression.

Conclusion
A person's cognitive vulnerability can affect the cognitive vulnerability of those around them, particularly when people are going through changes in their environment such as starting college.

Evaluation of Haeffel & Hames (2014)
Strengths
- ✓ The study has good ecological validity as the researchers did not manipulate any variables and used actual roommates, giving a natural condition.
- ✓ The use of a baseline assessment questionnaire meant that the researchers were able to compare their results to the initial findings so as to look for real changes in mood.

Limitations
- X The change in depression levels of the participants may have been due to other factors e.g. family circumstances, adjusting to life as a student, rather than from the 'contagion effect'.
- X A predominantly white sample makes it difficult to generalise the findings to other races and cultures.

Reference
Haeffel, G. J., & Hames, J. L. (2014). Cognitive vulnerability to depression can be contagious. *Clinical Psychological Science, 2*(1), pp.75-85.

****

TOPIC 2: ETIOLOGY OF ABNORMAL PSYCHOLOGY

Content 5: Explanations for disorder(s) – Major depressive disorder (MDD)
Sociocultural.

Key study 5.7: *Brown & Harris (1978). Social Origins of Depression: A Study of Psychiatric Disorder in Women*

Brief Summary
Investigated the psychosocial causation of depression. Proposed 4 'vulnerability factors' that interact with 'provoking agents' to increase the risk of depression in women.

Aim
To investigate the psychosocial causes of depression in women.

Participants
This was an opportunity sample of 458 women living in Camberwell, London.

Procedure
The participants were interviewed using semi-structured interviews asking biographical details about life events and difficulties such as relationship difficulties, poverty and unemployment. They were also asked if they had ever been diagnosed with depression.

Results
37 (8%) of all the women had become clinically depressed in the previous year. 33 of these women had experienced an adverse life event (such as the loss of a loved one) or a serious difficulty – some of them were in abusive relationships. 70% of the women who did not become depressed suffered from no such problems. Only 4 of the 37 women who became depressed had not experienced any adversity.

The researchers found that *vulnerability factors* predisposed women to depression: early maternal loss; lack of a confiding relationship; more than three children under the age of 14 at home, and unemployment. However, these are not a direct cause of depression, but can interact with *provoking agents* like poverty or a lack of a supportive partner or friends, to increase the risk of depression.

Conclusion
They concluded that low socio-economic status leads to increased exposure to both vulnerability factors and provoking agents, whereas high social status was associated with protection from both of these.

Evaluation of Brown & Harris (1978)
Strengths
- ✓ This study had high internal validity, as the semi-structured interviews were used to gain an in-depth understanding of the bibliographical details of the women's lives.
- ✓ The sample size of the original study was large, making the results potentially more reliable.

Limitations
- X The study is based on self-reporting and it is impossible to accurately determine the actual extent of depression each woman suffered.
- X While the research shows a correlation between stressful events and depression, it cannot determine that it is a cause and effect relationship. It is possible that biological vulnerability may combine with the social vulnerability identified by Brown and Harris.

Reference
Brown, G.W. & Harris, T.O. (1978). *Social Origins of Depression: A Study of Psychiatric Disorder in Women.* London: Tavistock Publications.

****

PSYCHOLOGY SORTED: KEY RESEARCH FOR STUDENTS AND TEACHERS
BOOK 2 – APPLIED PSYCHOLOGY

TOPIC 2: ETIOLOGY OF ABNORMAL PSYCHOLOGY

Content 5: Explanations for disorder(s) – Major depressive disorder (MDD)
Sociocultural.

Key study 5.8: *Auerbach et al. (2011). Conceptualizing the prospective relationship between social support, stress, and depressive symptoms among adolescents.*

Brief Summary
Examined the relationship between stress, social support and depression. Suggested that a lack of parental and classmate support was played a greater role in adolescent depression than any lack of peer support outside of this.

Aim
To examine the relationship between social support, stress, and depressive symptoms in adolescents.

Participants
258 adolescents (12-18 years old) from Montreal, Canada (57% female; 43% male). 79% of the participants were white, 8% Asian, 5% African American, 2% Hispanic, 6% 'other'.

Procedure
The participants filled in a series of questionnaires comprising the following:

- **Center for Epidemiologic Studies Depression Scale:** this is a questionnaire using 20 questions with a 0-3 scale of agreement which assesses levels of depressive symptoms. Examples of questions include, 'I felt hopeless about the future', and 'I felt lonely'.
- **Multidimensional Anxiety Scale for Children:** 10 statements using a 0-3 scale of agreement to measure the severity of anxious symptoms in the past week. Example of statements used include, 'I feel restless or on edge', 'I'm afraid that other kids will make fun of me'.
- **Adolescent Life Event Questionnaire:** 57 items that are designed to measure a broad range of possible stressors that have happened to or involve the participant in some way.
- **Social Support Scale for Children and Adolescents:** 18-statement questionnaire based on how liked/supported/involved the participant feels with parents, friends, classmates. The participant has to choose between two statements that most accurately expresses the type of person they are more like. Then, the participant is asked to determine whether the chosen statement is 'really true for me' or 'sort of true for me'. Examples of the statements include, 'Some kids have classmates they can become friends with' versus, 'Other kids don't have classmates that they can become friends with'.

The researchers conducted follow-up assessments every 6 weeks for 6 months after the initial assessments had been conducted.

Results
Participants who reported low levels of support from parents, friends and classmates reported higher levels of stress and subsequent development of depression. It was found that having supportive parents and classmates is very important for adolescents' mental health, particularly maternal support during early adolescence with supportive classmates and friends becoming more important for older adolescents.

Conclusion
The supportive role played by parents and classmates/friends is crucial for adolescents and can ultimately help them to avoid experiencing stress and depression.

Evaluation of Auerbach et al. (2011)
Strengths
- ✓ The study used a good-sized sample which did not reduce over the course of the repeated follow-up assessments which means that the findings are robust.
- ✓ The use of multiple questionnaires means that the researchers obtained a large amount of data which they were able to correlate to show patterns and trends in the data.

Limitations
- X Using a series of questionnaires to gather data is problematic as it could give rise to some forms of bias e.g. response bias, social desirability bias, which could affect the validity of the findings.
- X There are potential issues with the subjectivity of the participants' responses: questions/statements may be interpreted differently per participant so that an absolutely objective idea of what 'stressful' means is elusive and difficult to pin down exactly.

Reference
Auerbach, R. P., Bigda-Peyton, J. S., Eberhart, N. K., Webb, C. A., & Ho, M. H. R. (2011). Conceptualizing the prospective relationship between social support, stress, and depressive symptoms among adolescents. *Journal of Abnormal Child Psychology, 39*(4), 475-487.

****

TOPIC 2: ETIOLOGY OF ABNORMAL PSYCHOLOGY

Content 5: Explanations for disorder(s) – Major depressive disorder (MDD) *Sociocultural.*

Key study 5.9: *Bryant et al. (2016). Mental health and social networks after disaster.*

Brief Summary
Assessed the extent to which depression after a disaster is associated with social network structures. Found that depression appears to co-occur in linked individuals, and MDD is associated with a lack of social networks.

Aim
To investigate the extent to which social networks can offer mental health support for those who have experienced a disaster.

Participants
558 adults who had participated in the "Beyond Bushfires: Community, Resilience, and Recovery" study living in 25 communities in 10 rural locations in Australia that had been affected by bushfires, some of them very badly, in 2009. 241 men and 317 women were in the sample with a mean age was 57 years. Most of the sample had a good level of education.

Procedure
The participants answered a series of questions during an interview with a researcher, comprising the following:

- **Network name generator:** this measure involved each participant naming individuals to whom they felt particularly close and who could offer them social support in times of crisis.
- **PTSD checklist:** symptoms of PTSD were assessed using a standardised, itemised checklist.
- **Depression score:** a standardised, well-known depression inventory was used to assess the extent of depressive symptoms per participant.
- **Disaster exposure:** the severity of each participant's exposure to the bushfire was assessed in terms of fear for life (yes/no), death of loved ones (yes/no), property loss (ranging from 0=nothing to 10=everything
- **Subsequent life events:** major life events occurring since the bushfires were assessed, including stressors classed as non-traumatic e.g. negative changes in employment, loss of income, livelihood and traumatic stressors e.g. assault/violence, serious accident. Relocation away from community after the fires was indicated by comparing past and current residential addresses.

Results
The rate of probable PTSD in the sample was 16% (N=87), and the rate of probable depression was 39% (N=215). The researchers found that the participants who had difficulty naming significant others who might offer them support were more likely to suffer from PTSD i.e. fewer ties to others meant increased PTSD. Those participants who were close to someone who had experienced significant property loss were also more likely to develop PTSD i.e. individuals who were significantly linked to someone who had suffered from the bushfires then suffered themselves. Depression was experienced more by those participants who had fewer social ties or significant social support than others.

Conclusion
Contact with others who have experienced their own trauma and social disruption may make PTSD symptoms worse in an individual.

Evaluation of Bryant et al. (2017)
Strengths
- ✓ The study used standardised measurements which means that each participant was assessed using the same, unbiased criteria.

✓ The study used participants who had experienced a real disaster which means that the findings have some generalisability and could be applied to survivors of similar disasters.

Limitations
X This research used cross-sectional data which does not reveal as much as a longitudinal study would about the longer-term effects of exposure to a disaster.
X There may be other explanations for the onset of PTSD and/or depression e.g. a family history of mental illness; similar experience in the past; age, gender, level of health generally.

Reference
Bryant, R. A., Gallagher, H. C., Gibbs, L., Pattison, P., MacDougall, C., Harms, L., ... & Richardson, J. (2016). Mental health and social networks after disaster. *American Journal of Psychiatry*, *174*(3), pp.277-285.

****

TOPIC 2: ETIOLOGY OF ABNORMAL PSYCHOLOGY

Content 6: Explanations for disorder(s) – Post-traumatic stress disorder (PTSD)
Biological.

Key study 6.1: *Geracioti et al. (2001). CSF norepinephrine concentrations in posttraumatic stress disorder.*

Brief Summary
Investigated noradrenaline levels in cerebro-spinal fluid (CSF) of participants with chronic PTSD. Found that the levels were significantly higher in participants with PTSD than in a control group of those with no PTSD. There was a positive correlation between the levels and the severity of the PTSD symptoms.

Links to
Biological approach: Neurotransmitters and their effect on behaviour – neurotransmitters and mood and memory. (Noradrenaline mainly acts as a neurotransmitter - in the brain, between the synapses - rather than as a hormone in the blood).

Aim
To assess the levels of CSF noradrenaline in patients with PTSD.

Participants
11 men who were suffering from PTSD (mean age 42 years) and 8 non-PTSD healthy men. All of the 11 men with PTSD had suffered severe combat-related trauma, nine in Vietnam and two in Iraq during the Desert Storm operation in 1991.

Procedure
The severity of the participants' PTSD symptoms was measured with the clinician-administered PTSD scale. Participants had CSF withdrawn from their spinal cord every hour for 6 hours through a catheter. Thus, the researchers could measure the hourly levels of noradrenaline under baseline

(unstressed) conditions and compare the levels of those with PTSD with the levels of those without PTSD. The participants fasted throughout the period of CSF withdrawal.

Results
The PTSD patients had higher levels of CSF noradrenaline compared to the healthy control group, with the most severe PTSD cases showing the highest levels. The researchers noted that the baseline levels of CSF noradrenaline were akin to those that would be seen in highly fear-related situations e.g. war.

Conclusion
Heightened levels of CSF noradrenaline may be linked to chronic PTSD.

Evaluation of Geracioti et al. (2001)
Strengths
- ✓ The study used a clinical, objective measure free of bias which increases the reliability of the findings.
- ✓ The findings of the study could be used to inform future treatment for war veterans or others with chronic PTSD.

Limitations
- X The usefulness of the findings is limited somewhat due to the small sample used.
- X The researchers themselves point out that, although the setting for the study should not have induced fear in the participants it is still possible that confinement to a hospital bed for several hours before and during CSF withdrawal might have triggered a stress reaction.

Reference
Geracioti Jr, T. D., Baker, D. G., Ekhator, N. N., West, S. A., Hill, K. K., Bruce, A. B., ... & Kasckow, J. W. (2001). CSF norepinephrine concentrations in posttraumatic stress disorder. *American Journal of Psychiatry*, *158*(8), pp.1227-1230.

****

TOPIC 2: ETIOLOGY OF ABNORMAL PSYCHOLOGY

Content 6: Explanations for disorder(s) – Post-traumatic stress disorder (PTSD)
Biological.

Key study 6.2: *Klaassens et al. (2012). Adulthood trauma and HPA-axis functioning in healthy subjects and PTSD patients: a meta-analysis.*

Brief Summary
Conducted a meta-analysis into the relationship between hypothalamic-pituitary-adrenal axis (HPA-axis) function and PTSD. Neither adulthood trauma exposure nor PTSD were associated with differences in HPA-axis functioning. More evidence on other dynamic tests of HPA-axis functioning in PTSD and adulthood trauma exposure is needed.

Aim
To provide a meta-analysis of studies on the relationship between adulthood trauma, HPA-axis functioning and PTSD.

Procedure
The researchers conducted a meta-analysis of studies on trauma and PTSD. A total of 37 studies (21 giving a sample of 2468 participants) were included.

Results
The researchers found that participants with PTSD had the same levels of cortisol as non-PTSD healthy participants. Cortisol was measured in saliva, blood plasma and urine and no real differences between PTSD and non-PTSD participants were found. War veterans without PTSD appear to have enhanced suppression of cortisol which may indicate a long-term alteration in glucocorticoid regulation in response to an acute or chronic stressor. Increased sensitivity of the HPA-axis to corticosteroids after trauma exposure may be a mechanism of the body to protect itself against the detrimental effects of sustained high cortisol levels.

Conclusion
In the light of these rather inconclusive findings more evidence on other dynamic tests of HPA-axis functioning in PTSD and adulthood trauma exposure is needed.

Evaluation of Klaassens et al. (2012)
Strengths
- ✓ The study attempted to find a biological basis for behaviour via use of a clinical method which can be easily replicated.
- ✓ The researchers included studies on basal cortisol sampling as well as studies of cortisol reactivity which provides a more complete picture of HPA-axis functioning in relation to exposure to adulthood trauma.

Limitations
- X The researchers point out that they cannot rule out the possibility that they missed some studies meeting the inclusion criteria for the meta-analysis which would limit the findings if this is in fact the case.
- X Not all of the studies used in the meta-analysis stated whether they assessed lifetime psychiatric illness of their participants so some may have included participants with psychiatric disorders e.g. mood disorders, acute stress disorder etc.

Reference
Klaassens, E. R., Giltay, E. J., Cuijpers, P., van Veen, T., & Zitman, F. G. (2012). Adulthood trauma and HPA-axis functioning in healthy subjects and PTSD patients: a meta-analysis. *Psychoneuroendocrinology, 37*(3), pp.317-331.

****

TOPIC 2: ETIOLOGY OF ABNORMAL PSYCHOLOGY

Content 6: Explanations for disorder(s) – Post-traumatic stress disorder (PTSD)
Biological.

Key study 6.3: *Nicholson et al. (2014). Interaction of noradrenaline and cortisol predicts negative intrusive memories in posttraumatic stress disorder.*

Brief Summary
Suggested that release of cortisol (hormone) and noradrenaline (neurotransmitter) together lead to greater intrusive memories in PTSD.

Aim
To investigate the idea that the interaction of cortisol and noradrenaline predicts negative recall and intrusive thoughts in PTSD sufferers.

Participants
A self-selecting sample of 58 participants was obtained. 20 participants, (12 women, 8 men, mean age 22 years) as the control group. 20 participants, (14 women, 6 men, mean age 29 years) were classified as trauma-exposed controls (TE), i.e. they had experienced events such as car accidents, sexual assault, natural disasters. 18 participants were classified as PTSD (13 women, five men, mean age 31) having experienced a traumatic event and reported symptoms consistent with PTSD. In the PTSD group, 4 participants were war veterans, 11 experienced interpersonal or sexual assault and 3 reported traffic accidents.

Procedure
The participants had samples of their saliva taken to extract baseline noradrenaline cortisol. Participants were then instructed to view a series of images on a computer screen. 60 images were presented: 20 of a negative nature; 20 of a neutral nature and 20 of a positive nature. A second saliva sample was taken immediately after presentation of the negative images then a third saliva sample was taken to measure cortisol after the negative images had been presented.

Two days later, participants returned and were instructed to write down as many of the images they recalled from the first testing session. They then filled out an intrusive memory diary in which they recorded the number and content of intrusive memories of the images they had seen during the first testing session.

Results
The interaction between noradrenaline and cortisol significantly predicted negative intrusive memories in the PTSD group, who showed increased noradrenaline levels and a greater number of negative intrusive memories of the negative images they had seen.

Conclusion
Understanding how unwanted and intrusive memories are manifested is crucial in the quest to help PTSD sufferers. By better understanding the biological and cognitive processes that lead to intrusive

memories in PTSD, potential early intervention strategies may be applied that minimise the factors that are shown to lead to intrusive memories of upsetting and fear-inducing experiences.

Evaluation of Nicholson et al. (2013)

Strengths
- ✓ The study used a variety of measures to obtain data which increases its internal validity.
- ✓ The use of memory diaries provides some valuable qualitative data which is a good source of insight and depth compared to quantitative data.

Limitations
- ✗ It is unclear as to whether the interaction of noradrenaline and cortisol contributes to the risk of intrusive thoughts in PTSD or whether it is a predisposing tendency to someone developing PTSD.
- ✗ The use of a retrospective diary may produce unreliable data if participants were prone to retrospective memory bias or to social desirability bias.

Reference
Nicholson, E. L., Bryant, R. A., & Felmingham, K. L. (2014). Interaction of noradrenaline and cortisol predicts negative intrusive memories in posttraumatic stress disorder. *Neurobiology of Learning and Memory, 112*, pp.204-211.

****

TOPIC 2: ETIOLOGY OF ABNORMAL PSYCHOLOGY

Content 6: Explanations for disorder(s) – Post-traumatic stress disorder (PTSD)
Cognitive.

Key study 6.4: *Beck & Haigh (2014). Advances in Cognitive Theory and Therapy: the Generic Cognitive Model.*

See above, under **TOPIC 2: ETIOLOGY OF ABNORMAL PSYCHOLOGY,** *Content 5: Explanations for disorders - MDD. Cognitive.* This study may also be used for discussing PTSD.

****

PSYCHOLOGY SORTED: KEY RESEARCH FOR STUDENTS AND TEACHERS
BOOK 2 – APPLIED PSYCHOLOGY

TOPIC 2: ETIOLOGY OF ABNORMAL PSYCHOLOGY

Content 6: Explanations for disorder(s) – Post-traumatic stress disorder (PTSD)
Cognitive.

Key study 6.5: *El Leithy et al. (2006). Counterfactual thinking and posttraumatic stress reactions.*

Brief Summary
Pre-occupation with alternative outcomes after trauma (counter-factual thinking) was positively correlated with the continuation of post-traumatic stress.

Aim
To investigate the extent to which counterfactual thinking can be distinguished from general rumination (thinking over a problem or issue) and whether a detailed examination of its different aspects might provide insights into the process of adjustment to a trauma

Participants
46 people (37 male; 9 female) who had been victims of physical assault 3-15 months prior to the start of the investigation. The participants had all been treated at a hospital in London.

Procedure
The participants answered a series of questions during an interview with a researcher, comprising the following:

- **Impact of events scale:** this measure is designed to assess the psychological consequences of traumatic events in terms of how much distress the participant has experienced over the previous week.
- **World assumptions scale:** this is a list of 32 statements which measures the assumptions made by an individual as to their beliefs regarding trauma and threat.
- **Thought control questionnaire:** this assesses the ways in which each individual uses strategy to control their thoughts about their recovery from trauma.
- **Thought-listing tasks:** these tasks were used to generate data on the availability of counterfactual thoughts regarding the assault. Participants were asked to list as many words as they could that begin with each of the letters F, A and S in one minute. Participants were then asked to generate in the same way different types of thoughts or behavioural plans to complete specific sentence stems relating to trauma.

Results
The researchers found that a critical consideration of the situation/issue is the basic response strategy used by participants when distressing or unpleasant thoughts occur to them. Responding to unpleasant thoughts by actively reappraising them and testing the reality of those thoughts was associated with greater ease in generating counterfactual thoughts soon after the assault but fewer counterfactual thoughts long-term. Strategies aimed at interrupting unpleasant emotional states by

focusing on other negative thoughts or through "thought stopping," were not associated with improvement and may be associated with continued counterfactual thinking.

Conclusion
Counterfactual thinking may play a complex role in posttraumatic stress reactions.

Evaluation of El Leithy et al. (2006)
Strengths
- ✓ The study used a naturalistic sample, comprising people who had a broad range of experiences with differing degrees of adjustment from the trauma.
- ✓ The use of a range of different measures means that the researchers were able to compare the responses across the different measures which should ensure reliability.

Limitations
- X The participants were not assessed during the first three months after their trauma which excludes some potentially crucial data which could have been gathered early on in the participants' experiences of the assault.
- X The small sample size and gender imbalance limits the generalisability of the findings.

Reference
El Leithy, S., Brown, G. P., & Robbins, I. (2006). Counterfactual thinking and posttraumatic stress reactions. *Journal of Abnormal Psychology, 115*(3), pp.629-635.

****

TOPIC 2: ETIOLOGY OF ABNORMAL PSYCHOLOGY

Content 6: Explanations for disorder(s) – Post-traumatic stress disorder (PTSD) *Cognitive.*

Key study 6.6: *Wild et al. (2016). A prospective study of pre-trauma risk factors for post-traumatic stress disorder and depression.*

Brief Summary
Conducted a study into paramedics to identify which risk factors best predicted future PTSD or MDD. Found that participants at risk of developing episodes of PTSD or depression could be identified within the first week of paramedic training, using cognitive predictors.

Aim
To identify a range of risk factors that might influence the development of post-traumatic stress disorder (PTSD) or major depressive disorder (MDD) and which might successfully be treated with resilience interventions.

Participants
453 trainee paramedics who had just started a three-year training course with the London Ambulance service. This was an opportunity sample as the researchers approached all of the trainees at the beginning of the course and asked which of them were interested in taking part in the study.

Procedure
The researchers used a range of measures – known as predictor variables as these measures are designed to assess an individual's propensity to develop PTSD and MDD – throughout the course. Every 4 months, participants completed questionnaires which assessed their exposure to trauma and a questionnaire which assessed the degree of their potential symptoms for PTSD and/or MDD. If a participant responded in a way that suggested they had been exposed to a stressful event, they were assessed by interview for PTSD and MDD.

At 12 and 24 months, all participants were interviewed to identify any further exposure to stressful events and PTSD or MDD during the past year and whether or not they had received treatment. They also completed a set of questionnaires assessing burn-out (i.e. physical, emotional and psychological overload and strain), days off work, their weight, any insomnia and their overall quality of life.

Results
8.3% participants (a significant result) had experienced PTSD, and 10.6% had experienced MDD to the point that they felt extreme distress which interfered with their ability to function on a day-to-day basis. At 2-year follow-up these participants reported more days off work, poorer sleep, greater burn-out, lower quality of life and greater weight gain (PTSD only), indicating that episodes of PTSD and MD are predictive of long-term poorer well-being and physical health. Participants at risk of developing an episode of PTSD or depression were identified within the first week of their paramedic training programme. The strongest risk factors for developing PTSD and MDD were attributional style (i.e. how you explain the causes of events and what has happened to you), maladaptive post-traumatic cognitions (i.e. going over the trauma constantly using negative thought patterns), avoidant coping (i.e. not facing the problem, pretending it didn't happen), neuroticism (i.e. feelings of anxiety, worry, fear, anger, frustration, envy, guilt) and low social support.

Conclusion
There is a real need for adequate support for emergency workers who are exposed to potentially traumatic events and who may be prone to developing PTSD and MD.

Evaluation of Wild et al. (2016)
Strengths
- ✓ The study is high in ecological validity as the participants were reporting real symptoms of real-life events over a number of years.
- ✓ The use of a range of different measures means that the researchers were able to compare the responses across the different measures which should ensure reliability.

Limitations
- The researchers assessed alcohol, drug and tobacco use at the beginning of the study and at the 2-year follow-up, but they did not assess daily exercise or caffeine consumption, which could have had an impact of mental and physical health of the participants.
- The use of an opportunity sample from a specific geographical location limits the generalisability of the findings.

Reference
Wild, J., Smith, K. V., Thompson, E., Béar, F., Lommen, M. J. J., & Ehlers, A. (2016). A prospective study of pre-trauma risk factors for post-traumatic stress disorder and depression. *Psychological Medicine*, *46*(12), pp.2571-2582.

****

TOPIC 2: ETIOLOGY OF ABNORMAL PSYCHOLOGY

Content 6: Explanations for disorder(s) – Post-traumatic stress disorder (PTSD)
Sociocultural.

Key study 6.7: *Silva et al. (2000). Stress and Vulnerability to Posttraumatic Stress Disorder in Children and Adolescents*

Brief Summary
Investigated a stress-diathesis model of interaction between experiences and pre-existing vulnerability that contribute to the development of post-traumatic stress disorder (PTSD) in children and adolescents.

Aim
To investigate experiences and interacting vulnerabilities that contribute to PTSD syndrome after exposure to a source of stress. Four questions relating to a stress-diathesis model were asked:

1. Do different types of trauma vary in their potential for producing PTSD symptoms?
2. Are different symptoms of PTSD equally likely to develop?
3. Do pre-existing clinical conditions moderate the severity of the PTSD?
4. Do factors such as age, gender, or IQ modify the development of PTSD?

Participants
59 children and adolescents (ages 3 to 18 years, 39 male and 20 female) identified as having experienced a traumatic event were selected from 100 consecutive referrals to a children's psychiatric unit. The participants' demographic characteristics reflected those of the psychiatric clinic: 47% were Hispanic, 46% African American, 5% Caucasian and 2% Asian American.

Procedure
The evaluation was based on approximately 6 hours of semi-structured interviews with parents and children, using the PTSD module of the Children's Structured Clinical Interview for DSM-IV. Cognitive and IQ tests were administered separately by a clinical psychologist. Demographic and

clinical variables included age, gender, ethnicity, premature birth, and factors such as anxiety, depression, aggression, and sleep disorders in the child/young person.

Results
Children who experienced traumatic events were assigned to three outcome groups:
1. Those with no symptoms of PTSD (N=27).
2. Those with subthreshold PTSD, who had symptoms of PTSD but did not show evidence of the required number for a DSM-IV diagnosis (N=19).
3. Those who met the full criteria for PTSD (N=13).

There were no differences in age, gender or ethnicity that were associated with the severity of the reaction to the traumatic event. Higher IQ appeared to be a protective factor against developing PTSD. 21% of those who were physically abused, 15% of those who reported being sexually abused, and 17% of those who witnessed domestic violence developed PTSD.

Witnessing domestic violence or being physically abused predicted severity of PTSD. Children with pre-existing aggressive behaviour were more likely to be victims of subsequent physical abuse and those with pre-existing anxiety were more likely to develop severe PTSD.

Conclusion
The results suggest that pre-existing conditions and individual cognitive factors interact in reaction to extreme stressors to differentially affect the level of PTSD. The strongest predictor of resilience was the child's IQ, but because low IQ may reflect early deprivation or even brain damage, the exact mechanism of protection is unclear. Witnessing serious domestic violence (usually against the mother) was a powerful predictor of PTSD. A vulnerable anxious child exposed to serious domestic violence is most at risk of developing PTSD and therefore identification of a child at risk in a violent home situation is important.

Evaluation
Strengths
- ✓ Standardised testing was used, adding to the reliability of the findings.
- ✓ DSM-IV criteria were used to identify PTSD, with the difference between subthreshold and diagnosed PTSD carefully defined, again adding to the reliability.

Limitations
- X This is a small sample of children and adolescents from one inner-city US psychiatric facility and cannot therefore be generalised beyond similar facilities in similar cities, and samples with the same demographic characteristics.
- X Standardised testing and semi-structured interviews are self-report methods, and so are subject to misremembering and social desirability bias, which may limit their validity.

Reference
Silva, R.R., Alpert, M., Munoz, D.M., Singh, S., Matzner, F. & Dummit, S. (2000). Stress and vulnerability to posttraumatic stress disorder in children and adolescents. *American Journal of Psychiatry, 157*(8), pp.1229–1235.

****

PSYCHOLOGY SORTED: KEY RESEARCH FOR STUDENTS AND TEACHERS
BOOK 2 – APPLIED PSYCHOLOGY

TOPIC 2: ETIOLOGY OF ABNORMAL PSYCHOLOGY

Content 6: Explanations for disorder(s) – Post-traumatic stress disorder (PTSD)
Sociocultural.

Key study 6.8: *Kilpatrick et al. (2003). Violence and risk of PTSD, major depression, substance abuse/dependence, and comorbidity: results from the National Survey of Adolescents.*

Links to
- **Abnormal Psychology: Explanations for disorders** - Sociocultural etiology of PTSD.

Brief Summary
Exposure to interpersonal violence (i.e. physical assault, sexual assault, or witnessed violence) increases the risk of PTSD and of comorbidity with a major depressive episode (MDE) and/or substance abuse or dependence SA/D).

Aim
To investigate the prevalence, comorbidity, risk and protective factors associated with adolescent PTSD, MDE, SA/D. The researchers hypothesised that adolescents who had been exposed to interpersonal violence would be more at risk from these disorders.

Participants
4,023 adolescents aged between 12 and 17 years old (2,002 male; 1,904 female). The researchers used stratified sampling methods which produced a representative sample of adolescents from the U.S.A.

Procedure
The researchers conducted structured interviews by telephone which asked each participant about his/her family background, school, trauma history (e.g., sexual assault, physical assault), and their experience of PTSD, MDE and SA/D (whether they had used specific substances e.g. alcohol, drugs or witnessed their use within their families). The interview used closed-ended questions, most of which elicited either a "yes" or "no", or other one-word or phrase answers.

Results
15.5% of boys and 19.3% of girls had at least one of the identified disorders – PTSD, MDE or SA/D. Almost 75% all adolescents diagnosed with PTSD had at least one comorbid diagnosis (i.e. they had been diagnosed with another disorder as well). Being the victim of or witnessing interpersonal violence increased the risk of developing the disorders identified and of being comorbid. SA/D was identified in 8.2% of boys and 6.2% of girls. Older adolescents (aged 15-17) were more likely to show SA/D (10.3% of girls and 15.2% of boys).

The researchers found that their hypothesis that interpersonal violence would be associated with increased risk of PTSD, MDE, and SA/D was supported by the results.

Conclusion
A high percentage of American adolescents experience traumatic events and as a consequence suffer significant emotional responses associated with these events which may in turn contribute to PTSD, MDE, and SA/D.

Evaluation of Kilpatrick et al. (2003)
Strengths
- ✓ The researchers were careful to protect their participants by asking them if it was safe to talk on the phone to them: the use of the closed questions also meant that if the participants were overheard during the interview, they would not be revealing any sensitive information.
- ✓ The use of a structured interview means that the data is easily converted into statistics which can be analysed and compared.

Limitations
- X The researchers point out that their study would have benefited from using a longitudinal design as a one-off collection of data is less meaningful than data gathered over time.
- X The use of 'yes/no' responses means that the interviews lacked depth or detail which was perhaps a missed opportunity that the researchers could have used to gather more insightful data.

Reference
Kilpatrick, D. G., Ruggiero, K. J., Acierno, R., Saunders, B. E., Resnick, H. S., & Best, C. L. (2003). Violence and risk of PTSD, major depression, substance abuse/dependence, and comorbidity: results from the National Survey of Adolescents. *Journal of Consulting and Clinical Psychology, 71*(4), pp.692-700.

****

TOPIC 2: ETIOLOGY OF ABNORMAL PSYCHOLOGY

Content 6: Explanations for disorder(s) – Post-traumatic stress disorder (PTSD) *Sociocultural.*

Key study 6.9: *Bryant et al. (2016). Mental health and social networks after disaster.*

See above, under **TOPIC 2: ETIOLOGY OF ABNORMAL PSYCHOLOGY,** Content 5: Explanations for disorders - MDD. Sociocultural. This study may also be used for discussing PTSD.

****

PSYCHOLOGY SORTED: KEY RESEARCH FOR STUDENTS AND TEACHERS
BOOK 2 – APPLIED PSYCHOLOGY

TOPIC 2: ETIOLOGY OF ABNORMAL PSYCHOLOGY

Content 7: Prevalence rates and disorder(s). Major depressive disorder (MDD).

Key study 7.1: *Levav et al. (1997). Vulnerability of Jews to Affective Disorders.*

Links to
- **Abnormal Psychology: Explanations for disorders** - sociocultural etiology of depression.

Brief Summary
The researchers explored the relationships between religion, gender, alcoholism, and major depression. Found that Jewish males had significantly higher rates of major depression (MDD), but lower rates of alcoholism, than Catholics, Protestants, and all non-Jews combined. This links diagnosis to prevalence.

Aim
To examine previous claims that Jews are at higher risk for affective mental health disorders than members of other groups.

Procedure
The researchers analysed data from a NIMH Epidemiological Catchment Area (ECA) study in Los Angeles and New Haven, Connecticut, to investigate the above claims and also to investigate any correlations between gender, alcoholism and major depression. The calculated rates were weighted according to the 1980 U.S. population census. Female-to-male rate ratios and rates of alcohol abuse/dependence were also obtained.

Results
While Jewish females had the same rates of MDD as Catholic, Protestant and all non-Jewish females, Jewish males had significantly higher rates of major depression than male Catholics, Protestants, and all non-Jewish males combined. This means that, instead of women having a higher prevalence of MDD than males, as is usual in the non-Jewish population, Jewish males and females had the same rate of MDD. Rates of alcohol abuse/dependence were negatively correlated with MDD.

Conclusion
The results support only in part the earlier reports that Jews have higher rates of MDD. The equal gender distribution of MDD among Jews may be associated with the lower rate of alcoholism among Jewish males, the inference being that depression triggers non-Jewish males to drink alcohol, rather than visit the doctor.

Evaluation of Levav et al. (1997)
Strengths
- ✓ The calculated rates of MDD were weighted according to the 1980 US population census, meaning that they can be generalised to the US Jewish population.
- ✓ Rates of alcoholism were also examined, which gives a possible explanation for the higher diagnosed MDD amongst Jewish males and increases the explanatory capacity of the study.

Limitations
- X This finding is limited to the US, though other studies in Israel and in the UK have provided supporting evidence. More extensive research is called for.
- X This study relied on the respondents' definition of their religious affiliation, and so Jews who do not identify with their religion may have been included in the other non-Jewish groups.
- X The structured interview method is a self-report method, and so the responses may have been subject t participant bias.

Reference
Levav, I.L., Kohn, R., Golding, J. M. & Weissman, M.M. (1997). Vulnerability of Jews to affective disorders, *American Journal of Psychiatry, 154* (7), pp.941-947.

****

TOPIC 2: ETIOLOGY OF ABNORMAL PSYCHOLOGY

Content 7: Prevalence rates and disorder(s). Major depressive disorder (MDD).

Key study 7.2: *Hankin & Abramson (2001). Development of gender differences in depression: An elaborated cognitive vulnerability–transactional stress theory.*

See above, under **TOPIC 2: ETIOLOGY OF ABNORMAL PSYCHOLOGY,** *Content 5: Explanations for disorders - MDD. Cognitive.* This study may also be used for discussing prevalence rates.

****

TOPIC 2: ETIOLOGY OF ABNORMAL PSYCHOLOGY

Content 7: Prevalence rates and disorder(s). Major depressive disorder (MDD).

Key study 7.3: *World Health Organization (2017). Depression and other common mental disorders. Global health estimates.*

Brief Summary
Global health estimates of depression and other common mental disorders: reliable estimates of the proportion of a global or a regional population affected by depression is necessary for effective health policy.

Aim
To provide a global prevalence rate for depression (and other mental disorders).

Summary

- The proportion of the global population suffering from depression in 2015 was estimated to be 4.4%.

- Depression was more common among females (5.1%) than males (3.6%).

- Prevalence rates varied by age, peaking in older adulthood (above 7.5% among females aged 55-74 years, and above 5.5% among males).

- The total estimated number of people living with depression increased by 18.4% between 2005 and 2015

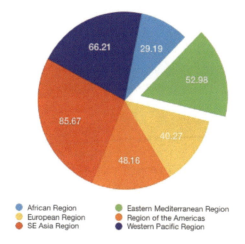

Cases of MDD in millions by WHO region, 2015 (Total 322M). Chart created from WHO statistics.

Conclusion

The increase in numbers reflects an increase in overall global population, but also a disproportionate increase in the age groups in which depression Is most common. Although depression can and does affect people of all ages, from all walks of life, the risk of becoming depressed is increased by poverty, unemployment, life events such as the death of a loved one or a relationship break-up, physical illness and problems caused by alcohol and drug use.

Evaluation of WHO (2017)
Strengths
- ✓ The data is high in reliability as the data is collected from worldwide epidemiology studies using agreed diagnoses of depression.
- ✓ It gives a useful, large-scale comparison of prevalence rates between countries and regions.

Limitations
- X Apart from suggesting that much of the increase observed between 2005 and 2015 is due to population increase, the study suggests no reasons for this increase in depression.

Reference
World Health Organisation (2017). *Depression and Other Common Mental Disorders. Global Health Estimates.* Geneva: WHO

****

TOPIC 2: ETIOLOGY OF ABNORMAL PSYCHOLOGY

Content 8: Prevalence rates and disorder(s). Post-traumatic stress disorder (PTSD).

Key study 8.1: *Mueser et al. (1998). Trauma and Post-traumatic Stress Disorder in Severe Mental Illness.*

Brief Summary
Discovered that several severe mental disorders had a comorbidity with PTSD. Their findings were that 43% of their sample had symptoms that fitted a diagnosis of PTSD, though only 2% had actually been diagnosed with this. This has implications for prevalence rates of PTSD.

Aim
To investigate lifetime occurrences of traumatic events and PTSD in a sample of people already diagnosed with severe mental disorders.

Participants
275 patients aged 18-60 already diagnosed with severe mental disorders, such as schizophrenia and bipolar disorder, who were receiving care through the public mental health services in New Hampshire and Maryland, USA. One-third of the sample was in-patients and two-thirds were out-patients. 56% were female and 44% male.

Procedure
All questionnaires were administered through trained interviewers at the hospitals and clinics that the patients were attending. Lifetime exposure to traumatic events was assessed with the Trauma History Questionnaire and selected items from the Community Violence Scale and PTSD was assessed with the PTSD checklist.

Results
98% of the patients reported exposure to at least one traumatic event over their lives, with patients experiencing an average of 3.5 different types of traumatic events (counting events that occurred in childhood and adulthood separately). Women were more likely to have experienced sexual abuse as a child (35% in men, 52% in women), and sexual abuse as an adult (26% in men, 64% in women). Men were more likely to have been attacked with a weapon (49% in men, 36% in women) and to have witnessed a killing or serious injury to another as an adult (43% in men, 24% in women). Gender differences in the other types of traumatic events were not significant.

43% of the sample had symptoms that fit a diagnosis of PTSD, though only 2% had actually been diagnosed with this. The rate of PTSD was highest in patients with depression (58%), and lowest in patients with schizophrenia (28%).

Conclusion
Considering that at the time of this study, the prevalence of PTSD in the general population was estimated at 8-9% this suggests that patients with severe mental illness are at increased risk for having PTSD, in line with their increased reported exposure to traumatic events. Comorbidity of PTSD and other mental disorders is high.

Clearly the incidence of PTSD is under-diagnosed in those with severe mental disorders, with only 2% of the sample being diagnosed with PTSD. This has implications for the prevalence rate of PTSD and, even more importantly, for assessment and management of their disorders.

Evaluation of Mueser et al. (1998)

Strengths
- ✓ The study generates valuable questions regarding the validity of statistics on prevalence rates for disorders. Co-morbidity can artificially lower the prevalence for PTSD amongst those already diagnosed with another disorder
- ✓ The use of standardized questions and participants with a diversity of different mental disorders should increase the replicability of the study and the reliability of the results.

Limitations
- X Retrospective self-reporting of traumas makes it impossible to identify the causal relationship between PTSD and other disorders: trauma and PTSD, especially at an early age, may increase vulnerability to the development of other disorders. Alternatively, persons with disoders such as depression might be more likely to remember past traumatic experiences and their effects, leading to PTSD symptoms that are at least partly secondary to other psychiatric symptoms.
- X Self-report methods, even using trained interviewers and standardised questioning, can be subject to participant bias.
- X The use of samples from specific USA geographical locations limits the generalisability of the findings.

Reference
Mueser, K.D., Goodman, L. B., Trumbetta, S. L., Rosenberg, S.D., Osher, F.C., Vidaver, R., Auciello, P. & Foy, D.W. (1998). Trauma and post-traumatic stress disorder in severe mental illness, *Journal of Consulting and Clinical Psychology, 66* (3), pp. 493-499.

****

TOPIC 2: ETIOLOGY OF ABNORMAL PSYCHOLOGY

Content 8: Prevalence rates and disorder(s). Post-traumatic stress disorder (PTSD).

Key study 8.2: *Kilpatrick et al. (2003). Violence and risk of PTSD, major depression, substance abuse/dependence, and comorbidity: results from the National Survey of Adolescents.*

See above, under **TOPIC 2: ETIOLOGY OF ABNORMAL PSYCHOLOGY,** *Content 6: Explanations for disorders - PTSD. Sociocultural.* This study may also be used for discussing prevalence rates.

****

PSYCHOLOGY SORTED: KEY RESEARCH FOR STUDENTS AND TEACHERS
BOOK 2 – APPLIED PSYCHOLOGY

TOPIC 2: ETIOLOGY OF ABNORMAL PSYCHOLOGY

Content 8: Prevalence rates and disorder(s). Post-traumatic stress disorder (PTSD).

Key study 8.3: *World Health Organization (2017). Depression and other common mental disorders. Global health estimates.*

See above, under **TOPIC 2: ETIOLOGY OF ABNORMAL PSYCHOLOGY,** *Content 7: Prevalence rates and disorder(s) - PTSD.* This study may also be used for discussing the prevalence rate of PTSD.

PTSD figures are included as part of the statistics for anxiety disorders, including generalised anxiety disorder (GAD), panic disorder, phobias, social anxiety disorder and obsessive-compulsive disorder (OCD). This again shows how problematic it can be to obtain reliable figures for one disorder.

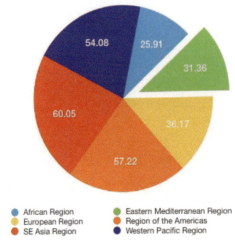

Cases of anxiety disorder in millions by WHO region (Total 264M) Chart created from WHO statistics.

****

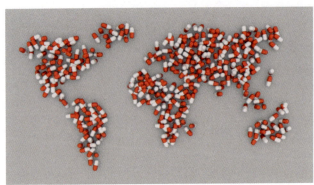

Mental disorders are a worldwide issue

PSYCHOLOGY SORTED: KEY RESEARCH FOR STUDENTS AND TEACHERS
BOOK 2 – APPLIED PSYCHOLOGY

TOPIC 2: ETIOLOGY OF ABNORMAL PSYCHOLOGY

Critical thinking points

When faced with an array of extraneous variables, is it possible to draw meaningful conclusions about a biological basis to mental illness?

Recent advances in science means that mental illness can now be investigated from a biological perspective much more closely and accurately than in decades and centuries past. From the use of brain-imaging technologies to DNA and hormone profiling, gaining access to what is going on inside the body is now easier than it has ever been. Research by Caspi et al. (2003) found that having two short alleles in the 5HTT transporter gene is linked to more depressive symptoms being reported in response to stressful life events than other allele combinations. Participants with two long alleles reported fewer depression symptoms. Participants with one or two short alleles who had been mistreated (e.g. abused or neglected) as children had scores that could be used to predict depression in adulthood. The fact that these biological findings were used in conjunction with self-reported stressors means that they do not offer a purely biological explanation of depression: it is impossible to know whether the short-allele participants had simply been prone to more stressors in life than the other groups in the study; it also possible that these depressed participants were simply more predisposed to depression because of their personality type or because they chose to over-report or possibly to invent their life stressors on the questionnaire. Building on this idea, Risch et al. (2009) found that there was a significant association between stressful life events such as bereavement or job loss with depression, which is a sociocultural explanation of depression. Furthermore, they did not find a biological association between depression and the 5HTT gene and no interaction was found between stressful life events and the 5HTT gene. Until technology advances even more it is still not possible to be absolutely confident that depression has a purely biological aetiology.

The depressed woman: a self-fulfilling prophecy?

Art, literature, history, psychiatry, are littered with examples of the 'depressed/hysterical' woman e.g. Picasso's weeping woman; Freud's writing on Dora and other 'hysterical' Viennese female patients; female Suffragists being depicted as out-of-control lunatics. As most of the history of the world/art/literature/politics has been written by (and mainly about) men, the telling of these tales has been biased: this is still true to some extent in the 21st century, with women being diagnosed and treated differently than men in terms of mental illness. As Hankin & Abramson's (2001) research points out, there is a gender imbalance in depression prevalence between girls and boys e.g. girls are far more likely than boys to develop depressive symptoms around the age of 13; girls tend to experience higher levels of anxiety and eating disorders than boys do. The higher levels of depression experienced by girls also contribute to the triggering of negative events which means that there is a bi-directional relationship between the two. Findings like this, although to some extent useful, are also responsible for perpetuating the idea that girls are more 'sensitive' and 'vulnerable' than boys, thus they may be viewed as weaker and less resilient perhaps. Similarly, Brown & Harris (1978) published research on depression that only included women as their participants, and which goes some way to presenting women as being more vulnerable to depression than men. Reading over Brown & Harris's findings one might conclude, 'I'm female, and therefore I must be depressed'. Which is depressing all round.

Comorbidity complicating the issue.
Kilpatrick et al. (2003) investigated how exposure to interpersonal violence (i.e. physical assault, sexual assault, or witnessed violence) increases the risk of PTSD and of comorbidity with a major depressive episode and/or substance abuse or dependence. Almost 75% all adolescents diagnosed with PTSD had at least one comorbid diagnosis (i.e. they had been diagnosed with another disorder as well). Findings such as this one means that treating PTSD becomes a complex and multi-layered procedure because if a patient is severely depressed, anxious or even psychotic in response to the trauma then one treatment which should on the surface suit PTSD may not be appropriate for their other conditions/disorders. It may be difficult for doctors to ascertain which symptoms are purely PTSD, which symptoms are shared between disorders and which symptoms are evidence of something else entirely. Mueser et al. (1998) discovered that several severe mental disorders had a comorbidity with PTSD (43% of their sample had symptoms that fitted a diagnosis of PTSD, though only 2% had actually been diagnosed with this). Clearly the incidence of PTSD is under-diagnosed in those with severe mental disorders which has implications for the prevalence rate of PTSD and, even more importantly, for assessment and management of their disorders. It is vital that PTSD be recognised in its early stages as it can lead to the development of other disorders if left undiagnosed and untreated.

****

Depressed woman - unfair stereotype or self-fulfilling prophecy?

TOPIC 3: TREATMENTS FOR DISORDERS

Key Idea: Treatments vary according to beliefs in etiology and according to culture.

Content 9: Treatments. Major depressive disorder (MDD)
Biomedical treatment (Biological)

KEY STUDY 9.1: *Kroenke et al. (2001). Similar Effectiveness of Paroxetene, Fluoxetene, and Sertralene in Primary Care.*

Brief Summary
Although selective serotonin reuptake inhibitors are the most common treatment for depression, it is not known whether one is more effective than another. This study used a randomized trial design to compare the effectiveness of three common SSRIs and found that all were equally effective in treating MDD.

Aim
To compare the effectiveness of three SSRIs (paroxetine, fluoxetine and sertraline) in treating MDD, using a large-scale randomized clinical trial.

Participants
573 depressed adult patients, from 37 clinics whose main physicians thought they would benefit from anti-depressants. The mean age was 46 years (range 18-96) and 79% were women. The ethnic distribution was 84% white, 13% black and 3% other.

Procedure
Participants completed a baseline assessment over the telephone and were randomly assigned to receive one of the SSRIs for 9 months. Physicians were allowed to change their patient to another SSRI if they had a bad response, or if they did not improve at all, when taking the one to which they were originally assigned.

At 1, 3, 6 and 9 months each participant completed a 36 item Mental Component Summary Score health scale with standardised questions and also multiple measures of, for example, social and work functioning, physical functioning, sleep, memory and pain.

Results
79% of participants completed all measurements for the whole 9 months. All participants improved similarly, by a mean of between 15 and 17 points on the health scale, and those in each group had similar rates of side-effects and discontinuation. In the entire sample, the % of patients who met criteria for MDD dropped from 74% at baseline (others had less severe depression at baseline) to 32% at 3 months and 26% at 9 months.

Conclusion
This showed that paroxetine, fluoxetine and sertraline were similar in effectiveness for treatment of MDD over a 9-month period.

Evaluation of Kroenke et al (2001)

Strengths
- ✓ Outcomes were measured 4 times during treatment, giving a comprehensive longitudinal assessment through telephone interview using standardised questions to reduce researcher bias and improve reliability.
- ✓ Drop-out rate was very small.
- ✓ Patients were from multiple clinics across the USA, which increases the generalisability of the findings.

Limitations
- X The interviewers were not blinded to the group, and so knew which SSRI the participant was receiving.
- X The relationship of any participant with their main prescribing physician is an uncontrolled variable and may have impacted the drop-out rate.

Reference
Kroenke, K., West, S.I., Swindle, R., Gilseman, A., Eckert, G.J., Dolor, R., Stang, P....& Weinberger, M. (2001). Similar Effectiveness of Paroxetene, Fluoxetine, and Sertralene in Primary Care. *JAMA, 286* (23), pp.2947-2955.

****

TOPIC 3: TREATMENTS FOR DISORDERS

Content 9: Treatments. Major depressive disorder (MDD)
Biomedical treatment (Biological)

KEY STUDY 9.2: *Kirsch et al. (2008). Initial severity and antidepressant benefits: a meta-analysis of data submitted to the Food and Drug Administration.*

Brief Summary
Drug–placebo differences in antidepressant effectiveness increase with more severe MDD, but are relatively small even for this group. The increase is attributable to decreased responsiveness to placebo among very severely depressed patients, rather than to increased responsiveness to medication.

Aim
To examine the efficacy of four types of antidepressant medication compared to the use of placebos in clinical trials.

Procedure
The researchers conducted a meta-analysis of 35 clinical trials for the antidepressants fluoxetine, venlafaxine, nefazodone and paroxetine. These trials had been submitted to the US Food and Drug Administration (FDA). The findings involved a total of 5,133 patients, 3,292 of whom had been randomly allocated the medication and 1,841 of whom had been randomly allocated a placebo.

Main comments and findings

- The findings (including data that had previously been unpublished) showed that overall the effect of the antidepressants does not reach the threshold criteria to be able to claim statistical significance i.e. the antidepressant medication was found to be ineffective in the trials studied in the meta-analysis.
- It was found that the efficacy of the antidepressants studied only reached a statistically significant level with the most severely depressed patients and that this was due to a decrease in response to the placebo rather than the antidepressant medication having an increased beneficial effect.
- There appears to be a link between early severe symptoms of depression and effective treatment from antidepressants although this does not increase with time i.e. the treatment may show early promise but this may tail off after some time.
- Moderately depressed and severely depressed patients showed a 'substantial' response to treatment using a placebo and this was even true for patients with extremely severe levels of depression.
- Moderately depressed and extremely depressed patients showed overall less improvement from antidepressant medication than patients who were categorised as being at the lower end of the 'severely depressed' scale.

Conclusion

Antidepressants and placebos used in the treatment of depression bring about relatively small benefits, even for those patients diagnosed as severely depressed.

Evaluation of Kirsch et al. (2008)

Strengths

- ✓ The study's findings suggest that the widespread prescribing of antidepressants in the USA may not actually be addressing the needs of depressed patients.
- ✓ The use of a meta-analysis means that the data can be analysed using statistical methods and the findings displayed graphically which makes for a clear and straightforward view of the findings as a whole.

Limitations

- X The researchers point out that the FDA data did not include examples of clinical trials with patients who reported initially severe depression symptoms and only one study was used with moderately depressed patients which means that the data may be biased due to its incompleteness.
- X Treating depression is a complex and multi-layered process which cannot be fully explored in a 'cold' method such as a meta-analysis.

Reference

Kirsch, I., Deacon, B. J., Huedo-Medina, T. B., Scoboria, A., Moore, T. J., & Johnson, B. T. (2008). Initial severity and antidepressant benefits: a meta-analysis of data submitted to the Food and Drug Administration. *PLoS medicine*, *5*(2), e45.

****

TOPIC 3: TREATMENTS FOR DISORDERS

Content 9: Treatments. Major depressive disorder (MDD)
Biomedical treatment (Biological)

KEY STUDY 9.3: *Singh et al. (2016). A double-blind, randomized, placebo-controlled, dose-frequency study of intravenous ketamine in patients with treatment-resistant depression.*

Brief Summary
Double-blind study evaluating the effectiveness of ketamine for MDD that had resisted previous treatment. Found intravenous ketamine to be equally effective at treating depression, as measured after 15 days of the trial, whether administered twice or three times weekly. In both cases it was significantly more effective than a placebo.

Aim
To assess the effectiveness of ketamine (administered via intravenous drip) two or three times a week on patients with depression on whom other treatments had proved ineffective.

Participants
67 adults aged 18-64 years old (45 female; 22 male) from the USA who had been diagnosed with MDD.

Procedure
The researchers used a randomised double-blind procedure which meant that the researchers, the patients and anyone else connected to the study were 'blind' (i.e. unaware of which condition each participant had been randomly assigned to). The conditions were:

- Intravenous administration of ketamine two or three times a week over a four-week period.
- Intravenous administration of a placebo two or three times a week over a four-week period.

The patients were asked to refrain from eating for 8 hours before the onset of the drug administration and to wait for an additional 2 hours after having received the drug before resuming eating. Blood samples were taken at the start and end of the testing phase to measure the levels of ketamine in the blood per patient. Each patient filled in a questionnaire designed to measure the degree of their depression throughout the study's duration.

Results
The depression scores for the ketamine condition showed improvement compared to the placebo condition, with ketamine appearing to enhance the effect of antidepressants and to lessen the severity of symptoms. By day 29 of the testing phase most patients in the placebo group had dropped out because they did not feel any benefit from the treatment.

Conclusion
The intravenous administration of ketamine either twice or thrice weekly can prove effective in enhancing the effects of antidepressants in patients who have shown resistance to other forms of treatment.

Evaluation of Singh et al. (2016)
Strengths
- ✓ This is a highly controlled study with effective use of the double-blind procedure which minimises possible researcher bias.
- ✓ The finding that by day 29 most of the placebo group had dropped out serves to strengthen the study design and to validate the findings.

Limitations
- X The sample is small and is gender-biased, having more females than males.
- X Participant variables may have confounded the results, particularly as this was an independent groups design: the participants in the ketamine condition may have reported improved depression scores for reasons other than the effects of ketamine.

Reference
Singh, J. B., Fedgchin, M., Daly, E. J., De Boer, P., Cooper, K., Lim, P., ... & Kurian, B. (2016). A double-blind, randomized, placebo-controlled, dose-frequency study of intravenous ketamine in patients with treatment-resistant depression. *American Journal of Psychiatry*, *173*(8), pp.816-826.

****

TOPIC 3: TREATMENTS FOR DISORDERS

Content 9: Treatments. Major depressive disorder (MDD)
Psychological treatment (Cognitive)

KEY STUDY 9.4: Beck (2005). The Current Sate of Cognitive Therapy. A Forty Year Retrospective.

Background
Cognitive behavioural therapy (CBT) as treatment for major depressive disorder. Review of the last 40 years of CBT.

Links
Cognitive approach: schema theory – role of negative schemas.
Abnormal psychology: etiology of disorders - cognitive explanations.

Aim
To review progress in the development of CBT and in the empirical testing of this.

Procedure
Summary of a review of 15 meta-analyses of 332 studies of treatment outcomes of CBT for MDD, between 1967 and 2003.

Results
Large effect sizes were found for CBT as a treatment for MDD, in comparison with placebo. CBT was found to be equal or superior to antidepressant medication, in treating symptoms, and superior when it came to relapse, with fewer patients treated with CBT suffering relapse. Short-term CBT after long-term antidepressant medication also showed a significant reduction in the recurrence of depression.

Conclusion
CBT can be recommended as a treatment for mild/moderate depression, and in combination with antidepressant medication for severe depression (MDD).

Evaluation of Beck (2005)
Strengths
- ✓ Randomised controlled trials have shown similar outcomes, which adds to the credibility of these statistics.
- ✓ While this summary focused on MDD, it also gave similar statistics for PTSD and other anxiety disorders, suggesting the reliability of research.

Limitations
- X Limitations of the meta-analysis approach are the assumptions of uniformity across the studies in the samples, both in the content of therapy and the approach of therapists.

Reference
Beck, A. T. (2005). The current state of cognitive therapy. A 40-year retrospective. *Archives of General Psychiatry, 62,* pp.953-959.

****

TOPIC 3: TREATMENTS FOR DISORDERS

Content 9: Treatments. Major depressive disorder (MDD)
Psychological treatment (Cognitive)

KEY STUDY 9.5: *Keller et al. (2000). A comparison of Nefazodone, the Cognitive Behavioral-Analysis System of Psychotherapy, and their combination for the treatment of chronic depression.*

Background
Comparison of treatment outcomes between CBT, antidepressants or a combination of both in patients with chronic MDD.

Aim
To compare three different treatment paths for MDD in terms of remission and response to treatment. CBT, antidepressant medication and a combined approach were compared.

Participants
681 adults, of whom 662 attended at least one treatment session and so were included in the results. All participants had a score of at least 20 on the Hamilton Rating Scale for Depression (HRSD), which indicates clinically significant MDD.

Procedure
Participants were randomly assigned to 12 weeks of outpatient treatment with either nefazodone, CBT or both. Remission was defined as a score of 8 or less on the HRSD at weeks 10 and 12, and a satisfactory response was defined as a reduction in the score by at least 50% from their initial assessment and a score of 15 or less. Raters were blind to the patients' treatment group.

Results
Drop-out rates were similar for all 3 groups, and this gave 519 participants at the end of 12 weeks, with rates of response (remission and satisfactory response) of 55% in the nefazodone group, 52% in the CBT group and 85% in the combined-treatment group. Nefazodone produced results within 4 weeks, while CBT had a greater effect by the second part of the study.

Conclusion
The combination of CBT and antidepressant medication is significantly more effective than either treatment alone.

Evaluation of Keller et al. (2000)
Strengths
- ✓ The use of a single-blind design increased reliability, as the raters did not know the treatment group of the participants they interviewed.
- ✓ The HRSD relies on self-report and so is subject to participant bias in the responses.

Limitations
- X A limitation was a lack of a placebo (control) group, though if introduced this may have reduced the number of willing participants.

Reference
Keller, M.B., McCullough, J.P. & Klein, D.N. (2000). A comparison of Nefazodone, the Cognitive Behavioral-Analysis System of Psychotherapy, and their combination for the treatment of chronic depression. *The New England Journal of Medicine, Vol 342,* p. 1462.

****

TOPIC 3: TREATMENTS FOR DISORDERS

Content 9: Treatments. Major depressive disorder (MDD)
Psychological treatment (Cognitive)

KEY STUDY 9.6: *Kuyken et al. (2016). Efficacy of Mindfulness-based Cognitive Therapy in Prevention of Depressive Relapse. An Individual Patient Data Meta-analysis from Randomized Trials.*

Background
Research into the effectiveness of mindfulness-based cognitive therapy (MBCT) in preventing remission in people with recurrent depression.

Aim
To conduct a meta-analysis of patient data to examine the efficacy of MBCT compared with usual care and antidepressants in treating people with recurrent depression.

Participants
1258 patients, 944 (75%) female, with a mean age of 47.1 years described in 9 studies.

Procedure
Meta-analysis of 9 studies of individual patient data, with a total of 1258 participants. Data was gathered on relapse rates within a 60-week follow-up period.

Results
Patients receiving MBCT had a reduced risk of depressive relapse within this period, compared both with those who received no treatment, and those who received antidepressants. MBCT seemed to have a larger effect if the depression was severe. Age, sex, education, and relationship status had no influence on the effectiveness of MBCT. Psychiatric variables, such as age at onset of depression and number of previous episodes of depression also showed no statistically significant interaction with MBCT treatment.

Conclusion
MBCT appears effective as a treatment for relapse prevention for those with recurrent depression, particularly those with more serious symptoms.

Evaluation of Kuyken et al. (2016)
Strengths
- ✓ The comparison with active antidepressant treatment as well as with no treatment increases the validity of the findings.

Limitations

X   Some background variables, such as ethnicity and employment status, were not collected, and may have been relevant. This limits the generalisability of the findings.
X   Studies varied in the way that data was collected, with age at onset of depression being collected in some cases informally through self-report and in other cases through structured clinical interview. This limits the reliability of the results.

Reference

Kuyken, W., Warren, F.C., Taylor, R.S.....et al. (2016). Efficacy of Mindfulness-Based Cognitive Therapy in Prevention of Depressive Relapse. An Individual Patient Data Meta-analysis from Randomized Trials. *JAMA Psychiatry, 73*(6), pp. 565-574.

****

TOPIC 3: TREATMENTS FOR DISORDERS

Content 10: Treatments. Post-traumatic stress disorder (PTSD)
Biomedical treatment (Biological)

KEY STUDY 10.1: *Davidson et al. (2001). Multicenter, double-blind comparison of sertraline and placebo in the treatment of Post-traumatic Stress disorder.*

Background

Because few large trials of treatment for Post-traumatic Stress disorder (PTSD) have been conducted, this research tried to remedy this. Conducted a multicentre, double-blind comparison of sertraline (an SSRI) and a placebo in the treatment of PTSD.

Aim

To compare the efficacy of sertraline and a placebo in the treatment of PTSD.

Participants

208 US participants, 108 placebo-treated and 100 sertraline-treated. Ages ranged from 18-69 years, with 75% under 45 years of age. Women constituted the majority (156 participants) and over 80% in each group were of a white European background.

Procedure

Outpatients with a DSM diagnosis of moderate-to-severe PTSD were randomized to 12 weeks of double-blind treatment with either sertraline or a placebo. Outcome was measured through the Clinician-Administered PTSD Scale (CAPS-2), patient-rated impact of event scale and the clinical global impression-severity and improvement ratings.

Results

Significantly steeper improvement slopes were found for sertraline compared with placebo on all scales, with 60% of the participants responding to sertraline and 38% responding to placebo. Side effects of insomnia, fatigue, diarrhoea, nausea, fatigue and decreased appetite were all significantly more common in sertraline participants than in the placebo participants.

Conclusion
Sertraline appears to be a safe, well-tolerated and effective treatment for PTSD.

Evaluation of Davidson et al. (2001)
Strengths
✓ The double-blind design increased the validity of the study, as neither participants nor clinicians knew the assignations to groups.

Limitations
✗ Some subjects in each group were concurrently being treated with another antidepressant, and the illness duration ranged from 23 to 61 months, which decreases the reliability of the results.
✗ The trial was limited to 12 weeks, so the long-term effectiveness of the treatment is not measured.

Reference
Davidson, J.R.T., Rothbaum, B.O., van der Kolk, B.A., Siles, C.R. & Farfel, G.M. (2001). Multicenter, double-blind comparison of sertraline and placebo in the treatment of Post-traumatic Stress disorder. *Archives of General Psychiatry, 58,* pp. 485-492.

****

TOPIC 3: TREATMENTS FOR DISORDERS

Content 10: Treatments. Post-traumatic stress disorder (PTSD)
Biomedical treatment (Biological).

KEY STUDY 10.2: *Davidson et al. (2006). Treatment of Post-traumatic Stress disorder with venlafaxine extended release. A 6-month randomized controlled trial.*

Background
To evaluate the long-term efficacy of venlafaxine (a serotonin norepinephrine reuptake inhibitor) in treatment of PTSD.

Aim
To evaluate the long-term efficacy of venlafaxine in the treatment of PTSD.

Participants
329 adult outpatients from 56 treatment clinics internationally, who had DSM-defined symptoms for 6 months or more and who scored 60 or more on the Clinician-Administered PTSD scale.

Procedure
6-month, double-blind, placebo-controlled trial, where participants were randomly assigned to either a venlafaxine or placebo treatment group for 24 weeks. The main measure was their change from baseline on the Clinician-Administered PTSD scale, and a secondary measure was remission, which was defined as a score on this scale of 20 or lower. Measures of stress vulnerability, resilience, depression, quality of life, functioning and global illness severity were also taken.

Results
In this study, venlafaxine was effective for patients with PTSD, with remission rates of 50.9% for venlafaxine and 37.5% for placebo.

Conclusion
Venlafaxine appears to be a safe, well-tolerated and effective short-term and ongoing treatment for PTSD. Improvement on all other measures was significantly greater for the venlafaxine group.

Evaluation of Davidson et al. (2001)
Strengths
- ✓ The double-blind design increased the validity of the study, as neither participants nor clinicians knew the assignations to groups.
- ✓ Standardised measurements of other factors, such as resilience and stress vulnerability improved the reliability of the results.

Limitations
- X The maximum dose, although approved by clinicians, was higher than the dose recommended on the product label and therefore these results may not be generalisable to a real-life situation.

Reference
Davidson, J., Baldwin, D., Stein, D.J., Kuper, E., Benattia, I., Ahmed, S., Pedersen, R. & Musgung, J. (2006). Treatment of Post-traumatic Stress disorder with venlafaxine extended release. A 6-month randomized controlled trial. *Archives of General Psychiatry (63),* pp. 1158-1165.

****

TOPIC 3: TREATMENTS FOR DISORDERS

Content 10: Treatments. Post-traumatic stress disorder (PTSD)
Biomedical treatment (Biological).

KEY STUDY 10.3: *Boggio et al. (2010). Noninvasive brain stimulation with high-frequency and low-intensity repetitive transcranial magnetic stimulation treatment for post-traumatic stress disorder.*

Background
Repetitive transcranial magnetic stimulation (rTMS) -a method of noninvasive neuromodulation - has been emerging as a potentially effective technique in the treatment of PTSD. This study compares high-dose rTMS with a placebo.

Aim
To evaluate the efficacy of 20 Hz rTMS of either right or left dorsolateral prefrontal cortex (DLPFC) as compared to a placebo (sham rTMS) for the relief of PTSD symptoms.

Participants
30 participants diagnosed with PTSD

Procedure
This was a double-blind, placebo-controlled trial. Participants were randomly assigned to receive 1 of the following treatments: active 20 Hz rTMS of the right DLPFC, active 20 Hz rTMS of the left DLPFC, or sham rTMS. Treatments were administered in 10 daily sessions over 2 weeks. Raters (who were not aware of the treatment group of participants) assessed severity of core PTSD symptoms, depression, and anxiety before, during, and after completion of the treatment. In addition, a series of neuropsychological tests was administered before and after treatment.

Results
Both active treatment conditions resulted in a significant decrease in PTSD symptoms as measured by the PTSD checklist, and PTSD treatment outcome PTSD scale. Right rTMS induced a larger decrease in symptoms than did left rTMS. In addition, there was a significant improvement of mood after left rTMS and a significant reduction of anxiety following right rTMS. Improvements in PTSD symptoms were long lasting; effects were still significant at the 3-month follow-up. Finally, neuropsychological evaluation showed that active 20 Hz rTMS was not associated with cognitive worsening and is safe for use in patients with PTSD.

Conclusion
This suggests that modulation of the pre-frontal cortex can reduce the symptoms of PTSD, and that high-frequency rTMS of right DLPFC may be the best treatment strategy.

Evaluation of Boggio et al (2010)

Strengths
✓ The double-blind design increased the validity of the study, as neither participants nor clinicians knew the assignations to groups.

Limitations
X It is possible that participants guessed if they were in the sham rTMS group, as the equipment was not identical to the real rTMS equipment.

Reference
Boggio, P.S., Rocha, M., Oliveira, M.O....et al. (2010). Noninvasive brain stimulation with high-frequency and low-intensity repetitive transcranial magnetic stimulation treatment for post-traumatic stress disorder. *Journal of Clinical Psychology, 71*(8), pp. 992-999.

****

TOPIC 3: TREATMENTS FOR DISORDERS

Content 10: Treatments. Post-traumatic stress disorder (PTSD)
Psychological treatment (Cognitive).

KEY STUDY 10.4: *Foa et al. (2005). Randomized trial of prolonged exposure for post-traumatic stress disorder with and without cognitive restructuring: outcome at academic and community clinics.*

Background
Wide range of PTSD symptoms suggest that multiple treatment techniques may be more effective than a single approach.

Aim
To investigate and compare the efficacy of prolonged exposure (PE) alone, PE plus cognitive restructuring (PE/CR), or wait-list (WL) conditions in reducing PTSD symptoms.

Participants
179 female assault survivors with a primary diagnosis of PTSD related to a sexual or non-sexual assault that occurred at least 3 months prior to the evaluation or related to childhood sexual abuse.

Procedure
Participants were referred by police departments or other professionals, or they were recruited through advertisements in newspapers and flyers. Enrolment was either through the Center for the Treatment and Study of Anxiety (CTSA), an academic centre, or through Women Organized Against Rape (WOAR), a Philadelphia community clinic for rape survivors where therapists had no prior experience with CBT.

Weighted randomization was used, with fewer participants allocated to the WL condition. 26 participants were assigned to WL, 74 to PE/CR and 79 to PE only. 121 completed, with WL having a dropout of only one participant, but the other two conditions having dropout rates of 40.5% and 34.2% respectively. The 17-item PTSD scale was used to interview participants and as a primary measure of change in PTSD symptoms. A self-report version of this scale was also used. The Beck Depression Inventory (BDI) measured depression.

The measures were used pre-treatment, and at 3, 6 and 12 months post-treatment.

Results
Both active treatment conditions resulted in a significant decrease in PTSD symptoms as measured by the PTSD scale and depression (measured by the BDI). The addition of CR to PE did not improve the treatment outcome. Social functioning was improved in all who completed treatment. Treatment gains were maintained at long-term follow-up.

Conclusion
Treatment with PE alone and PE/CR was superior to WL in reducing PTSD and depression. In addition, participants who completed treatment showed significant improvement in social functioning. The addition of CR to PE did not enhance treatment outcome

Evaluation of Foa et al (2010)
Strengths
- ✓ The combination of several standardised measures, using interview and self-assessment, increased the reliability of the study.

Limitations
- X There was no active control group, but instead a wait list group, which is not as reliable as a double-blind study using a placebo group (which actually would have been impossible in this case).

Reference
Foa, E.B., Hembree, E.A., Cahill, S.P., Rauch, S.A.M., Riggs, D.S. & Feeny, N.C. (2005). Randomized trial of prolonged exposure for post-traumatic stress disorder with and without cognitive restructuring: outcome at academic and community clinics for post-traumatic stress disorder. *Journal of Consulting and Clinical Psychology, 73*(5), pp. 953-964.

****

TOPIC 3: TREATMENTS FOR DISORDERS

Content 10: Treatments. Post-traumatic stress disorder (PTSD)
Psychological treatment (Cognitive).

KEY STUDY 10.5: *Rothbaum et al. (1999). Virtual reality exposure therapy for PTSD Vietnam veterans: a case study.*

Links
Cognitive approach HL extension:
1. **Methods used to study the interaction between digital technology and cognitive processes** – case study of emotion and cognition (memory).
2. **The influence of digital technology on cognitive processes** – emotion and cognition (memory).

Background
Posttraumatic stress disorder (PTSD) is one of the most disabling mental disorders affecting the veteran population. Virtual reality therapy (VRET) is a type of exposure therapy that gives patients the chance to relive their experience when it is impractical for them to do it in reality.

Aim
To investigate the use of VRET as treatment for PTSD in a controlled treatment case study.

Participants
One participant – a 50-year-old US Caucasian male who had served as a helicopter pilot in Vietnam 26 years previously. He met DSM-IV criteria for PTSD and MDD and had suffered past alcohol abuse.

Procedure
A pre-treatment evaluation was conducted by an independent assessor who reviewed the inclusion criteria, explained the procedures in detail and scheduled the initial treatment session. Treatment was delivered in fourteen, 90-min individual sessions conducted twice weekly over 7 weeks.

Results
Pre-, mid- and post-treatment analyses using clinician-rated and self-report measures of PTSD showed significant improvement from baseline at each stage. Following the treatment, assessments were also conducted at 3 months and 6 months and showed that the immediate post-treatment improvements had been maintained. His depression decreased from severe to moderate and his anger score also dropped, showing an improvement in negative emotion.

Conclusion
This was the first known Vietnam veteran to undergo VRET and the results suggest that the treatment was beneficial in decreasing the symptoms of PTSD.

Evaluation of Rothbaum et al (1999)

Strengths
- ✓ The participation of the MBCT patients in their homework and in session exercises was individually monitored to show any correlation with the reduction in PTSD symptoms.

Limitations
- ✗ This was only a brief 8-week intervention, with no long-term follow-up, so it is not known if the improvements were long-lasting.
- ✗ Patients were not randomly assigned to different treatments. Thus, the reported results must be considered as lacking reliability, and these findings have to be replicated in random assignment design

Reference
Rothbaum, B.O., Hodges, L., Alarcon, R., Ready, D.... et al. (1999). Virtual reality exposure therapy for PTSD Vietnam veterans: a case study. *Journal of Traumatic Stress, 12*(2), pp. 263-271.

****

TOPIC 3: TREATMENTS FOR DISORDERS

Content 10: Treatments. Post-traumatic stress disorder (PTSD)
Psychological treatment (Cognitive).

KEY STUDY 10.6: *King et al. (2013). A pilot study of group mindfulness-based cognitive therapy (MBCT) for combat veterans with post-traumatic stress disorder (PTSD).*

Background
Mindfulness-based Cognitive Therapy (MBCT) is effective for prevention of depression relapse but has been less studied in anxiety disorders. This study investigated the use of MBCT group intervention adapted for combat PTSD.

Aim
To investigate MBCT group therapy for combat PTSD.

Participants
Patients seeking treatment for chronic (over 10 years' duration) PTSD at an outpatient clinic. Total of 36 participants in all, with 20 spread over 4 MBCT groups and 16 spread among the 3 treatment as usual groups. Patients did not differ in terms of PTSD symptom severity (CAPS), co-morbidity, age, marital or employment status, time from combat trauma, or psychiatric service-connected disability. Assignment to groups was not randomized, but only one group was recruited at a time.

Procedure
Pre- and post-therapy psychological assessments with clinician administered PTSD scale (CAPS) were performed with all patients, and self-report measures were administered in the MBCT groups. The intervention lasted 8 weeks in all cases.

Results
Pre- to post-treatment analysis demonstrated that patients who completed MBCT (N=15) showed significant improvement in PTSD symptoms when compared with those in the treatment as usual groups.

Conclusion
These data suggest group mindfulness-based cognitive therapy as an acceptable therapy to combat PTSD.

Evaluation of King et al (2013)
Strengths
✓ The participation of the MBCT patients in their homework and in session exercises was individually monitored to show any correlation with the reduction in PTSD symptoms.

Limitations
X This was only a brief 8-week intervention, with no long-term follow-up, so it is not known if the improvements were long-lasting.

X Patients were not randomly assigned to different treatments. Thus, the reported results must be considered as lacking reliability, and these findings have to be replicated in random assignment design

Reference
King, A.P., Erickson, T.M., Giardino, N.D....et al. (2013). A pilot study of group Mindfulness-Based Cognitive Therapy (MBCT) for combat veterans with Post-traumatic Stress Disorder (PTSD). *Depression and Anxiety, (30)*7, pp. 638-645.

****

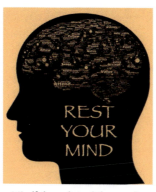

Mindfulness-based therapy for PTSD

TOPIC 3: TREATMENTS FOR DISORDERS

Content 11: Treatments. MDD & PTSD.

The role of culture in treatment (Sociocultural)

Key study 11.1: *Smith & Griner (2006). Culturally adapted mental health interventions: a meta-analytic review*

Background
There is a responsibility to improve the availability and quality of mental health services provided to persons from diverse ethnic groups. Many previous authors have advocated that traditional mental health treatments be modified to better match clients' cultural contexts. Numerous studies evaluating culturally adapted interventions have appeared, and the present study used meta-analytic methodology to summarise these data.

Aim
To summarise the findings from studies evaluating culturally-adapted therapies.

Procedure
Meta-analysis of 76 studies evaluating culturally-adapted therapies. The research also evaluated whether culturally adapted interventions were more or less effective across differences in participant age, gender, ethnicity, and acculturation level. The majority of research studies (82%) involved experiments or quasi-experiments.

Results
Therapies targeted to a specific cultural group were 4 times more effective than interventions provided to groups consisting of clients from a variety of cultures. Interventions conducted in participants' native language (if other than English) were twice as effective as interventions conducted in English.

Conclusion
The findings provide evidence of the benefits of culturally adapting mental health interventions – particularly when the interventions are targeted to a specific racial/ethnic group and when the interventions are conducted in participants' preferred language.

Reference
Griner, D., & Smith, T. B. (2006). Culturally adapted mental health interventions: a meta-analytic review. *Psychotherapy: Theory, Research, Practice & Training, 43,* pp. 531-548.

Evaluation of Smith & Griner (2006)
Strengths
- ✓ Analysis of any possible moderating effects of demographic variables such as age, gender ethnicity and acculturation level (as outlined about) add to the robustness of the data.

Limitations

- ✗ The use of a meta-analysis involves analysing secondary data over which the researchers have had no control: several of the studies did not provide detailed descriptions of the specific adaptations. This could mean that reliability is compromised somewhat.
- ✗ It is possible that the positive client outcomes associated with culturally adapted mental health interventions in this meta-analysis may be more related to participants' increased sense of comfort than to the adaptations themselves. This decreases the validity of the findings.

Reference
Smith, T.B. & Griner, D. (2006). Culturally adapted mental health interventions: a meta-analytic review. *Psychotherapy: Theory, Research, Practice & Training, 43*, pp. 531-548.

****

TOPIC 3: TREATMENTS FOR DISORDERS

Content 11: Treatments. MDD & PTSD.

The role of culture in treatment (Sociocultural)

Key study 11.2: *Hinton et al. (2005). A randomized controlled trial of cognitive-behavior therapy for Cambodian refugees with treatment-resistant PTSD and panic attacks: a cross-over design*

Background
Refugees often have severe PTSD resulting from various traumas and research needs to be conducted to investigate the efficacy of different treatment methods for refugees from different cultures. In the United States, in the late 1990s, Cambodians without knowledge of the local culture or language, had to adjust to urban environments. Cambodian refugees attending psychiatric clinics have high rates of PTSD.

Aim
To examine the therapeutic efficacy of culturally adapted CBT for Cambodian refugees with treatment-resistant PTSD and panic attacks.

Participants
40 participants who had survived the Cambodian genocide between 1975-1979 and had been at least 6 years old at the beginning of this. They all also still met the PTSD criteria, despite receiving counselling and having taken an SSRI for at least a year.

Procedure
All participants continued supportive psychotherapy, which consisted of a meeting with a social worker every 2 weeks, and medications, which consisted in all cases of a combination of an SSRI and the benzodiazepine clonazepam. Participants were randomly allocated to either an initial treatment (IT) condition or delayed treatment (DT) condition, with 20 participants in each

condition. Their anxiety and distress symptoms were measured at baseline, after the IT group had undergone 12 sessions of CBT, after the DT group had undergone 12 sessions of CBT and 12 weeks after the completion of therapy. Thus, the IT group was compared to the DT group, which functioned initially as a waitlist group. This was done by a bilingual Cambodian worker who did not know which treatment condition the participants were in, using clinician-administered standardised tests for PTSD and general anxiety disorder (GAD), panic attacks - including those triggered somatically by neck pain - and a flashback severity scale.

The CBT was modified culturally to be appropriate to the Cambodian participants, for example with visualization of a lotus bloom that spins in the wind at the end of a stem (an image encoding key Asian cultural values of flexibility) and framing relaxation as mindfulness. Because a lot of the symptoms were somatic, such as neck pain and dizziness accompanying the flashbacks, the CBT also involved Sensory Reprocessing Therapy (SRT), focusing on sensations and decreasing general arousal and stress through muscle relaxation and breathing training.

Results
The participants in the IT condition improved significantly in comparison to those in the DT condition. By the second assessment, 12/20 of the IT patients no longer met PTSD criteria and 11 of these also no longer met GAD criteria. The DT patients, unsurprisingly, all met the criteria for both. At the third assessment, 10/20 of the DT patients no longer met the PTSD criteria and 9 of these no longer met the GAD criteria. In the final assessment, these improvements had been maintained.

Conclusion
In this study of traumatised Cambodian refugees, culturally adapted CBT focusing on PTSD and panic attacks was effective in reducing symptoms and distress for at least 50% of the patients treated.

Evaluation of Hinton et al (2005).
Strengths
- ✓ Participants were measured on a broad range of standardised scales that increased the reliability of the study.
- ✓ The CBT was culturally modified to be appropriate for the types of traumatic experiences and distress undergone by the Cambodians, thus increasing the cultural relevance of the therapy.

Limitations
- X It is possible that there was a 'therapist effect', as the same bilingual therapist provided all treatment.
- X There was no comparison of the culturally modified CBT with an unmodified CBT. A comparative study would need to be carried out to see if the modifications were necessary and improved the CBT.

Reference
Hinton, D.E., Chhean, D., Pich, V., Safren, S., Hofmann, S.G. & Pollack, M.H. (2005). A randomized controlled trial of cognitive-behavior therapy for Cambodian refugees with treatment-resistant PTSD and panic attacks: a cross-over design. *Journal of Traumatic Stress, 18* (6), pp. 617–629.

****

TOPIC 3: TREATMENTS FOR DISORDERS

Content 11: Treatments. MDD & PTSD.
The role of culture in treatment (Sociocultural)

Key study 11.3: *Hodge & Nadir (2008). Moving toward culturally competent practice with Muslims: modifying cognitive therapy with Islamic tenets.*

Background
Little information is available regarding the provision of culturally adapted services for Muslims. 4 common therapeutic models are discussed in light of their level of congruence with Islamic values - psychoanalytic, group, strength- based, and cognitive.

Aim
To investigate the implications of the values underpinning Western-style counselling.

Procedure
Literature review of research based on 4 therapeutic approaches - psychoanalytic, group, strength-based, and cognitive.

Results
Two therapeutic models may be problematic for Muslim clients, for the following reasons:
- **Psychoanalytic approaches** – these are based on individual introspection. In contrast, Islam highlights the importance of community, and rather than looking inwards to analyse themselves, Muslims tend to look outwards, grounding their identity in religious teachings, culture and family.
- **Group therapy** – some Muslins may feel uncomfortable sharing personal details with a group, particularly in a mixed-gender group.

Two models are more suitable:
- **Strengths-based approach** – in this approach, strengths are identified, drawn from one's faith, family, culture and community, and therefore this is more congruent with Islamic values.
- **Cognitive therapy** - the underlying principles on which cognitive therapy rests are congruent with Islamic values. However, this individualistic, autonomous approach could be modified to substitute traditional self-statements with statements drawn from clients' spiritual traditions. This approach has been successful using Taoist, Christian and Muslim traditions.

This adaptation to cognitive therapy in order to align it with Muslim values is necessary, as from an Islamic perspective, although the individual is responsible for change, the ultimate success of these efforts is dependent upon God.

Conclusion
Social workers and psychologists will encounter Muslims in a variety of settings, including schools, hospitals, and community mental health centres. The use of adaptations that align with the client's values help endue positive outcomes.

Evaluation of Hodge & Nadir (2008).

Strengths
- ✓ Analysis of a large number of cross-cultural studies into the modification of psychological interventions to be congruent with the spiritual values of clients from different religious backgrounds.

Limitations
- ✗ This review is an analysis of secondary data over which the researchers have had no control, and therefore reliability has been compromised.
- ✗ The researchers note that not all Muslims would agree with modifications made, as Islam is a broad religion with many narratives. This may limit the value of the modifications for some Muslim clients.

Reference
Hodge, D.R. & Nadir, A. (2008). Moving toward culturally competent practice with Muslims: modifying cognitive therapy with Islamic tenets. *Social Work, 53,* pp. 31-41

****

Note: All of the studies in **TOPIC 3: TREATMENTS FOR DISORDERS** can be used for *Assessing the effectiveness of treatment(s)*. Therefore, we have not written a separate section on this.

****

TOPIC 3: TREATMENTS FOR DISORDERS

Critical thinking points

The placebo effect – better than the real thing?
Research on the efficacy of antidepressants – along with myriad other types of medication – is mixed, to say the least. Researchers have long been occupied by the question of whether antidepressants really do that which they are supposed to do i.e. reduce/eliminate the symptoms of depression via 'tinkering' with brain chemicals, or whether it is simply the result of the placebo effect i.e. 'I am on antidepressants therefore my depression must be diminishing, and I must be feeling better.' Kroenke et al. (2001) concluded that a range of antidepressants (both SSRI and non-SSRI) are of equal effectiveness in the treatment of depression but this in itself does not really tell us anything: if antidepressants work via the placebo effect then any antidepressant medication will be just as successful as any other. Kirsch et al. (2008) found that overall the effect of antidepressants does not reach the threshold criteria to be able to claim statistical significance and that even severely depressed patients show a 'substantial' response to treatment using a placebo. Could it be possible that antidepressants don't actually do anything in terms of actually treating depression and that it is the mindset of the patient, their belief that 'the drugs do work' that is in fact responsible for the observed improvements in the depressed patient?

PSYCHOLOGY SORTED: KEY RESEARCH FOR STUDENTS AND TEACHERS
BOOK 2 – APPLIED PSYCHOLOGY

Can new therapies such as mindfulness actually work as a treatment?
Some of the research cited in this chapter focuses on the use of alternative forms of therapy for mental illnesses; 'alternative' in this sense meaning non-drug-based. Kuyken et al. (2016) used a sample of depressed patients taken from a meta-analysis comprising 9 studies and found that a Mindfulness Based Cognitive Treatment Programme was particularly effective at reducing the symptoms of severe depression. Mindfulness has become quite a 'buzz word' in both therapeutic and wider media circles with many self-help books, TV programmes, apps and community classes using it as a means to a better understanding of the self, the world and as a relaxation technique. Scientists may doubt the efficacy of mindfulness as it is not based on any, real 'scientific' criteria i.e. it is difficult to measure, it lacks objectivity and it is unfalsifiable. The practice of being 'mindful' is very like what has been taught for centuries by religions such as Buddhism and in countries such as India where meditation and reflection are key components in the pursuit of a balanced, healthy mind and body. So, it might be the case that mindfulness is nothing new but is being packaged as an alternative treatment for mental illnesses such as depression: and if it works then surely it is something to be welcomed?

Culture is a vital aspect of any treatment.
We live in an increasingly multi-cultural world with a wide range of ethnic groups rubbing shoulders with each other, particularly in large urban areas. Treating mental disorders, however, may fall prey to an ethnocentric approach, particularly if a patient is an immigrant or comes from a cultural background with very different values, attitudes and behaviours to that of the dominant culture. Research by Hinton et al. (2005) found that a modified form of CBT which addressed and was sensitive to the cultural background of the traumatised Cambodian refugee in the US, was effective in reducing symptoms of PTSD, panic attacks and distress for at least 50% of the patients treated. Hodge & Nadir (2008) similarly found that adapting CBT in order to align it with Muslim values is necessary, as from an Islamic perspective the ultimate success of any treatment is dependent upon God rather than on an individual (be that the self or the therapist).

****

Mindfulness-based therapy

Developmental Psychology

Ethics ⬇

Methods ⬇

⬇

Developing as a learner
- Brain development
- Cognitive development

Influences on cognitive and social development
- Role of peers and play
- Childhood trauma and resilience
- Poverty/socio-economic status

Developing an identity
- Attachment
- Gender identity and social roles
- Development of empathy and theory of mind

Evaluate   *To what extent?*   *Discuss*

Contrast

DEVELOPMENTAL PSYCHOLOGY

Topic 1: Developing as a learner
Key Idea: Changes in the brain and cognition underlie childhood development

Content	Research	Use in Developmental Psychology	Links to
Brain development	Classic **Chugani (1998)**	PET scan of babies and children, measuring cerebral glucose metabolism, identified biological stages of brain development that peaked at 10 years old, providing a 'window of opportunity' for learning.	**Biological approach: The brain and behaviour –** neuroplasticity.
	Critique/Extension **Gotgay et al. (2004)**	Neural pruning is the process carried out in the brain to increase its efficiency: neurons and synaptic connections that are no longer used are eliminated. Neural branching strengthens the brain and extends the network of synapses within it much the same way as muscles are strengthened by repeated exercise.	**Biological approach: The brain and behaviour –** neuroplasticity.
	Recent **Luby et al. (2013)**	Exposure to poverty in early childhood impacts cognitive development by school age, showing neuroplasticity of the brain in the area of the limbic system (amygdala and hippocampus). These effects are mediated positively by good caregiving and negatively by stressful life events.	**Biological approach: The brain and behaviour –** neuroplasticity.

Further resources
ASAP Science film (2016). Why are Teens so Moody?
https://youtu.be/du8siPJ1ZKoZKo

Why are Teens so Moody?

Hardach, S. (28 March 2018). The secret world of babies. *BBC Future.*
https://tinyurl.com/y6b6747w

TED talk by Sarah-Jayne Blakemore (2012). The mysterious workings of the adolescent brain.
https://tinyurl.com/pab6vub

TedxYouth talk by Jill Bolte Taylor (2013). The neuroanatomical transformation of the teenage brain. https://www.youtube.com/watch?v=PzT_SBl31-s

DEVELOPMENTAL PSYCHOLOGY

Topic 1: Developing as a learner
Key Idea: Changes in the brain and cognition underlie childhood development

Content	Research	Use in Developmental Psychology	Links to
Cognitive development	Classic **Piaget (1952)**	Claimed that children's development progresses through a series of cognitive stages, with each stage having distinctly different qualities. The stages are a way to describe changes in the logic of thinking. His view was that the sequence of stages was the same for all humans, and therefore the way in which we develop is universal. Cognitive theory.	
	Critique/Extension **Samuel & Bryant (1984)**	Re-worked Piaget's conservation task, with 5-8 year-old children (at the pre-operational stage and beginning of the concrete operational stage) and found that asking the same question twice – both before and after the transformation – is a confounding variable as it suggests that the first answer given was incorrect. With this modification the children were able to conserve to a greater extent than Piaget claimed.	
	Classic **Vygotsky (1962)** (Written nearly 30 yrs. earlier. This is the English translation).	Theorised that a child develops through interaction with a 'more knowledgeable other.' This could be a parent, sibling, teacher or peer who has a better understanding than the learner. The child seeks to understand the instructions of the tutor and then internalizes the information.	
	Critique/Extension **Conner & Cross (2003)**	Scaffolding can enable a child to make good progress and to develop the skills needed to problem-solve. Found that children who were given scaffolding as and when required made good progress with the task. This is a social theory of developmental learning.	

	Recent **Paulus et al. (2014)**	Examined longitudinal relationship between early measures of prosocial action in infancy as well as cognitive and social-cognitive abilities, and the sharing behaviour of preschool children. Found that inhibitory control and social-cognitive abilities play an important role in the early development of prosocial action.	**Human Relationships: Social responsibility** – pro-social behaviour.

Further resources
Crash course psychology film by Hank Green (2015). No.18. The Growth of Knowledge.
https://www.youtube.com/watch?v=8nz2dtv--ok

The Growth of Knowledge

TED talk by Laura Schulz (2015). The surprisingly logical minds of babies. *(This is also good for methods, representativeness and generalization).*
https://tinyurl.com/y3nbq7fs

TED talk. Laura Schulz

Scaffolding support for learning.

PSYCHOLOGY SORTED: KEY RESEARCH FOR STUDENTS AND TEACHERS
BOOK 2 – APPLIED PSYCHOLOGY

DEVELOPMENTAL PSYCHOLOGY

Topic 2: Influences on cognitive and social development
Key Idea: A child's social and cognitive development is affected by environmental factors.

Content	Research	Use in Developmental Psychology	Links to
Role of peers and play	Classic **Elias and Berk (2002)**	Vygotsky theorised that make-believe play encourages healthy cognitive and social development. These researchers investigated whether or not participation in make-believe play influences socially responsible behaviour (social measure) and attentiveness (cognitive measure).	
	Critique/Extension **Fiorelli & Russ (2012)**	Longitudinal study investigating the relationship between emotional themes in pretend play and positive mood in daily life. Found that imagination and organization in play related to coping ability. Their results also support the stability of imagination and organization in pretend play over time	
	Recent **Silva et al. (2015)**	Late adolescents tested with peer observers engaged in more exploratory behaviour, learned faster from both positive and negative outcomes, and evinced better task performance than those tested alone. Suggests spending time with peers during adolescence may increase the odds that adolescents will behave recklessly, but also that they will learn from the consequences of their actions.	

Further resources

Kennedy-Moore, E. (2010). How children make friends. *Psychology Today* blog.
https://tinyurl.com/y3xvx726

Narvaez, D. (1 April 2014). Is pretend play good for kids? *Psychology Today* blog.
https://tinyurl.com/y3bvdekl

Youtube film clip (2012). Studying Imagination in Children's Play.
https://youtu.be/sQb95itdoCM

Imagination in Children's Play

PSYCHOLOGY SORTED: KEY RESEARCH FOR STUDENTS AND TEACHERS
BOOK 2 – APPLIED PSYCHOLOGY

DEVELOPMENTAL PSYCHOLOGY

Topic 2: Influences on cognitive and social development
Key Idea: A child's social and cognitive development is affected by environmental factors.

Content	Research	Use in Developmental Psychology	Links to
Childhood trauma and resilience	Classic **Rutter et al. (1999)**	Investigated the effects of profound deprivation in an on-going longitudinal case study of Romanian orphans adopted into UK families. In this smaller case study, found that 6% of 111 children so adopted, at 4 and 6 years old showed a quasi-autistic pattern of behaviour associated with severe deprivation and a level of cognitive impairment.	
	Critique/Extension **Boyden (2003)**	A review article challenging assumptions about children's resilience related to their experiences of living in a war zone. Concludes that children should not be viewed as vulnerable and incompetent victims but as agents of their own fate and should be accorded a level of respect based on their ability to be resilient in the face of terrible odds.	
	Recent **Werner (2005)**	Summary of Werner & Smith's earlier work: the **Kaui Longitudinal Study** into the impact of a series of different stressors and traumatic events on a multi-ethnic cohort of 698 children on Kauai, Hawaii. Found that early childhood trauma or adversity can be overcome if one or more protective factors are in place to encourage resilience.	

Further resources
Howard, M. (6 Feb 2007). Children of war. The generation traumatised by violence in Iraq. *The Guardian.* https://tinyurl.com/y5rhactd

Children of War

TED talk on health effects of childhood trauma, by Nadine Burke Harris (2014). How childhood trauma affects health across a lifetime.
https://tinyurl.com/op5odrb

TEDx talk on resilience in the face of childhood trauma, by Charles Hunt (2016). What trauma taught me about resilience. https://www.youtube.com/watch?v=3qELiw_1Ddg

DEVELOPMENTAL PSYCHOLOGY

Topic 2: Influences on cognitive and social development

Key Idea: A child's social and cognitive development is affected by environmental factors.

Content	Research	Use in Developmental Psychology	Links to
Poverty/socio-economic status	Classic **Werner (2005)**	Summary of Werner & Smith's earlier work: the **Kaui Longitudinal Study** into the impact of a series of different stressors and traumatic events on a multi-ethnic cohort of 698 poor children on Kauai, Hawaii. Found that early childhood trauma or adversity can be overcome if one or more protective factors are in place to encourage resilience. Suggested that, at least partly, dispositional rather than situational factors are responsible for varying levels of resilience to the effects poverty.	
	Critique/Extension **Kar et al (2008)**	Investigated effect of malnutrition on cognitive performance in a sample of 20 Indian children from 5 to 7 years old and between 8 and 10. Malnourished children in both groups scored lower in attention, working memory and visuospatial tasks than a control group. But older children showed less impairment. Kar developed a theory of delayed cognitive development rather than permanent impairment.	
	Recent **Luby et al. (2013)**	Exposure to poverty in early childhood impacts cognitive development by school age, showing neuroplasticity of the brain in the area of the limbic system (amygdala and hippocampus). These effects are mediated positively by good caregiving and negatively by stressful life events.	**Biological approach:** The brain and behaviour – neuroplasticity.

Further resources

Balter, M. (30 March 2015). Poverty may affect the growth of children's brains. *Science.* https://tinyurl.com/yyb2nxjp

Jensen, E. (May 2013). How poverty affects classroom engagement. *Educational Leadership,* ASCD. https://tinyurl.com/kub763j

Poverty affects brain growth

DEVELOPMENTAL PSYCHOLOGY

Topic 3: Developing an identity
Key Idea: Identity is the result of an interaction between biological, cognitive and social factors.

Content	Research	Use in Developmental Psychology	Links to
Attachment	Classic (1) **Ainsworth & Bell (1970)**	Identified three different attachment styles (secure, insecure-avoidant, insecure-resistant /ambivalent) and concluded that attachment style can be seen in the behaviour exhibited by caregiver and child with the majority of children showing a secure and positive relationship with the caregiver.	
	Classic (2) **Bowlby (1988)**	Analysis of the past, present and future of attachment theory, with reference to Harlow, Ainsworth and Rutter.	
	Critique/Extension **Van Ijzendoorn & Kroonenberg (1988)**	Meta-analysis of 32 studies carried out in eight different countries that had replicated Ainsworth's method. The researchers combined all the results of the 32 studies and looked at attachment differences *within* cultures and countries as well as *between* them. Found cultural variations in attachment styles.	
	Recent **Gross et al. (2017)**	Reported on the nature of the link between secure attachment and prosocial behaviour. Found that there was a connection, broadly defined, but results vary across comforting, sharing, and helping.	

Further resources

Crash course psychology film by Hank Green (2015). No.19. Monkeys and Morality.
https://www.youtube.com/watch?v=YcQg1EshfIE

Shemmings, D. (15 Feb 2016). A quick guide to attachment theory. *The Guardian.*
https://tinyurl.com/yabwnsv8

Monkeys and morality

DEVELOPMENTAL PSYCHOLOGY

Topic 3: Developing an identity

Key Idea: Identity is the result of an interaction between biological, cognitive and social factors.

Content	Research	Use in Developmental Psychology	Links to
Gender identity and social roles	Classic (sociocultural) **Whiting & Edwards (1973)**	Studied children aged 3 - 11 in six different countries. In the majority of these societies, girls were more nurturing. Boys were more aggressive, dominant, and engaged in more rough-and-tumble play. The researchers interpreted the gender differences in the six cultures as differences in **socialization.**	**Sociocultural approach:** Cultural influences on individual attitudes, identity and behaviours – enculturation.
	Classic (biological) **Imperato-McGinley et al. (1974)**	Case study of the Batista family in the Dominican Republic. Due to genetic mutation, some children were born with what appeared to be the genitalia of girls, but physically developed into men at puberty. Throughout their childhood, they were raised as girls. As adults, they demonstrated masculine gender roles and heterosexual behaviour. Seems to indicate a strong biological origin of gender identity. (This is one of 27 affected families, due to an inherited mutant gene).	
	Classic (cognitive) **Bem (1981)**	Gender schema theory suggests that children gradually form their gender identity as they learn about the network of themes and associations within their own culture. In addition, gender schema is closely linked to self-concept. Children engage in gender appropriate behaviour because they are motivated by the desire to be good girls or boys.	
	Critique/Extension **Sroufe et al. (1993)**	Observed that children aged 10-11 who did not behave in a gender-stereotyped way were the least popular with their peers. These studies indicate that children establish a kind of social control in relation to gender roles very early, and it may well be that peer socialization is an important factor in gender development.	**Sociocultural approach:** Cultural influences on individual attitudes, identity and behaviours – enculturation.

	Recent **Halpern & Perry-Jenkins (2016)**	Used longitudinal, self-report data from a sample of 109 dual-earner, working-class couples and their 6 year-old children living in the USA to investigate the relative importance of parents' gender ideology and their actual behaviour in predicting children's development of gender role attitudes. Found that mothers' and fathers' behaviours were better predictors of children's gender-role attitudes than parents' ideology.	

Further resources

Crash course psychology film by Hank Green (2015). No.20. Adolescence.
https://www.youtube.com/watch?v=PzyXGUCngoU

Tedx talk on gender and identity by Alice Dreger (2010). Is anatomy destiny?
https://www.ted.com/talks/alice_dreger_is_anatomy_destiny

Gender and identity

TEDx talk on girls' and boys' toys and stereotyping by Elizabeth Sweet (2015). Beyond the blue and pink toy divide. *(Also good for sociocultural approach: stereotypes).*
https://www.youtube.com/watch?v=xdHJGH97vyo

Girls' Toys and Boys' Toys?

DEVELOPMENTAL PSYCHOLOGY

Topic 3: Developing an identity
Key Idea: Identity is the result of an interaction between biological, cognitive and social factors.

Content	Research	Use in Developmental Psychology	Links to
Development of empathy and theory of mind	Classic **Baron-Cohen et al. (1985)**	False belief testing of the representational stage of theory of mind, using the Sally-Ann task. Found that 11 year-old children on the autistic spectrum were not able to correctly identify that others had a different view from their own, while 10 year-old children with Down syndrome and 4 year-old children with neither autism nor Down syndrome were able to detect this.	
	Critique/Extension **Repacholi and Gopnik (1997)**	The researchers wanted to get a better understanding of when children are able to understand that other people may have a belief or desire that is different from their own. Children who were only 14 months old offered foods that they themselves liked, but those who were 18 months old were able to separate the experimenters' wishes from their own.	
	Recent **Cowell et al. (2015)**	The current study examined the role of early theory of mind in sharing in a large sample of preschool aged children. Found a contradictory relationship between early false-belief understanding and sharing behaviour, whereby competence in false-belief understanding was correlated with less sharing. It was the children who could engage in theory of mind that decided to share less with others.	

Further resources

Etchells, P. (23 Jan 2017). The Sally Anne task: a psychological experiment for a post-truth era? *The Guardian*. https://tinyurl.com/hhbdjtd

TED talk by Alison Gopnik (2011). What do Babies Think?
https://tinyurl.com/y6j6mlof

What do Babies Think?

DEVELOPMENTAL PSYCHOLOGY KEY STUDIES

TOPIC 1: DEVELOPING AS A LEARNER

Key Idea: Changes in the brain and cognition underlie childhood development

Content 1: Brain development

KEY STUDY 1.1: *Chugani (1998). A critical period of brain development: studies of cerebral glucose utilization with PET.*

Links to:
- **Biological approach: The brain and behaviour** – neuroplasticity.

Background
The use of brain imaging technology on babies and younger children can give insights into the correlation between brain development and learning. PET scans of babies and children, measuring cerebral glucose metabolism, identified biological stages of brain development that peaked at 10 years old, providing a 'window of opportunity' for learning.

Aim
To investigate glucose metabolism in the human brain from birth to late adolescence.

Procedure
The article reviews the overall development of the human brain, using findings from research into PET scans: areas of the brain were scanned, and resultant active areas showed up via radioactive tracers indicating where glucose was being metabolised.

Main comments and findings
- Research using PET scans on the brains of newborn babies highlighted which areas showed signs of activity and thus development. Chugani found that there was reduced activity in the cerebral cortex, which is associated with executive functioning e.g. planning, reflection, decision-making. There was, however, activity of amygdala and cingulate cortex which suggests that the limbic system (which regulates emotional responses) plays an important role in newborn babies' interactions and, possibly, in emotional development.

- Lower levels of the brain develop first, and over time glucose consumption can be registered in higher levels of the brain. For example, from age six to nine months, activity begins to increase in the frontal lobes, prefrontal areas of the cortex and evidence of improved cognitive competence. This theory of brain development states that activity grows outward from the brain stem to the cortex, as the child develops.

- The following table sums up the 'windows of opportunity' regarding brain development in children. If any window is missed then it may have devastating, long-term consequences for the child.

Brain function	Window of opportunity
Motor skills	Pre-birth-6 months
Vision	0-6 months
Emotion regulation	0-3 years
Vocabulary and speech	0-3 years
Logic including mathematical skills	0-4 years

- There appears to be a 'critical period' of brain plasticity during the first 10 years of a child's development, particularly for the development of language (specifically, the learning of grammatical structures rather than individual words).

Evaluation of Chugani (1998)
Strengths
- ✓ PET scan studies are replicable – as long as you have access to the equipment and skilled, trained staff who can operate the machines and analyse the scans. This increases the reliability of these studies.
- ✓ Chugani's findings have been supported by other research into brain development identifying the prefrontal cortex as being the last part of the brain to develop: this provides useful insight into behaviours associated with the immature brain.

Limitations
- ✗ PET scans do not account for other important influences on cognitive development e.g. upbringing, peers, environment, which may all play an important role in brain and cognitive development.
- ✗ It is notoriously difficult to isolate cause and effect in an organ as complex as the brain: cognitive neuroscience is still in its infancy and there is still a huge amount of information to be learned about the brain.

Reference
Chugani, H. T. (1998). A critical period of brain development: studies of cerebral glucose utilization with PET. *Preventive Medicine*, *27*(2), pp. 184-188.

****

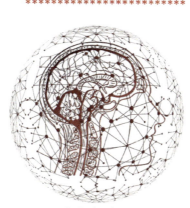

Brain development

PSYCHOLOGY SORTED: KEY RESEARCH FOR STUDENTS AND TEACHERS
BOOK 2 – APPLIED PSYCHOLOGY

TOPIC 1: DEVELOPING AS A LEARNER

Content 1: Brain development

KEY STUDY 1.2: *Gotgay et al. (2004). Dynamic Mapping of Human Cortical Development During Childhood Through Early Adulthood.*

Links to:
- **Biological approach: The brain and behaviour** – neuroplasticity.

Background
Research which covered neural pruning (the process whereby neurons and synaptic connections that are no longer used are eliminated) and neural branching (extends the network of synapses within the brain).

Aim
To chart brain development using MRI scans in children from age the age of 4 to 21 years.

Participants
13 children and teenagers from the USA. Every two years of the study's duration (10 years per child) the children were scanned using MRI technology, enabling the researchers to amass a large amount of data spanning years of brain development.

Procedure
MRI scans were used to highlight the ways in which the grey matter of the cortex had been affected due to neural pruning, which showed up on the scans as diminished areas (unused neuronal connections that were no longer used were evident on the scans). Neural branching was evident in the volume of grey matter observed as increasing with age in areas that are linked to cognitive and functional milestones in human development.

Results
The first areas of the brain to mature were those associated with the most basic of functions e.g. the motor cortex in the frontal lobe of the brain which controls voluntary movements. Areas that involve spatial orientation and language were the next to develop in the parietal lobes. Areas with more advanced and sophisticated cognitive functioning in the prefrontal cortex develop last (at some point in a person's early 20s).

Conclusion
The brain only reaches full maturity in adulthood, with more emotional and impulsive behaviour (of the type seen in young children) being largely due to the lack of development in the pre-frontal cortex, the area of the brain that is in charge of executive functioning (e.g. impulse control, inhibiting of emotional responses). More reasoned thought is possible with a mature prefrontal cortex, which goes some way towards explaining development as a learner.

Evaluation of Gotgay et al. (2004)

Strengths
- ✓ The use of a longitudinal design in this study means that the researchers were able to track changes over time which increases the internal validity of the research.
- ✓ Using MRI scans to measure brain development is a reliable way of analysing volume of grey matter in the brain as it eliminates researcher bias in the process of obtaining the data and it is a precise and clinical method.

Limitations
- X The use of such objective, clinical methodology means that the study lacks ecological validity and explanatory power: it is not clear as to *why* brain areas develop according to the study's findings, only that they appear to follow the same pattern.
- X The ways in which the participants of the study functioned as learners was not measured so it is unclear as to how able they were cognitively when compared to their brain development.

Reference
Gotgay, G., Giedd, J., Lusk, L., Hayashi, K., Greenstein, D., Vaituzis, A., Nugent III, T., Herman, D., Clasen, L., Toga, A., Rapoport, J., Thompson, P. (2004). Dynamic Mapping of Human Cortical Development During Childhood Through Early Adulthood. *Proceedings of the National Academy of Sciences, 101*(21), pp. 8174-8179.

****

TOPIC 1: DEVELOPING AS A LEARNER

Content 1: Brain development

KEY STUDY 1.3: *Luby et al. (2013) The effects of poverty on childhood brain development: the mediating effect of caregiving and stressful life events.*

Links to
- **Neuroplasticity.** The effects of caregiving on brain development.

Brief Summary
Exposure to poverty in early childhood impacts cognitive development by school age, showing neuroplasticity of the brain. These effects are mediated positively by good caregiving and negatively by stressful life events.

Aim
To investigate whether poverty experienced in childhood is shown in delayed brain development and to investigate the extent to which mediating factors may influence early deprivation.

Participants
Children who were already enrolled on a 10-year longitudinal study of Preschool Depression comprised the target population for this study: a sample of 145 children (right-handed) was drawn from this population. The children were from the USA.

Procedure
Prior to being scanned via MRI the children had undergone regular testing: once a year (for a duration of 3-6 years) the children had taken part in a series of tests aimed to measure their cognitive, emotional and social aptitudes. The involvement of significant adults in their lives was also recorded (e.g. how close they were to their caregivers) as well as the occurrence of any negative and stressful events in their lives. Once this collection of information had been amassed per child, each one underwent two MRI scans. The whole brain was scanned on one of the MRI sessions and the other MRI session looked only at the hippocampus and the amygdala.

Results
Both the hippocampus and the amygdala showed less white and grey matter in the MRI scans of the children in this study. While both the hippocampus and amygdala showed less development in poverty-affected children the researchers found that in cases where the child experienced positive care there was less negative effect on the hippocampus. Difficult and stressful life events only affected the left hippocampus.

Conclusion
Poverty does appear to have a negative effect on brain development in childhood. The quality of caregiving, however, can mediate against some of these harmful effects.

Evaluation of Luby et al. (2013)
Strengths
- ✓ The measurement of non-clinical variables prior to the MRI scanning provided the researchers with a great deal of background data (triangulation) which contributed to the internal validity of the study: this means that the researchers could check the behavioural, cognitive, and social measures against the MRI results.
- ✓ The study's findings highlight the importance of good quality care in childhood. These findings could be used to help children of all economic backgrounds by implementing early intervention strategies for children at risk of not receiving proper caregiving.

Limitations
- X Attempting to measure complex variables (e.g. nature of caregiving, behavioural responses) is beset with difficulties as these variables are not exact and may be prone to researchers interpreting them in subjective ways.
- X The sample is relatively small and difficult to generalise from, plus it only represents pre-school children who exhibit symptoms of depression so it cannot explain how poverty may affect non-depressed children.

Reference
Luby, J., Belden, A., Botteron, K., Marrus, N., Harms, M. P., Babb, C., ... & Barch, D. (2013). The effects of poverty on childhood brain development: the mediating effect of caregiving and stressful life events. *JAMA pediatrics*, *167*(12), pp. 1135-1142.

****

PSYCHOLOGY SORTED: KEY RESEARCH FOR STUDENTS AND TEACHERS
BOOK 2 – APPLIED PSYCHOLOGY

TOPIC 1: DEVELOPING AS A LEARNER

Content 2: Cognitive development

KEY STUDY 2.1: *Piaget (1952). The origins of intelligence in children.*

Background
Claimed that children's development progresses through a series of cognitive stages, with each stage having distinctly different qualities. The stages are a way to describe changes in the logic of thinking. His view was that the sequence of stages was the same for all humans, and therefore the way in which we develop is universal. This is a cognitive theory.

Aim
To present a theory of cognitive development that demonstrated that children think in qualitatively different ways to that of adults.

Piaget's stage theory of cognitive development
Piaget claimed that children go through a maturational process of cognitive development, with each threshold of skill development being linked to their biological age. Piaget's theory tends to fall on the 'nature' side of the nature/nurture debate as he stated that all children – regardless of upbringing, environment, culture, IQ – go through each stage at the same time and that none of the stages could be skipped. In this way his theory falls in line with his approach to the study of behaviour, known as *genetic epistemology*, in other words, using a biological basis as the foundation to question what we know and how we know it.

The sensorimotor stage (0-2 years): Characterised by physicality: learning through actions and senses via exploration of the baby's environment e.g. sucking, crawling, touching; having a 'here and now' concept of the world. Skills deficits at this stage is lack of object permanence (not realising that something continues to exist even if it cannot be seen).

The pre-operational stage (2-7 years): Characterised by symbolic thought e.g. being able to form mental representations of objects; pretend play, particularly involving anthropomorphism e.g. attributing human traits/behaviour to toys, animals etc; an understanding of past and future. Skills deficits at this stage are egocentrism – the inability to see the world from another's perspective and lack of conservation – the inability to appreciate that objects or materials remain the same even when their appearance changes.

The concrete operational stage (7-11 years): Characterised by the ability to conserve; the use of props and other 'concrete' items to aid their logical thinking; a lack of egocentrism. Skills deficits at this stage are the inability to deal with abstract concepts or to carry out hypothetical tasks.

The formal operational stage (11 years +): Characterised by the ability to use abstract concepts and hypothetical situations and to solve problems using logic in a systematic way. By this stage there should be no obvious skills deficit.

Procedure - testing the pre-operational stage

Piaget claimed that children in this stage, aged 2-7 years, lack the ability to conserve – to understand that the superficial change of an object's appearance does not mean that the object itself has changed. To demonstrate this idea, he devised a series of tests known as conservation tasks:

1. The child is shown, for example, two containers identical in size, containing the same volume of liquid each.

2. The child is then asked, *'Do each of these containers have the same amount of liquid or does one have more than the other?'*

3. The researcher then pours one of the containers into another container that is of a different size (e.g. wider or taller) than the remaining container. The child watches this take place.

4. The child is then asked, *'Do each of these containers have the same amount of liquid or does one have more than the other?'*

Results

The results tend to be that the child will say that the containers have different amounts of liquid in even though they have observed the transformation take place, thus they lack the ability to conserve.

Piaget used the results of these conservation tasks to argue that pre-operational children cannot conserve, although he did concede that this is seen more in the younger children in this stage and that older children show increased ability to conserve.

Evaluation of Piaget (1952)

Strengths
- ✓ Piaget's theory has been highly influential in educational contexts and its influence can still be seen today in the way that children are set specific tasks according to their stage of cognitive development.
- ✓ Piaget was the first researcher to be interested in *how* children think rather than just *what* they think.

Limitations
- X Piaget published very little data so his theory cannot be supported by strong empirical evidence.
- X Piaget's stage theory is restrictive as it does not account for children moving swiftly through or even skipping some stages or that some children may experience developmental delays.

Reference

Piaget, J., & Cook, M. (1952). *The Origins of Intelligence in Children* (Vol. 8, No. 5). New York: International Universities Press.

****

TOPIC 1: DEVELOPING AS A LEARNER

Content 2: Cognitive development

KEY STUDY 2.2: *Samuel & Bryant (1984). Asking only one question in the conservation experiment.*

Background
Re-worked Piaget's conservation task, with 5-8 year-old children (at the pre-operational stage and beginning of the concrete operational stage) and found that asking the same question twice – both before and after the transformation – is a confounding variable as it suggests that the first answer given was incorrect. By only asking one question after the alteration was observed the children were able to conserve to a greater extent than Piaget claimed.

Aim
To challenge the standard Piagetian conservation task by changing parts of the procedure.

Participants
252 children aged between 5 years 3 months to 8 years 3 months from Crediton, Devon, UK.

Procedure
The participants were tested on their ability to conserve number (coins), volume (liquid) and mass (clay). They took part in 12 trials each. There were three conditions of the IV – the standard Piagetian task in which the child is asked the same two questions: one *before* and one *after* the transformation of the material; the 'one judgement' condition in which the child is asked only one question *after* the transformation; the 'fixed array' condition in which the child only sees the materials *after* they have been transformed and is then asked only one question. The question was the same for each condition: *'Do each of these containers/rows of coins/lumps of clay have the same amount of liquid/number of coins/amount of clay or does one have more than the other?'*

Results
The results showed that all children made fewer errors in the one-judgement condition. The older children made fewer errors and number was found to be the easiest material for the children to conserve, as shown in the table below:

MEAN ERRORS PER GROUP			
AGE	STANDARD	ONE JUDGEMENT	FIXED ARRAY
5	8	7	9
6	6	4	6
7	3	3	5
8	2	1	2

Conclusion

Asking the same question twice – both before and after the transformation – is a confounding variable as it suggests that the first answer given was incorrect, thus the child is more likely to change their answer when asked a second time. By only asking one question after the transformation was observed the children were able to conserve to a greater extent than Piaget claimed they could within this stage of development.

This study still supports Piaget's theory, however, as the older the child was, the fewer errors were made - showing that biological maturation brings with it increased cognitive skills.

Evaluation of Samuel & Bryant (1984)
Strengths
- ✓ This was a well-designed study with three conditions of the IV, using a standardised procedure which would make it straightforward to replicate which means that it is high in reliability.
- ✓ The quantitative data also adds to the study's reliability and the fact that the children took part in 12 trials each adds to the study's *internal validity* meaning that the procedure contains in-built 'checks' as to what is being measured. In practical terms this was done in the form of checking that the child could actually judge amounts accurately by asking them to judge whether an amount was equal or not - by starting the task with the material in either an equal or unequal condition (hence the 12 trials per condition). If the child could not judge the amount, then the researchers would not include their data in their research as it would invalidate the results.

Limitations
- X The study lacks ecological validity as it tested the ability to conserve in an artificial and contrived way. The fact that each child took part in 12 trials each may also give rise to practice effects, fatigue or boredom with the procedure, which could bias the results.
- X The sample is not generalisable beyond its setting of Devon: such a culturally homogeneous and rural population may not represent the ways in which children from big cities or different cultural groups might think.

Reference
Samuel, J. & Bryant, P. (1984). Asking only one question in the conservation experiment. *Journal of Child Psychology and Psychiatry*, 25, pp 315-18.

****

TOPIC 1: DEVELOPING AS A LEARNER

Content 2: Cognitive development

KEY STUDY 2.3: *Vygotsky (1962). Language and thought.*

Background
Theorised that a child develops through interaction with a 'more knowledgeable other.' This could be a parent, sibling, teacher or peer who has a better understanding than the learner. The child seeks to understand the actions or instructions of the tutor and then internalizes the information.

Aim
To present a theory of cognitive development that demonstrated that children develop cognitive skills in social contexts, relying on the guidance and help of adults.

Vygotsky's social interaction theory of cognitive development
Lev Vygotsky (1896-1934) proposed a theory of cognitive development that differed in many ways to Piaget's. His main assertion was that the social world of the child played a key role in the child's development as a learner, with adults playing a key role in the process. Where Piaget saw cognitive development as an innate maturation-based process Vygotsky placed social interaction at the centre of cognitive development. His ideas can be summarised as follows:

The Zone of Proximal Development: This is based on the idea that each child has a potential for going beyond his/her current level of achievement and – with the help of a *More Knowledgeable Other* (e.g. a teacher) – reach even higher levels of progress and attainment. Vygotsky believed that children can only reach the ZPD if they have an adult to help them.

Scaffolding: This is the process by which the *More Knowledgeable Other* offers constructive help and guidance to the child in order for a particular task or skill to be completed or practised. This type of guidance is designed to be specific to the needs of each individual child, giving them the opportunity to achieve success in ways that might have not been possible without it. Scaffolding includes strategies such as maintaining the child's interest in a task; simplifying complex ideas or actions; giving specific verbal instructions; demonstrating the task.

Language and culture: Vygotsky claimed that children are able to pick up the rudiments of communication at home via interaction and in the context of the child's culture. He thought that culture played a role in teaching children how to think and to make sense of their experiences, a process he called 'social construction'.

Evaluation of Vygotsky (1962)
Strengths
- ✓ Vygotsky acknowledged the importance of environment to a child's learning, particularly of the influential role played by adults e.g. parents and teachers, which makes his theory more holistic than Piaget's theory.
- ✓ Vygotsky's idea of the More Knowledgeable Other can be seen widely in educational contexts with the use of teaching assistants, mentors and differentiated classroom seating plans implemented to enhance the progress of all students, particularly those with specific learning requirements.

Limitations
- X There is not a great deal of research based on Vygotsky's theory as his ideas are difficult to operationalise with any degree of reliability.
- X Vygotsky does not address the issue that scaffolding could actually *hamper* the progress of some children if they are given too much help from an adult. It has always to be appropriate.

Reference
Vygotsky, L. S. (1962). *Language and Thought.* Ontario, Canada: Massachusetts Institute of Technology Press.

TOPIC 1: DEVELOPING AS A LEARNER

Content 2: Cognitive development

KEY STUDY 2.4: *Conner & Cross (2003). Longitudinal analysis of the presence, efficacy and stability of maternal scaffolding during informal problem-solving interactions.*

Background
Scaffolding, if used appropriately, can enable a child to make good progress and to develop the skills needed to problem-solve. Found that children who were given scaffolding as and when required made good progress with the task. This is a social theory of developmental learning.

Aim
To investigate the effect of using scaffolding from the perspective of mother-child interactions when engaged in problem-solving tasks.

Participants
45 mother and child pairs (the children were aged 16, 26, 44 and 54 months per observation period over a total of three years).

Procedure
The mother and child pairs were observed more than one researcher as they took part together in a series of informal problem-solving tasks. The observations took place over a period of three years, with four observational sessions carried out during this period. The mothers were observed in terms of how they used scaffolding: which strategies were most successful; the consistency of the strategies employed and their outcomes; how much direct help was offered; the independence displayed by the children.

Results
The mothers were seen to increase the level of support and guidance to their children in the initial, early stages of the study, when the children were less sure of what to do, being younger and not as capable as in the later stages of the study. The researchers observed that the use of *contingent instruction* e.g. providing more help when needed but holding back when the child appeared confident, increased as the child became more adept and skilled at a task (i.e. when the child progressed then he/she would be given more independence and less help from the mother).

Conclusion
Scaffolding, when used appropriately, can enable a child to develop expertise at a task and a degree of independence.

Evaluation of Conner & Cross (2003)
Strengths
- ✓ The longitudinal design of this research means that the researchers were able to check their findings against each sampled session, increasing the validity of the results.
- ✓ The use of mother-child pairs and the young age of the children at the commencement of the

research gives the study some ecological validity as the participants were engaging in the type of behaviour that is frequent and natural when mothers help their children learn.

Limitations
X The small sample size of 45 and the fact that the participants were all from the USA makes the findings difficult to generalise to those outside of this demographic.
X The observational method can produce a type of demand characteristic (the observer effect) which would affect the validity of the findings if the participants felt self-conscious or produced artificial behaviour when being observed. Observational data can also be subject to researcher bias as it can be prone to interpretation rather than objective analysis.

Reference
Conner, D. B., & Cross, D. R. (2003). Longitudinal analysis of the presence, efficacy and stability of maternal scaffolding during informal problem-solving interactions. *British Journal of Developmental Psychology, 21*(3), pp. 315-334.

****

TOPIC 1: DEVELOPING AS A LEARNER

Content 2: Cognitive development

KEY STUDY 2.5: *Paulus et al. (2014). Social understanding and self-regulation predict pre-schoolers' sharing with friends and disliked peers: A longitudinal study.*

Links to:
- **Human Relationships: Social responsibility** – pro-social behaviour.

Background
Examined longitudinal relationship between early measures of prosocial action in infancy as well as cognitive and social-cognitive abilities, and the sharing behaviour of preschool children. Found that inhibitory control and social-cognitive abilities play an important role in the early development of prosocial action.

Aim
To investigate the relationship between prosocial behaviour in infancy along with cognitive and social skills with sharing behaviour.

Participants
72 children (35 female; 37 male) from white, middle-class families in urban areas of Germany. The children had a mean age of 61 months at the end of the study: they were tested at the age of 7 months; 18 months; 24 months; 30 months and 48 months.

Procedure
This was a longitudinal study with the children being tested on a variety of measures over the time span of the study's duration.

The measures used were as follows:
- **Goal-encoding:** this was used when the children were 7 months old to test their ability to anticipate the goal-directed action of another person e.g. reaching in a familiar place for an object or in a new place to which the object had just been moved.

- **Working memory:** the children, aged 7 months, were tested to see whether they could recall the location of visual cues, using working memory (i.e. short-term memory).

- **Instrumental helping:** the children, now aged 18 months, were tested to see whether or not they would pick up an object that the experimenter had dropped, and which was out of her reach and give it to her.

- **Empathic reasoning:** the children were tested for this measure at the age of 24 months: it involved them responding to their mother's (fake) pain at having trapped her finger in a clipboard.

- **Gift Delay:** the children were tested at 24 months: they were left alone with a gift for 3 minutes to see whether or not they would be tempted to open it.

- The children were also tested on inhibitory control/attention skills and how well they could take another person's perspective at 30 months; their verbal IQ at 48 months and their sharing behaviour (with a friend and also a disliked peer) at 60 months.

Results
A correlation was found between gratification delay (24 months) and inhibitory control (30 months) and sharing behaviour (60 months). The children who, at 24 months, understood their mother's distress (at her fake accident with the clipboard) shared well with friends at the age of 60 months. Children who had good goal-encoding scores at 7 months were willing to share with a disliked peer at 60 months. No relationship was found between early prosocial behaviour and later sharing behaviour.

Conclusion
Children who show early signs of being able to inhibit their responses and control their behaviour and who also have good social-cognitive skills are more likely to develop prosocial behaviour as they get older.

Evaluation of Paulus et al. (2014)
Strengths
- ✓ This was a well-designed study with in-built checks on reliability: all observational sessions were carried out by more than one observer, giving the procedure inter-rater reliability and tasks were counter-balanced so as to avoid order effects e.g. practice with the task, boredom, fatigue.
- ✓ The use of a longitudinal design means that real changes in the children's development could be tracked over time so that their performance at one age could be compared to their performance at other ages.

Limitations

- X The sample is small and is difficult to generalise as the demographic was white, middle-class Germans: it would be interesting to see how other social and cultural groups performed in a similar piece of research.
- X The tasks lack ecological validity: it is possible that the children did not behave as they would in real-life situations and as they got older, they may have been 'on their best behaviour' as they would become increasingly aware that they were being observed.

Reference

Paulus, M., Licata, M., Kristen, S., Thoermer, C., Woodward, A., & Sodian, B. (2015). Social understanding and self-regulation predict pre-schoolers' sharing with friends and disliked peers: A longitudinal study. *International Journal of Behavioral Development, 39*(1), pp. 53-64.

****

TOPIC 1: DEVELOPING AS A LEARNER

Critical thinking points

What are the possible applications of the findings of research into brain development?
Chugani (1998) found that there appears to be a 'critical period' for the development of crucial functions such as language in the first 10 years of a child's life. Having this information could help to inform the work of paediatricians, health visitors and other professionals who work closely with young children and are responsible for identifying possible signs of developmental delay. The findings of Gotgay et al. (2004) could be used to check for signs of developmental delay in young children. For example, if a child is slow to walk, talk, read etc. then this could be investigated using brain imaging to see if their brain is under-developed with regards to neural branching and pruning in the regions associated with such functions. Early interventions for children who have delayed brain and cognitive development is essential: there are definite 'windows of opportunity' in terms of brain development and the cognitive abilities linked to them so it is vital for clinicians, teachers, parents to be alert to any signs of impaired development in infants.

Are 'stage' theories of cognitive development, such as Piaget's, too restrictive? *According to Piaget, children pass through the developmental milestones (thresholds) when they reach a specific age and exit that stage when they hit the next age-based threshold. There are clearly some flaws with this idea. Not all children will reach the stage thresholds at the same time. e.g. some children may be advanced or may attain particular skills later than others. It is also possible that there are adults who are not capable of abstract thought, which Piaget claimed everyone became able to do at the age of 11. This is a 'one size fits all' theory that, particularly in today's world, needs to be revised in line with the significant influence that technology and mass media have on children's developing minds. The ways in which children experience family life are very different from when Piaget first proposed his theory (there are more single-parent families; blended families; gay parents for example) and the fact that Piaget did not even acknowledge the role that the family has on cognitive development is an oversight that is difficult to reconcile with any full account of a child's cognitive development.*

Could using children as participants actually confound the research process?
There is a saying in showbusiness: 'Never work with children or animals' and this is a sentiment with

which psychologists may, to some extent, agree. (In fact, they would probably argue that working with obedient lab rats is far preferable to any attempt to try to get a two-year-old child's attention!) When measuring a young child's behaviour, the researcher is at the mercy of a range of potentially study-wrecking variables: a lack of consistency in the child's responses; mood; time of day; hunger; illness; to say nothing of the potentially overbearing influence of the parents. The unpredictable and possibly contradictory nature of young children presents a problem when trying to form meaningful conclusions as to the behaviour under investigation. Researchers must be mindful of the pitfalls involved in measuring the behaviour of young children and so they should do as much as they can to eradicate the variables that may confound and ultimately invalidate their results.

****

Children learn through play

PSYCHOLOGY SORTED: KEY RESEARCH FOR STUDENTS AND TEACHERS
BOOK 2 – APPLIED PSYCHOLOGY

TOPIC 2: INFLUENCES ON COGNITIVE AND SOCIAL DEVELOPMENT

Key Idea: A child's social and cognitive development is affected by environmental factors

Content 3: Role of peers and play

KEY STUDY 3.1: *Elias & Berk (2002). Self-regulation in young children: is there a role for sociodramatic play?*

Background
Vygotsky theorised that make-believe play encourages healthy cognitive and social development. This study investigates whether or not participation in make-believe play influences socially responsible behaviour (social measure) and attentiveness (cognitive measure).

Aim
To investigate the role played by participation in make-believe play in terms of its influence on socially responsible behaviour (social measure) and attentiveness (cognitive measure).

Participants
51 children aged three to four years old from the USA.

Procedure
The children were observed in their classrooms during two terms of one school year. The children were observed in four 10-minute sessions by more than one observer. The quantity and the quality of their play was observed, with examples of fantasy and make-believe play episodes being of special interest to the observers. The social measure was based on how well they self-regulated their behaviour by willingly taking part in such socially responsible tasks as helping others, cleaning the classroom etc. The cognitive variable was measured via the children's attentiveness during circle time when they were listening to the teacher.

Results
Make-believe play was found to correlate positively with self-regulation and socially responsible behaviour: the more time a child spent in make-believe play – particularly with peers – the higher the number of socially responsible behaviours they performed. The results for the cognitive measure of attention were less conclusive as the teachers tended to regulate the children's behaviour during circle-time.

Conclusion
Make-believe play may contribute to a child's development of self-regulatory behaviour.

Evaluation of Elias & Berk (2002)
Strengths
- ✓ The use of time-sampling using an agreed scale, method of coding and more than one observer means that the study has inter-rater reliability.
- ✓ Young children tend to be less conscious of being observed than older children or adults, so it is possible that their behaviour was natural and unforced.

Limitations
- ✗ The cognitive variable of attentiveness is particularly difficult to measure as what appears to be attentiveness could, in fact, be something else e.g. daydreaming, tiredness.
- ✗ It is possible that researcher bias could have interfered with the recording of the data, with more importance being given to behaviours which supported the research hypothesis, or some behaviours being misinterpreted by the observers.

Reference
Elias, C.J. & Berk, L.E. (2002). Self-regulation in young children: is there a role for sociodramatic play? *Early Childhood Research Quarterly 17*, pp. 216–238.

****

TOPIC 2: INFLUENCES ON COGNITIVE AND SOCIAL DEVELOPMENT

Content 3: Role of peers and play

KEY STUDY 3.2: *Fiorelli & Russ (2012). Pretend play, coping, and subjective well-being in children: A follow-up study.*

Background
Longitudinal study investigating the relationship between emotional themes in pretend play and positive mood in daily life. Found that imagination and organization in play related to coping ability. Their results also support the stability of imagination and organization in pretend play over time.

Aim
To investigate relationships between pretend play, coping and subjective well-being/positive mood.

Participants
49 girls from a private girls' school who had originally participated in a study conducted by the researchers on private play and coping strategies in stressful situations.

Procedure
The girls participated in a series of tasks alongside an experimenter, with the following measures being used:

- **The Affect in Play Scale** (designed for ages 6-10 years): during a 25-minute session the experimenter observed the participant playing with two glove puppets and some coloured blocks.

- **The School Coping Scale:** 10 items on a self-report which asks the participant how they deal with potential problems at school e.g. *'What would you do if you were going to be late for school?'*

- **The Positive and Negative Affect Schedule for Children:** 30 items on a self-report that assess a child's positive and negative moods.

- **The Multidimensional Student Life Satisfaction Scale for Children**: 34 items asking about subjective well-being e.g. *'I wish I had different neighbours.'* The scale asks children to rate their satisfaction with friends, family, school, environment and themselves.

Results
Pretend play was significantly related to subjective well-being and coping at school. The girls who expressed themselves using emotions in pretend play were found to report a more positive mood on a daily basis and girls who showed imagination and were organised in their play had better coping mechanisms than those who did not.

Conclusion
Children who engage in expressive pretend play experience more positive moods and emotions in daily life and those who are organised in play show better coping ability.

Evaluation of Fiorelli & Russ (2011)
Strengths
- ✓ This was a highly controlled study, using well-established measures that had been tested for their reliability and validity: the use of correlational analysis also contributes to the objective nature of the data analysis.
- ✓ The fact that this was a follow-up study using a longitudinal design gives the findings validity as the researchers were able to check their findings against earlier results.

Limitations
- X The use of self-report scales is artificial and may have produced social desirability bias which would invalidate the responses of participants.
- X It is possible that some of the questions may have caused some distress to participants as they were being asked directly about their mood and about their feelings related to personal issues such as family relationships and potential problems at school.

Reference
Fiorelli, J. A. & Russ, S. (2012). Pretend play, coping, and subjective well-being in children: A follow-up study. *Journal of Play*, 5(1), pp. 81-103

****

The role of pretend play

TOPIC 2: INFLUENCES ON COGNITIVE AND SOCIAL DEVELOPMENT

Content 3: Role of peers and play

KEY STUDY 3.3: *Silva et al. (2016). Peers increase late adolescents' exploratory behavior and sensitivity to positive and negative feedback.*

Background
Late adolescents tested with peer observers engaged in more exploratory behaviour, learned faster from both positive and negative outcomes, and evinced better task performance than those tested alone. Suggests spending time with peers during adolescence may increase the odds that adolescents will behave recklessly, but also that they will learn from the consequences of their actions.

Aim
To investigate how peers affect older adolescents' exploratory behaviour; their ability to learn from the consequences of their actions and how they are able to use feedback to adjust their behaviour so as to experience positive long-term effects.

Participants
101 males aged 18-22 years old from the USA obtained using a self-selecting sampling method. 91% of the sample were college students; 67% were white; 12% were black; 15% were Asian; 4% were Latino and 2% was other/mixed race.

Procedure
The participants were randomly allocated to one of two conditions: the 'alone' condition in which they completed the task alone or the 'peer' condition in which one randomly-allocated participant completed the task while being observed by three other participants. The task was the Modified Iowa Gambling Task which involved the player either making a play or passing the decision to one of four randomly-assigned decks. Two of the decks (C and D) were positive, generating modest immediate rewards and relatively small losses, and ultimately resulting in long-term financial gains over repeated play. The other two decks (A and B) were negative, generating larger immediate rewards but large losses, and resulting in long-term loss over repeated play. In addition, within each type of deck there was one deck in which the losses were infrequent but relatively large and one in which they were consistent and relatively small.

Results
The results showed that participants in the 'peer' condition had a greater tendency to explore the environment in terms of making decisions to play more frequently than those in the 'alone' condition, particularly early on in the task when they did not have information as to the payoff of each deck. Those in the 'peer' condition were also more responsive to feedback than 'alone' participants, making them quicker to learn which choices led to rewards and which to costs in the game.

Conclusion
The presence of peers seems to increase the extent to which adolescent males learn from feedback and in turn are able to see the positive and negative consequences of their actions.

Evaluation of Silva et al. (2016)
Strengths
- ✓ The findings of this study are refreshing as they cast a different light on the behaviour of adolescents when with their peers, with some research finding that risk-taking and reckless behaviour increases when adolescent males are with their peers.
- ✓ The study uses a standardised procedure which is replicable and so could generate reliable results.

Limitations
- X The demographic of the sample comprises some ethnic diversity, but it is predominantly white and as the sample is all-male and almost all college students it is not fully representative of a wider population, making it difficult to generalise the findings.
- X The procedure was conducted in lab conditions, using an artificial task, meaning that it is difficult to know how peers might influence male adolescents in real-life, thus the study lacks external validity.

Reference
Silva, K., Shulman, E. P., Chein, J., & Steinberg, L. (2016). Peers increase late adolescents' exploratory behavior and sensitivity to positive and negative feedback. *Journal of Research on Adolescence*, 26(4), pp. 696-705.

****

TOPIC 2: INFLUENCES ON COGNITIVE AND SOCIAL DEVELOPMENT

Content 4: Childhood trauma and resilience

KEY STUDY 4.1: *Rutter et al. (1999). Quasi-autistic patterns following severe early global privation.*

Background
Investigated the effects of profound deprivation in an on-going longitudinal case study of Romanian orphans adopted into UK families. In this smaller case study, found that 6% of 111 children so adopted, at 4 and 6 years old showed a quasi-autistic pattern of behaviour associated with severe deprivation and a level of cognitive impairment.

Aim
To assess the long-term effects of profound deprivation (in this case as a result of living in a Romanian orphanage from a very early age) on cognitive and social development.

Participants
165 randomly selected children from Romanian orphanages who had been adopted by English families before the age of 42 month. 111 of the sample were assessed at the age of four and the ages of 4 and 6 years old; the remaining 54 were assessed at the age of 6 years old. A control group was used which consisted of 52 non-deprived British children who had been adopted before the age of 6 months.

Procedure
Social, behavioural and emotional functioning was assessed using interviews with the children's parents and questionnaires that parents and teachers completed. One questionnaire used was the Autism Screening Questionnaire which includes questions such as, *'Has X ever used odd phrases or said the same thing over and over?'* The children were also video-recorded during a play session. 26 of the children also took part in a more detailed clinical evaluation led by Rutter.

Results
6% of the 111 Romanian children assessed at 4 years and 6 years old showed signs of autism; no child in the British control group showed any such signs. The Romanian children who exhibited the autistic traits had markedly impaired cognitive skills compared to the other Romanian children in the study and showed signs of a deep, abiding long-term psychological distress due to early privation (never having established an attachment with an adult care-giver).

Conclusion
Healthy social and cognitive development is strongly influenced by early experience and can be impaired massively through deprivation and privation.

Evaluation of Rutter et al. (1999)
Strengths
- ✓ The researchers state that, *'The resemblance to autism was clearly demonstrated through the use of a well-validated, reliable, standardised diagnostic interview employed by an investigator very well experienced in its use and in the clinical manifestations of autism'* (p. 544).
- ✓ The use of a control group of non-deprived adoptees means that the study has good reliability as the variables of interest can be clearly identified and compared between the groups by the researchers.

Limitations
- X It is possible that, due to the traumatic early experiences of the Romanian children, those diagnosed with autism may in fact have been exhibiting signs of other disorders e.g. PTSD, OCD, rather than autism.
- X It remains unclear as to what the cause of the Romanian children's autism might be: they could simply have been born with a genetic predisposition to autism rather than the autism having been a result of their early privation.

Reference
Rutter, M., Andersen-Wood, L., Beckett, C. et al. (1999). Quasi-autistic patterns following severe early global privation. *The Journal of Child Psychology and Psychiatry and Allied Disciplines*, *40*(4), pp.537-549.

****

TOPIC 2: INFLUENCES ON COGNITIVE AND SOCIAL DEVELOPMENT

Content 4: Childhood trauma and resilience

KEY STUDY 4.2: *Boyden (2003). Children under fire: challenging assumptions about children's resilience.*

Background
A review article challenging assumptions about children's resilience related to their experiences of living in a war zone. Concludes that children should not be viewed as vulnerable and incompetent victims but as agents of their own fate and should be accorded a level of respect based on their ability to be resilient in the face of terrible odds.

Aim
To challenge assumptions about children's resilience related to their experiences of living in a war zone.

Procedure
A review article in which traditional views of childhood and war are challenged by the author.

Main comments and findings

- **Research in child development may make assumptions that are not necessarily accurate:** The author takes issue with the fact that most research on child development focuses on the early years which has led to a dearth of information relating to middle and later childhood. It is this emphasis on very young children that has encouraged the idea that children are fragile, vulnerable creatures requiring a lot of care from adults if they are to thrive. Boyden argues that this may actually prevent children from developing a resilient 'shell' with which to deal with life's ups and downs.

- **War is not necessarily a rare or unusual thing:** Boyden claims that researchers from Western backgrounds have presented the world as a well-regulated, safe place in which war and conflict are aberrations that lie outside the range of normal human experience. Too much emphasis has been placed on psychological outcomes, she argues, with the assumption that children in war zones will necessarily show signs of PTSD and other pathologies – these come from an individualistic perspective and may not fully take into account the range of responses from different cultures.

- **Different cultures conceptualise childhood in ways which are not the same as a Westernised, industrialised, individualistic perspective:** Boyden argues that there is an overtly Westernised projection of childhood that follows a specific set of expected norms but that does not acknowledge that childhood is a shifting state, characterised by context-specific, changing variables. In Bangladesh, for example, a person stops being referred to as a 'child' the moment they start work, even if this is at the age of six, as may well happen in poorer countries.

- **The idea of what 'suffering' means should be re-defined:** What seems an unbearable hardship to one society may be regarded as nothing very serious by another and to use one framework to try to understand the other is flawed. There is a lot of anecdotal evidence that children flourish in adversity, often taking on caring roles, replacing adults, becoming the family 'breadwinner', keeping the family together, being resourceful.

- **Children should not be viewed as helpless victims as this can have a negative impact on their resilience:** Boyden claims that to assume that children in war zones are psychologically unwell, traumatised and weak (which, she also accepts, could be true given the awful circumstances of their lives) is a mistake. She claims that this assumption could seriously undermine children's resilience, creating a self-fulfilling prophecy of incompetence and inability to cope.

Conclusion
Children are active agents in their own resilience, and they should not be regarded as passive, helpless victims, at the mercy of decisions and actions made by adults. Children can and do have insights and opinions about their situation that may well be as informed and as valid as those of adults.

Evaluation of Boyden (2003)
Strengths
✓ Boyden's ideas may be controversial, but they shed a refreshing new light on the experience of children living in war zones – it is a view which may ultimately empower children not to feel as if they are victims but instead that they have some control over their lives
✓ By focusing on the Western-centric stance of much of the research in this field Boyden has made a good case for there being a need for a more emic approach to the topic.

Limitations
X A review article relies on secondary data that may not be reliable as it was obtained by other researchers, whose methodology the author cannot vouch for.
X This is a huge, far-ranging topic to offer an overview of and it is difficult to form meaningful conclusions that address the experience and needs of all children going through the trauma of living in a war zone.

Reference
Boyden, J. (2003). Children under fire: challenging assumptions about children's resilience. *Children Youth and Environments, 13*(1), pp. 1-29.

****

Children under fire

PSYCHOLOGY SORTED: KEY RESEARCH FOR STUDENTS AND TEACHERS
BOOK 2 – APPLIED PSYCHOLOGY

TOPIC 2: INFLUENCES ON COGNITIVE AND SOCIAL DEVELOPMENT

Content 4: Childhood trauma and resilience

KEY STUDY 4.3: *Werner (2005). Resilience and recovery: Findings from the Kauai longitudinal study.*

Background
Summary of Werner & Smith's earlier work: the **Kaui Longitudinal Study** into the impact of a series of different stressors and traumatic events on a multi-ethnic cohort of 698 children on Kauai, Hawaii. Found that early childhood trauma or adversity can be overcome if one or more protective factors are in place to encourage resilience.

Aim
To investigate the impact of a series of different stressors and traumatic events on one cohort of children on Kauai, Hawaii.

Participants
One cohort of 698 children born in 1955 on the Hawaiian island of Kauai, U.S.A.

Procedure
A longitudinal study which tracked the progress of the participants over decades. The participants' doctors, public health nurses, social workers and mental health workers carried out the investigation. They were studied as children, and then as adults, at ages 1, 2, 10, 18, 32, and 40 years. 30% of the sample had experienced trauma in their early years. e.g. a home life characterised by violence or disharmony; poverty; birth complications; parental mental health issues; childhood delinquency. These negative life events were termed 'risk factors' by Werner as they presented a definite threat to the children's physical, psychological and emotional development. The researchers distinguished between two types of participant in their sample

- Survivors: these were the children who were able to come through early childhood trauma and adverse, potentially traumatic circumstances and emerged positively, with good prospects, successful life choices and a productive lifestyle

- Victims: the children whose early traumatic, negative experiences resulted in them making negative choices e.g. turning to crime, substance abuse, unhealthy relationships.

Results
Two thirds of the sample, the 'victims' had already shown evidence of behaviour problems by the age of two; by the age of 10 there was evidence of them having mental health issues and some delinquency. The 'survivors' were successful at school, had good home and social lives, secured good jobs, had better physical health, fewer divorces and a lower death rate than the victims. What is even more surprising is that some of the children performed even better than children from an advantaged background.

Werner identified specific 'protective factors' that contributed to the resilience of the survivors:

- A 'sunny' disposition – this was identified as a personality type that worked as its own protective factor. *'Independent observers described the resilient toddlers as agreeable, cheerful, friendly, responsive, and sociable'* (Werner, 2005).

- An adult who takes an interest – the survivors tended to have at least one adult who took care of their emotional needs: if a parent could not fulfil this role then grandparents, extended family members, older siblings or teachers worked as effective parental substitutes.

- Education – some of the survivors became properly involved in education as a mature student which enabled them to 'turn over a new leaf' and make positive changes in their lives.

- A stable romantic relationship – the survivors tended to have someone in their life who was meaningful to them and a source of support e.g. a spouse or someone to whom they felt emotionally close.

- Religion – this was especially true for those survivors who found resilience later on in life, particularly those who had struggled with alcohol addiction or substance abuse.

Conclusion
Early childhood trauma or adversity can be overcome if one or more protective factors are in place to encourage resilience.

Evaluation of Werner (2005)
Strengths
- ✓ This massive longitudinal study amassed a large amount of data which could clearly show progress and changes over time, from a variety of sources, increasing validity in terms of the ability to triangulate data.
- ✓ There is real scope to use the findings from this research in practical contexts such as schools' intervention programmes, mentoring schemes and the identification of talent in at-risk children e.g. via sports clubs, drama clubs etc.

Limitations
- X While it may be true that the findings from this study have great applicability to practical and therapeutic settings it remains very difficult for some institutions such as schools to be able to actually implement such schemes due to a lack of resources or the skill needed in order to identify such children and provide suitable intervention for them.
- X The sample in this research was drawn from one Hawaiian island which means that the results are not easy to generalise to other populations.

Reference
Werner, E. (2005). Resilience and recovery: Findings from the Kauai longitudinal study. *Research, Policy, and Practice in Children's Mental Health, 19*(1), pp. 11-14.

****

TOPIC 2: INFLUENCES ON COGNITIVE AND SOCIAL DEVELOPMENT

Content 5: Poverty/socio-economic status

KEY STUDY 5.1: *Werner (2005). Resilience and recovery: Findings from the Kauai longitudinal study.*

See above, under **TOPIC 2: INFLUENCES ON COGNITIVE AND SOCIAL DEVELOPMENT**, *Content 4: Childhood trauma and resilience.* This study may also be used for the influence of poverty on cognitive and social development.

****

TOPIC 2: INFLUENCES ON COGNITIVE AND SOCIAL DEVELOPMENT

Content 5: Poverty/socio-economic status

KEY STUDY 5.2: *Kar et al. (2008). Cognitive development in children with chronic protein energy malnutrition.*

Background
Investigated the effect of malnutrition on cognitive performance in a sample of 20 Indian children from 5 to 7 years old and between 8 and 10 years old. The data from these two age groups was compared to children in a control group. Malnourished children in both groups scored lower in attention, working memory and visuospatial tasks than the control group. But older children showed less impairment. Kar developed a theory of delayed cognitive development rather than permanent impairment.

Aim
To investigate the effect of stunted growth on the development of cognitive processes in children.

Participants
Children aged 5-7 years old and 8-10 years old from Bangalore, India. All the children were right-handed. 20 of the children were identified as being 'adequately nourished' and 20 were identified as 'malnourished'.

Procedure
The children underwent a battery of tests designed to assess their neuropsychological functioning. The tests assessed their motor speed (finger-tapping test); attention (a test in which they had to trail two colours); executive functioning (verbal fluency: naming as many items beginning with the same letter as they could); visual-spatial ability (completing an object with a missing part); comprehension (understanding verbal commands); memory (having to recall abstract designs). The children underwent 13 separate tests in all, with some cognitive skills, such as memory, being tested more than once in different ways.

Results
The children who had been identified as 'malnourished' performed worse on most of the neuropsychological tests, apart from motor speed, the least cognitively demanding of the tests. These children also performed poorly on tests of higher cognitive functions such as attention, working memory, verbal comprehension and memory. The malnourished children showed less cognitive development than the adequately nourished group, with some cognitive functions e.g. executive functioning, working memory.

Conclusion
Malnourished children may experience cognitive impairments and developmental delay compared to adequately nourished children. Malnourished children's cognitive development may follow a different pattern to that of adequately nourished children.

Evaluation of Kar et al. (2008)
Strengths
- ✓ The findings of this study reflect prior research on malnourished children which gives the study concurrent validity.
- ✓ There is a real purpose and usefulness to this study: its findings could be used to help combat the negative impact of malnutrition as part of an intervention to help those in need.

Limitations
- X The children identified as 'malnourished' may have shown impaired cognitive functioning for reasons other than diet e.g. genetic conditions; family environment.
- X It is possible that the malnourished children in the study might have experienced fatigue or some distress carrying out so many tests to assess their cognitive functioning.

Reference
Kar, B. R., Rao, S. L., & Chandramouli, B. A. (2008). Cognitive development in children with chronic protein energy malnutrition. *Behavioral and Brain Functions, 4* (1), p.1

****

TOPIC 2: INFLUENCES ON COGNITIVE AND SOCIAL DEVELOPMENT

Content 5: Poverty/socio-economic status

KEY STUDY 5.3: *Luby et al. (2013) The effects of poverty on childhood brain development: the mediating effect of caregiving and stressful life events.*

See above, under **TOPIC 1: DEVELOPING AS A LEARNER,** *Content 1: Brain development.* This study may also be used for the influence of poverty on cognitive and social development.

****

TOPIC 2: INFLUENCES ON COGNITIVE AND SOCIAL DEVELOPMENT

Critical thinking points

Is it possible to measure play?
The nature of play is that it is spontaneous, joyful, adventurous, and something that possibly even defies description or categorisation. Attempting to categorise types of play and link these categories to social and cognitive development may, ultimately, be futile. Berk (1998) looked at the effect of make-believe play and concluded that make-believe play may contribute to a child's development of self-regulatory behaviour, but this is a very difficult idea to find concrete, empirical evidence for as there as so many possible explanations to account for self-regulation. Once a person stops being a child they tend to forget how to play or why they played, and it could be argued that children should just be left alone to enjoy their play. Perhaps this is a topic that cannot – and should not - be intellectualised.

Does every child necessarily need protective factors in place in order to be resilient?
Although there is no research (yet) to back up this idea, it could be argued that some children may survive trauma and become, in the words of Werner (2005) a 'survivor' without having any protective factors to account for their survival. In other words, they have a dour, rather than a 'sunny' disposition, they do not have the benefit of an interested adult in their life, they do not take to religion or education etc. And yet, they survive, and they may even flourish in adverse circumstances. One of the difficulties in attempting to measure survival behaviour is that there are myriad possible explanations as to why, how, and who survives – what is a protective factor for one child may register as zero for another child. It could be argued, therefore, that resilience is something which is not restricted to one set of protective factors, but which is flexible and which depends on the circumstances of the trauma.

Is it ethical to study children living in a war-zone? Boyden (2003) has focused on a controversial, highly emotive topic for her review and her conclusion that treating children in war-zones as 'victims' is detrimental to their resilience is certainly a worthy and noble one. It could also be true that she is in danger of dismissing the long-term impact that living in a war zone might bring - and, along with it, the idea that such children require special consideration from adults assigned to their care. Most researchers cannot relate to the experience of war-zone children so how can they possibly know what is best for these children? What is particularly problematic is that her article tends to under-play the importance of a secure and nurturing family environment to the emotional well-being of a child: while it may be true that some children can overcome a harsh or abusive family it seems counter-intuitive to suggest that such an environment (i.e. a loving one) might in some way be a negative influence on their development. By placing the emphasis on the idea that war-zone children are 'tough' and not in need of a nurturing family life Boyden may be guilty of creating a self-fulfilling prophecy about these children i.e. 'these children don't need love or affection, they've lived through a war zone'. This could, ultimately, mean that they are treated with less care and attention than children who have not experienced life in a war-zone, which is potentially damaging for them.

****

TOPIC 3: DEVELOPING AN IDENTITY

Key Idea: Identity is the result of an interaction between biological, cognitive and social factors.

Content 6: Attachment

KEY STUDY 6.1: *Ainsworth & Bell (1970). Attachment, exploration, and separation: illustrated by the behaviour of one-year-olds in a strange situation.*

Background
Identified three different attachment styles (secure, insecure-avoidant, insecure-resistant /ambivalent) and concluded that attachment style can be seen in the behaviour exhibited by caregiver and child with the majority of children showing a secure and positive relationship with the caregiver.

Aim
To investigate attachment styles between a young infant and his/her caregiver.

Participants
56 white middle-class infants from the USA, aged 49-51 weeks.

Procedure
A controlled observation lasting a total of 20 minutes in which the following procedure was set up and then observed by Ainsworth:

1. The mother enters the room with her baby and sits down. The room contains interesting toys but is unfamiliar to the baby. (i.e. it is a *strange situation*).
2. A stranger enters, talks to the mother and then approaches the baby with a toy.
3. The mother leaves quietly. The stranger attempts to interact with the infant. If the baby shows distress the stranger attempts to comfort them.
4. The mother returns and greets the infant. The stranger leaves. The mother then tries to engage the baby in play and then she leaves, saying goodbye to the baby.
5. The baby is left alone.
6. The stranger enters and tries to play with and speak to the baby. If the baby is upset the stranger will offer comfort.
7. The mother returns, greets the baby and picks them up. The stranger leaves quietly.

The observed behavioural categories included separation anxiety (signs of distress from the baby when the mother leaves); stranger anxiety (signs of distress when the stranger attempts to engage with the child); proximity-seeking and exploration (use of the mother as a secure base from which to confidently explore the environment); reunion behaviour (behaviour of the baby when the mother re-enters the room).

Results

Ainsworth categorised the attachment styles she observed as follows:

- **Insecure-avoidant attachment (Type A) - seen in 10-15% of strange situation studies:** Behaviours associated with this type of attachment include the child showing very little interest in the mother with little or no separation anxiety or joy when reunited. Stranger anxiety is also absent, in fact the child may actually show preference for the stranger over the mother. Children within this attachment style may grow into adults who are 'disconnected' from life, who struggle to show empathy and who cannot sustain intimate relationships.

- **Secure attachment (Type B) - seen in 70% of strange situation studies:** Behaviours associated with this type of attachment include a dependence on the mother, seeing her as a secure base, but still having the confidence to explore the environment. There is separation anxiety but the child calms down quickly when reunited with the mother: the child definitely prefers the mother to the stranger and will only be comforted by the mother. This is a highly healthy attachment type: both mother and child benefit from it. Securely attached children generally grow up to be well-adjusted, sociable and productive adults according to attachment theory.

- **Insecure-resistant/ambivalent attachment (Type C) - seen in 10-15% of strange situation studies:** Behaviours associated with this type of attachment include an unwillingness to explore the immediate environment, staying close to the mother, clingy behaviour even when the mother is in the room and extreme separation anxiety (they may not calm down even during the reunion phase). They appear angry as well as anxious and they do not seem to see the mother as a secure base.

Conclusion

Attachment style can be seen in the behaviour exhibited by caregiver and child with the majority of children showing a secure and positive relationship with the caregiver.

Evaluation of Ainsworth & Bell (1970)

Strengths

- ✓ This research uses controlled observation with a standardised procedure, which makes it replicable; plus the use of measurable quantitative data enhances the study's reliability. The use of qualitative observations also adds rich, in-depth data to the results.
- ✓ The study has been replicated many times with similar results, thus validating Ainsworth's categorisation of specific attachment styles.

Limitations

- X Ecological validity is low as the study took place in a lab setting that could have resulted in artificial or out-of-character behaviour from infant or mother.
- X Attachment is a complex and multi-layered phenomenon so it cannot be definitively measured using one 20-minute sample of mother-infant behaviour.
- X Using stranger anxiety as a measure of attachment is ethnocentric and does not allow for cultures where stranger-care is more common.

Reference

Ainsworth, M. D. S., & Bell, S. M. (1970). Attachment, exploration, and separation: illustrated by the behaviour of one-year-olds in a strange situation. *Child Development*, pp.49-67.

****

TOPIC 3: DEVELOPING AN IDENTITY

Content 6: Attachment

KEY STUDY 6.2: *Bowlby (1988). A Secure Base. Parent-Child Attachment and Healthy Human Development.*

Background
Analysis of the past, present and future of attachment theory, with reference to Harlow, Ainsworth and Rutter.

Aim
To present an overview of research into attachment.

Procedure
A review of research in the field of child attachment and the implications of different attachment styles – of the lack of attachment – on a child's social development.

Main comments and findings
- Concerns as to the detrimental effects of institutional care and maternal deprivation were being voiced by psychologists as early as the 1930s and 40s but was initially met with little interest by those outside of psychological research.

- The article cites key work carried out by Ainsworth and Harlow, whose research using rhesus monkeys dramatically demonstrated the extreme emotional, psychological and physical distress and trauma experienced by the animals who had been deprived of maternal care in their early years.

- Bowlby criticises early theories of attachment, particularly the behaviourist, 'cupboard love' theory that argues that a child forms an attachment to his/her mother because she feeds him/her.

- The work of Lorenz is highlighted in the article, whose work on imprinting in geese was highly influential: it caused Bowlby to consider the nature of human attachment and the extent to which attachment is a natural, instinctive response that has evolved to ensure the survival of the vulnerable human infant.

- Bowlby cites the work of Ainsworth in the field of attachment, specifically attachment styles, stating that it *'has led attachment theory to be widely regarded as probably the best supported theory of socio-emotional development yet available'* (p 23).

- He argues for a theory of monotropy – the idea that a child has one caregiver whom they prefer above all others.

- Children who have experienced maternal deprivation or other forms of dysfunctional attachment will go on to inflict a negative parenting style on their own children.

Conclusion
There is still much work to be done in the field of attachment: Bowlby argues that is an essential topic to study and that it could yield enormous benefits.

Evaluation of Bowlby (1988)
Strengths
- ✓ Bowlby writes at great length and in impressive detail about a whole host of issues that relate to attachment: his work is influential and is still being cited and applied to a variety of contexts today.
- ✓ Bowlby's work with juvenile delinquents (young offenders) highlighted the important finding that maternal deprivation may lead to something he termed *affectionless psychopathy*. Such findings could be used to inform intervention programmes for children who are at risk of becoming life-long criminals.

Limitations
- X Because the article is so far-reaching it is at times rather difficult to encapsulate the ideas concisely: perhaps fewer ideas in more depth would have improved this aspect of the article.
- X Some of Bowlby's ideas have been challenged and found to be less valid than at first supposed e.g. monotropy (children appear to form multiple attachments of equal value rather than just one).

Reference
Bowlby, J. (1988). *A Secure Base. Parent-Child Attachment and Healthy Human Development.* New York: Basic Books.

****

TOPIC 3: DEVELOPING AN IDENTITY

Content 6: Attachment

KEY STUDY 6.3: *Van Ijzendoorn & Kroonenberg (1988). Cross-cultural patterns of attachment: A meta-analysis of the strange situation.*

Background
Meta-analysis of 32 studies carried out in eight different countries that had replicated Ainsworth's method. The researchers combined the results of the studies and looked at attachment differences *within* cultures and countries as well as *between* them. Found cultural variations in attachment styles.

Aim
To investigate attachment styles across a range of cultures.

Procedure
A meta-analysis of 32 studies using the *Strange Situation*, carried out in eight different countries with a total sample of 1,990 participants. The researchers combined all the results of the 32 studies

and they also looked at attachment differences *within* cultures and countries as well as *between* them.

Results
The table below shows some of the scores from the meta-analysis.

Country	Insecure-Avoidant (Type A) %	Secure (Type B) %	Insecure-Resistant (Type C) %
Great Britain	22	75	3
Sweden	22	74	4
USA	21	65	14
Germany	35	57	8
Japan	5	68	27
Israel	7	64	29
China	25	50	25

The most common attachment type across all countries was found to be Secure (Type B). Insecure-Resistant attachment came as the lowest type for all of the countries tested. Findings *within* countries highlighted massive variation in some cases. Variation within one country/culture was nearly one and a half times higher than variation between countries/cultures.

Conclusion
Attachment style may depend on culture and may vary within cultures.

Evaluation of Van Ijzendoorn & Kroonenberg (1988)
Strengths
- ✓ This is an example of etic research as it takes a cultural dimension such as individualism/collectivism and provides a comparison of a range of countries using the variable of attachment as the measure by which to compare them.
- ✓ The study amassed a large amount of quantitative data, which means that the findings should be robust and reliable.

Limitations
- X As this research was carried out at least 30 years ago it would seem that the time is ripe to re-visit the Strange Situation cross-culturally, given the changes in technology and the family dynamic that have occurred in the intervening years (e.g. the emergence of the internet; the proliferation in single-parent families, gay parents, blended families.)
- X Using a meta-analysis is a rather cold and clinical way of trying to understand what is a complex and very human behaviour that may be subject to varying interpretations depending on the context in which the behaviour is observed.

Reference
Van Ijzendoorn, M. H., & Kroonenberg, P. M. (1988). Cross-cultural patterns of attachment: A meta-analysis of the strange situation. *Child Development*, pp. 147-156.

****

TOPIC 3: DEVELOPING AN IDENTITY

Content 6: Attachment

KEY STUDY 6.4: *Gross et al. (2017). The multifaceted nature of prosocial behavior in children: links with attachment theory and research.*

Background
Reported on the nature of the link between secure attachment and prosocial behaviour. Found that there was a connection, broadly defined, but results vary across comforting, sharing, and helping.

Aim
To offer a theoretical model of the ways in which attachment contributes to the development of prosocial behaviour, specifically in comforting, sharing and helping others and to review research in this field.

Procedure
A review of research in the field accompanied by the authors' own observations on the topic of attachment.

Main comments and findings

- The authors argue that research by renowned figures in the field such as Bowlby and Ainsworth identified that the secure attachment style is the most conducive to the development of prosocial behaviour. This hinges on the child, via their attachment behaviour with the caregiver(s) developing a strong Internal Working Model, being able to regulate their emotions and thus developing key traits such as empathy, kindness and consideration for others.

- Research using the *Strange Situation* on two-year olds found that those children who exhibited a secure attachment style at the age of two showed prosocial behaviour towards their peers at the age of five.

- Studies which have looked for a relationship between prosocial behaviour and secure attachment in middle childhood have shown widely varying results, with positive correlations between the two variables being found more in longitudinal studies rather than snapshot studies. Secure eight and nine-year old children in one study were rated as more prosocial than insecure-ambivalent children, however another study found that there was no difference between secure and insecure children in terms of their prosocial behaviour towards their younger siblings.

- The findings of research in this field differs in terms of who is reporting the prosocial behaviour: in some studies, a positive correlation between secure attachment and prosocial behaviour is reported by parents and in other research it is reported by teachers, often with contrasting results.
- Studies of adolescent participants using a standardised questionnaire (Inventory of Parent and Peer Attachment-Revised) link secure attachment with increased prosocial behaviour. Some

research shows that secure attachment with the mother but not the father is correlated to prosocial behaviour in adolescents, with emphasis being placed on empathy and self-control in the adolescents' reported behaviour.

Conclusion
There appears to be a relationship between secure attachment and prosocial behaviour, but it is inconclusive as the findings of research in this field vary widely.

Evaluation of Gross et al. (2017)
Strengths
- ✓ By reviewing research which uses measures such as the Strange Situation and the Inventory of Parent and Peer Attachment-Revised mean that the findings of the studies are easy to compare as they use standardised measures.
- ✓ There does appear to be some agreement across studies that secure attachment may be linked to prosocial behaviour.

Limitations
- X Linking secure attachment to prosocial behaviour is somewhat deterministic and it doesn't account for the wide range of other possible explanations for sharing, comforting, helping etc.
- X There is very little empirical evidence on attachment and prosocial behaviour in adolescence so the findings from these studies are quite weak and inconclusive.

Reference
Gross, J. T., Stern, J. A., Brett, B. E., & Cassidy, J. (2017). The multifaceted nature of prosocial behavior in children: Links with attachment theory and research. *Social Development, 26*(4), pp. 661-678.

****

TOPIC 3: DEVELOPING AN IDENTITY

Content 7: Gender identity and social roles

KEY STUDY 7.1: *Whiting & Edwards (1973). A cross-cultural analysis of sex differences in the behavior of children aged three through 11.*

Links to
- **Sociocultural approach:** Cultural influences on individual attitudes, identity and behaviours – enculturation.

Background
Studied children aged 3 - 11 in six different countries. In the majority of these societies, girls were more nurturing. Boys were more aggressive, dominant, and engaged in more rough-and-tumble play. The researchers interpreted the gender differences in the six cultures as differences in socialisation.

Aim
To investigate gender differences using a cross-cultural sample of children.

Participants
Children aged 3-11 years old from communities in Kenya, Japan, India, the Philippines, Mexico and the USA. A total of 31 girls and 31 boys made up the sample.

Procedure
Between 1954-1956 researchers who lived within the community they were observing conducted naturalistic observations over several months. Each child was observed one at a time by two observers for 5-minute sessions over a course of 6-14 months, totalling 17 observation periods per child.

Results
Boys in the 3-6 years age group exhibited more rough-and-tumble play, used more insults and showed more dominant and attention-seeking behaviour. Girls in this age group sought contact more, but in a prosocial rather than a rough manner; they were also found to be more nurturing than boys. Girls were given household and baby-minding tasks more than boys (although this was not seen in the sample from the USA) but as age increased so did the frequency of tasks assigned to boys, particularly in communities where animals and agriculture featured strongly. Girls, particularly in Kenya, spent more time in the home than boys did. Few gender differences were found in the sample from the USA, with girls having access to the same educational opportunities as boys and expressing similar career ambitions.

Conclusion
Socialisation may contribute to gender differences across cultures.

Evaluation of Whiting and Edwards (1973)
Strengths
- ✓ The aspect of this research which involved the researchers living within the communities they were observing shows an emic approach to considering cultural behaviours which is quite rare. Emic research is invaluable as it allows researchers to embed themselves within the culture they are studying so as to truly understand it and gain insight without prejudice or judgement.
- ✓ The observations were time-sampled and involved a strictly-agreed and adhered-to system of coding giving the study good inter-rater reliability.

Limitations
- X The samples per community were small which means that the data is unlikely to be robust.
- X It is possible that some of the participants may have succumbed to the observer effect, behaving in ways which were self-conscious as they knew they were being observed (this would be particularly true for the older children but less so for the younger ones).

Reference
Whiting, B., & Edwards, C. P. (1973). A cross-cultural analysis of sex differences in the behavior of children aged three through 11. *The Journal of Social Psychology, 91*(2), pp. 171-188.

****

TOPIC 3: DEVELOPING AN IDENTITY

Content 7: Gender identity and social roles

KEY STUDY 7.2: *Imperato-McGinley et al. (1974). Steroid 5α-reductase deficiency in man: an inherited form of male pseudohermaphroditism.*

Background
Case study of the Batista family in the Dominican Republic. Due to genetic mutation, some children were born with what appeared to be the genitalia of girls, but physically developed into men at puberty. Throughout their childhood, they were raised as girls. However, as adults, they demonstrated clearly masculine gender roles and heterosexual behaviour, as some of the physical characteristics of being a male also began to appear. This seems to indicate a strong biological origin of gender identity. (The family is one of 27 affected families, due to the inheritance of a mutant gene).

Aim
To investigate the role played by steroid 5a in the formation of male hormones (androgens) at the time of sexual differentiation in the womb and its subsequent expression in the male children from specifically selected families from the Dominican Republic.

Participants
13 families were selected from Salinas in the Dominican Republic on the basis that 24 males amongst the sample exhibited pseudo-hermaphroditic characteristics. The affected males had been born with genitalia that appeared ambiguous i.e. they appeared to be more female than male, and they were subsequently raised as girls.

Procedure
The males in the sample had been brought up as female due to the nature of their sexual organs, which resembled female characteristics more so than male characteristics. When the participants reached puberty at around the age of 12 however, it became obvious that they were not female as they began to present masculine puberty-related characteristics: a deeper voice; a more muscular frame; an emerging penis and testicles and no signs of the female characteristics of puberty. The researchers hypothesised that the affected males were all suffering from the same condition: a defect in the way that testosterone was metabolised due to malfunctioning of the 5a steroid. They therefore carried out analysis of the plasma testosterone in both affected and unaffected males so as to have a control group.

Results
The affected males had dihydrotestosterone concentrations that were well below the normal male range of 40 – 80 per 100ml. The affected males consistently measured lower on 5a, thus lowering their general levels of testosterone, which the researchers linked to their 'hidden' maleness pre-puberty.

Conclusion
During gestation (when the child is still in the womb) and at puberty it is necessary for the full range of testosterone-appropriate hormones and enzymes to be secreted in order for that child to exhibit full male secondary sexual characteristics.

Evaluation of Imperato-McGinley et al. (1974)
Strengths
- ✓ The procedure involved taking blood-plasma samples which is an unbiased, objective and clinical method high in reliability.
- ✓ The findings could be used to screen for possible birth defects in terms of ambiguity around gender. Suitable intervention could then be offered to affected families i.e. knowing to raise the affected child as male rather than female.

Limitations
- X The research can show *what* may happen when a family shares a defective testosterone metabolism, but it cannot explain *why* this happens.
- X The findings of this research – which really is in the form of a case study – can only be generalised to the selected families from the Dominican Republic.

Reference
Imperato-McGinley, J., Guerrero, L., Gautier, T., & Peterson, R. E. (1974). Steroid 5α-reductase deficiency in man: an inherited form of male pseudohermaphroditism. *Science, 186*(4170), pp. 1213-1215.

****

TOPIC 3: DEVELOPING AN IDENTITY

Content 7: Gender identity and social roles

KEY STUDY 7.3: *Bem (1981). Gender schema theory: a cognitive account of sex typing.*

Links to
- **Sociocultural approach:** Cultural influences on individual attitudes, identity and behaviours – enculturation.

Background
Gender schema theory suggests that children gradually form their gender identity as they learn about the network of themes and associations within their own culture. In addition, gender schema is closely linked to self-concept. Children engage in gender appropriate behaviour because they are motivated by the desire to be good girls or boys.

Aim
To investigate the extent to which gender schema is linked to the values associated with specific words.

Participants
48 females and 48 males, all undergraduate students from Stanford University, California, USA.

Procedure
The participants were presented with 61 words at 3-second intervals. The categories were:
- 16 proper names (8 female; 8 male)
- 15 animal names
- 15 verbs
- 15 items of clothing

In the animal, verb and clothing categories half of the words were chosen due to their overall rating of 'maleness' as measured on a previous test (e.g. *gorilla, trousers, hurling*) and half due to their previous rating of 'femaleness' (e.g. *blushing, bikini, butterfly*). One third of the words in this category were chosen due to their 'neutral' qualities (e.g. *sweater, ant, stepping*). After viewing the words, the participants were given 8 minutes to write down as many words as they could remember in free-recall conditions.

Results
Participants who had previously been labelled as identifying strongly with their own gender tended to cluster together the words from the categories that had the strongest associations with male/female values and qualities as determined by conventional, societal norms in the USA e.g. nurturing and passivity with femaleness; action and assertiveness with maleness.

Conclusion
Gender schemas may determine the ways in which individuals perceive the world, even extending to the ways in which neutral stimuli such as animal names or verbs are perceived.

Evaluation of Bem (1981)
Strengths
- ✓ Bem's article cites research findings and procedures from other studies so that her own research can be viewed in the light of other's findings, giving it validity.
- ✓ The procedure cited in this experiment would be easy to replicate and if done so with the same sample external reliability could be tested for.

Limitations
- X The procedure used by Bem is artificial and may have given rise to demand characteristics e.g. the participants may have responded according to how they thought they *should* respond rather than how they actually wanted to respond.
- X The findings of this research lack external validity as it is very difficult to make the leap between the participants' responses on this measure and the ways in which gender schema may influence behaviour in real life.

Reference
Bem, S. L. (1981). Gender schema theory: A cognitive account of sex typing. *Psychological Review, 88*(4), pp. 354-364.

****

TOPIC 3: DEVELOPING AN IDENTITY

Content 7: Gender identity and social roles

KEY STUDY 7.4: *Sroufe et al. (1993). The significance of gender boundaries in preadolescence: Contemporary correlates and antecedents of boundary violation and maintenance.*

Links to
- **Sociocultural approach:** Cultural influences on individual attitudes, identity and behaviours – enculturation.

Background
Children who did not behave in a gender-stereotypical way were the least popular with their peers. These studies indicate that children establish a kind of social control in relation to gender roles very early, and it may well be that enculturation by peers is an important factor in gender development.

Aim
To investigate if gender-stereotyped roles are influenced by enculturation by peers.

Participants
48 children who came from households where poverty was an issue and who tended to have young, single mothers with below-average high school completion rates, from Minnesota, USA. 80% were white; 14% were black; 6% were Native American or Hispanic. The children were allocated to one of three groups of 16 (equal numbers of males and females per group). Each group of 16 took part in a 4-week summer camp held on the university campus, at the rate of one group per year. (Each group had a mean age of 10 years at the time of taking part in the camp).

Procedure
The participants attended the camp 5 days a week for 4.5 hours per day, and during this time they took part in sporting activities, arts, circle time, singing and went on several day trips. The researchers made 317 observations on average per child and they recorded a total of 138 hours of video of each group of 16 with each child appearing more than once on the recording. Event sampling was used, and more than one observer coded the behaviours observed. The type of behaviours that the researchers were interested were based on gender and included categories such as no interest shown in the opposite gender; watching opposite members casually or with more intent; relaxed interactions. They were also particularly interested in what they termed 'Gender Boundary Violating Behaviour' such as 'hovering' near an opposite gender group for too long; a single child joining an opposite gender group; flirting and behaving in a provocative way towards the opposite gender. On the last day of camp, the children completed an exit poll, rating the popularity of each child at the camp.

Results
The researchers found that gender boundaries were rarely breached and that they appear to represent a valid social norm for children of this age (10 years). Most of the children associated with their own gender, with very little cross-gender interaction observed. This was particularly true for boys who tended to impose harsher sanctions for gender boundary violation. Children who violated gender boundaries were viewed as less popular and more socially incompetent than those who stuck to same-gender activities.

Conclusion
Understanding the rules of gender boundaries appears to determine the extent to which a child is seen as socially competent and it may be one of the products of enculturation.

Evaluation of Sroufe et al. (1993)
Strengths
- ✓ The use of naturalistic observation means that the findings are high in ecological validity.
- ✓ The observers used a strict coding method, with several checks being made on the videotaped observations particularly, which means that the research is high in inter-rater reliability.

Limitations
- X There are some ethical dilemmas with this study: filming under-16s is fraught with particularly sensitive issues and may have invaded their privacy; rating other children in terms of popularity may also perpetuate stereotypical views on a range of issues; the researchers would have had to ensure that the parents understood the aims and procedure of the research before giving their consent.
- X The use of naturalistic observation can produce findings that may be subjective or a result of misinterpretation. For example, 'hovering' may not actually be what the child was doing at the time – they may simply have been waiting for someone, daydreaming or deciding what to do next.

Reference
Sroufe, L. A., Bennett, C., Englund, M., Urban, J., & Shulman, S. (1993). The significance of gender boundaries in preadolescence: Contemporary correlates and antecedents of boundary violation and maintenance. Child Development, 64(2), pp. 455-466.

****

Breaking down gender boundaries

TOPIC 3: DEVELOPING AN IDENTITY

Content 7: Gender identity and social roles

KEY STUDY 7.5: *Halpern & Perry-Jenkins (2016). Parents' gender ideology and gendered behavior as predictors of children's gender-role attitudes: a longitudinal exploration.*

Background
Used longitudinal, self-report data from a sample of 109 dual-earner, working-class couples and their 6-year-old children living in the USA to investigate the relative importance of parents' gender ideology and their actual behavior, in predicting children's development of gender role attitudes. Found that mothers' and fathers' behaviours were better predictors of children's gender-role attitudes than parents' ideology.

Aim
To investigate the extent to the gendered behaviour as opposed to the stated gender ideology of parents could predict the gender-role development of their children.

Participants
109 working class couples (both of whom contributed to the family income) who had attended pre-natal parenting classes from Western Massachusetts. The females in the sample were on average 27 years old, the men were 29 years old on average and 95% of the sample were white. The couples in the sample earned less money and worked more hours than other families in the population from which they were obtained.

Procedure
The parents filled in a questionnaire designed to measure their gender ideology during the last 3 months of the mother's pregnancy and again when the baby was 6 months old. In a 6-year follow-up session the parents were interviewed, via a detailed rating-scale questionnaire regarding their attitudes towards women (e.g. women earning money, as carers etc.) The parents' gendered behaviour was assessed using questionnaires that focused on topics such as the division of housework; the division of child-care; the number of hours worked outside of the home and how traditional the occupation of the mothers and the fathers were. In the follow-up study the children, now aged 6, were asked questions and shown images of traditional gendered stimuli to assess the extent of their gender stereotyping.

Results
Girls at the age of 6 in the study showed more knowledge of female gender stereotypes if they had observed traditional female behaviours from their mothers, such as the mother taking on the burden of housework and childcare. Boys showed less knowledge of masculine behaviour when their mothers performed more stereotypically female tasks. The behaviour of the mother then, seemed to influence both girls and boys in terms of their gendered attitudes and knowledge. The more traditional the behaviour was from the mothers during the first year of the child's life, the more their children were likely to choose traditionally gendered occupations.

Conclusion
Children who receive more physical and emotional care from their mothers early in life in also receive messages about the roles of women and men which appear to strongly influence their attitudes towards gender.

Evaluation of Halpern & Perry-Jenkins (2016)
Strengths
- ✓ These findings are consistent with earlier research on mothers' behaviour and children's gender-role attitudes which gives the study concurrent validity.
- ✓ Using the follow-up study enabled the researchers to check the reliability of their initial findings and to check the validity of their hypotheses.

Limitations
- ✗ The sample is limited, being only from Western Massachusetts, predominantly white and working class – although the researchers do report that they are going to replicate the study using a more racially and ethnically diverse sample.
- ✗ The participants were paid $50 for their participation in each interview, making a total of $200 which represented a considerable amount to the couples sampled, which could bias the findings if the participants felt obliged to respond in a certain way.

Reference
Halpern, H. P., & Perry-Jenkins, M. (2016). Parents' gender ideology and gendered behavior as predictors of children's gender-role attitudes: A longitudinal exploration. *Sex Roles*, *74*(11-12), pp. 527-542.

****

TOPIC 3: DEVELOPING AN IDENTITY

Content 8: Development of empathy and theory of mind

KEY STUDY 8.1: *Baron-Cohen et al. (1985). Does the autistic child have a 'theory of mind'?*

Brief Summary
This was a test of the representational stage of theory of mind, using the Sally-Anne task (described below). Found that 11-year-old children on the autistic spectrum were not able to correctly identify that others had a different view from their own, while 10-year-old children with Down syndrome and 4-year-old children with neither autism nor Down syndrome were able to detect this.

Aim
To investigate whether or not children with autistic spectrum disorder (ASD) have theory of mind.

Participants
20 children with ASD (mean age of 11 years); 14 children with Down syndrome (mean age of 10.5 years); 27 normal children (mean age of 4.5 years).

Procedure
Each child participated in the false-belief test known as the Sally-Anne task which consists of the following procedure in which the children are presented with the following scenario:

- Sally and Anne are two dolls. Sally hides a marble in her basket: Anne is in the room with her when she does this so she can see where Sally has hidden the marble.
- Sally leaves the room. While Sally is gone, Anne hides the marble in a box.
- Sally comes back into the room and she can't find her marble. Where will she look for it?

If a child does not have theory of mind, they will say that Sally will look for the marble *in the box where Anne has hidden it*. This clearly demonstrates that they think that *Sally knows what they know i.e. that the marble has been moved.* They are unable to see the situation from Sally's perspective – *that she was out of the room when the marble was moved, and therefore will not know to look in the box.* If the child says that Sally will look for the marble in the basket *because that is where she originally put it* then the child has passed the false belief task and has shown evidence of having theory of mind.

Results
Results of the Sally-Anne task

Group	Number of correct answers
ASD	4 out of 20
Down Syndrome	12 out of 14
Normal	23 out of 27

Conclusion
Children with ASD may lack theory of mind, meaning that they do not have the cognitive capacity to understand that other people may have different thoughts, ideas and information from their own.

Evaluation of Baron-Cohen et al. (1985)
Strengths
- ✓ The use of two control groups, one comprising 'normal' children and other of children with Down syndrome provides good points of contrast with the ASD group, enabling the researchers to isolate theory of mind as the point of difference between the groups.
- ✓ The Sally-Anne task uses a standardised procedure, making it easy to replicate and increasing its reliability.

Limitations
- X It is possible that some children may have theory of mind but not be able to pass a false-belief task, because the task is artificial and is carried out in lab conditions, which would affect the validity of the findings.
- X The Sally-Anne task is conceptual and artificial: it does not reflect the ways in which children may apply theory of mind in real life.

PSYCHOLOGY SORTED: KEY RESEARCH FOR STUDENTS AND TEACHERS
BOOK 2 – APPLIED PSYCHOLOGY

Reference
Baron-Cohen, S., Leslie, A. M., & Frith, U. (1985). Does the autistic child have a 'theory of mind'? *Cognition, 21*(1), pp. 37-46.

****

TOPIC 3: DEVELOPING AN IDENTITY

Content 8: Development of empathy and theory of mind

KEY STUDY 8.2: *Repacholi & Gopnik (1997). Early reasoning about desires: evidence from 14-and 18-month-olds.*

Background
The researchers wanted to get a better understanding of when children are able to understand that other people may have a belief or desire that is different from their own. Children who were only 14 months old offered foods that they themselves liked, but those who were 18 months old were able to separate the experimenters' wishes from their own.

Aim
To investigate whether or not children as young as 14 and 18 months old can use reasoning to understand desire for a particular food.

Participants
81 children aged 14 months old (41 male; 40 female) and 78 children aged 18 months old (37 male; 41 female) from middle-class families where both parents were together. 72% of the sample were white.

Procedure
The procedure consisted of two conditions:

- The matched condition: this involved the experimenter showing pleasure when he/she tasted a sweet cracker and disgust when he/she tasted raw broccoli.
- The mismatched condition: this involved the experimenter showing pleasure when he/she tasted raw broccoli and disgust when he/she tasted a sweet cracker.

The experimenter then placed one hand with the palm upwards, between the two bowls of food (i.e. the sweet cracker and the broccoli) and requested of the participant, *'Can you give me some?'* so that it was not clear as to which food the experimenter was referring – the child had to make that decision on the basis of how they had seen the experimenter react to each food.

Results
The 18-month-old children offered the experimenter the food that he/she had shown pleasure tasting (i.e. the sweet crackers in the matched condition and the broccoli in the mismatched condition). In a baseline test the 18-month-olds had shown a preference for the sweet crackers but this did not appear to influence their choice of food in the mismatched condition: they still offered

the broccoli. The researchers state that this is evidence of the 18-month-olds using earlier emotional cues to infer which food the experimenter desired.

In contrast, the 14-month-olds offered the sweet crackers (i.e. the food they preferred), regardless of the experimenter's prior behaviour showing preference for the broccoli.

Conclusion
Children as young as 18 months old may have the ability to infer another person's desires based on their prior behaviour.

Evaluation of Repacholi & Gopnik (1997)
Strengths
- ✓ This was a well-controlled experiment which used counter-balancing of conditions to avoid order effects confounding the results.
- ✓ The findings shed some light on the remarkable ability of very young children to use theory of mind in order to ascertain what another person feels about a target object.

Limitations
- ✗ The 18-month-olds may simply have remembered which food the experimenter preferred and so they may have offered that food based on their superior recall to that of the 14-month-olds rather than on their inference of another person's desire for one food type over another.
- ✗ The sample demographic may have biased the results as it is probable that middle-class parents are more likely to expose their child to a range of emotions and situations in which the child is encouraged to interpret other people's behaviour than parents who may be less affluent, with more stressors in their lives and therefore will have less time to devote to encouraging their child's finer social skills.

Reference
Repacholi, B. M., & Gopnik, A. (1997). Early reasoning about desires: evidence from 14-and 18-month-olds. *Developmental Psychology*, *33*(1), pp. 12-21.

****

TOPIC 3: DEVELOPING AN IDENTITY

Content 8: Development of empathy and theory of mind

KEY STUDY 8.3: *Cowell et al. (2015). The curious relation between theory of mind and sharing in preschool age children.*

Background
The current study examined the role of early theory of mind in sharing in a large sample of preschool-aged children. Found a contradictory relationship between early false-belief understanding and sharing behaviour, whereby competence in false-belief understanding was correlated with less sharing. It was the children who could engage in theory of mind that decided to share less with others.

Aim
To investigate the role of early theory of mind and executive functioning in pre-schoolers' sharing behaviour.

Participants
98 children aged three to five years old from the greater Chicago area of the USA. The children came from a demographic that had a low socioeconomic status. 50% were African American; 36% were Hispanic and 14% were Caucasian.

Procedure
The children were tested using a series of measures which included:

- **Theory of Mind test**: a version of the Sally-Anne task was used for this test.

- **The Dictator game**: each child was given 6 stickers and told that these stickers were now theirs. They were then told that another child (not named or identified) in the study would not get any stickers but they could give that child any number of their own stickers if they chose to.

- **Something's the Same game**: this is a test of attentional shifting/flexibility. The children were shown pages with pictures on them that varied in size, colour, and type and they were then asked to identify pairs of pictures that were the same in size, colour, or likeness. Once they had identified two objects that matched on one dimension, they were told to match two other objects/pictures on another dimension.

- **Working memory**: the children were shown a drawing of an animal and a coloured dot, both located in a house. The child was told to name the colour and the animal. The experimenter then flipped to a blank house and asked the child which animal lived in this particular house.

Results
Children who passed the false-belief task, thereby showing Theory of Mind were less generous, sharing fewer of their stickers than children who failed the false-belief task. This result was not related to age but only to whether the child had passed or failed the false-belief task. Sharing behaviour was not related to executive functioning at all.

Conclusion
Pre-school children with Theory of Mind are less willing to share their resources than children of the same age without Theory of Mind.

Evaluation of Cowell et al. (2015)
Strengths
✓ The findings may pinpoint a possible window of development in the progression of theory of mind in young children as prior research has shown that theory of mind is associated with increased generosity in older children.
✓ The sample is of a good size and is representative of the target population from which it was drawn which makes the results generalisable to some extent.

Limitations

✗ This was a snapshot study of a young child's ability to take another person's perspective: it does not explain or reveal how each child might use Theory of Mind linked to sharing behaviour across time and in other situations.

✗ The researchers made inferences to the children's sharing behaviour, but without concrete evidence it remains unclear as to why the generous children were generous. Their generosity could have been due to factors such as social conditioning from their parents, a predisposition to be generous, or feeling that the experimenter expected them to share with another child, for example. (i.e. social desirability effects and participant expectations could have been present).

Reference

Cowell, J. M., Samek, A., List, J., & Decety, J. (2015). The curious relation between theory of mind and sharing in preschool age children. *PLoS One, 10*(2), e0117947.

****

TOPIC 3: DEVELOPING AN IDENTITY

Critical thinking points

Is some research into attachment culturally biased?

Mary Ainsworth's pioneering work, the 'Strange Situation' (1970) paved the way for numerous replications that have ultimately found her categorisation of the three attachment types to have some validity. Ainsworth's study has, however, been criticised due to the nature of the sample as it represented white, middle-class families with no allowance being made for alternative interpretations of attachment behaviours. Van Ijzendoorn & Kroonenberg's (1988) meta-analysis of cross-cultural replications of the 'Strange Situation' suggest that countries such as Japan have a higher number of insecure-resistant children. This may, however, be a misinterpretation of attachment behaviour as it is likely that Japanese children would have spent more time with their mother in 1988 than would children in countries such as the UK and Germany, as many Japanese mothers stayed at home with young children. Young babies in Japan at the time of the study may have expressed more separation anxiety than in Westernised countries as they may have been more used to being with their mother: this does not necessarily mean that they have an insecure attachment style. More up-to-date research is clearly needed on cross-cultural attachment behaviours.

Is it possible that the norms assumed of collectivist cultures and linked to gender roles are changing?

Whiting & Edwards (1973) research highlighted the very traditional gender roles observed within a range of collectivist cultures, but not seen in the New England community of the USA. While it would be foolish to argue that collectivist cultures have come to resemble individualistic cultures in the intervening years since this study it is nonetheless noticeable that some aspects of gender role expectation within some collectivist cultures are changing. With the strong presence of media (both mass and social) in the lives of so many people it may be the case that gender roles could change in collectivist cultures – despite the influence of parents, due to global communication)see globalization, in the Sociocultural Approach, and digital technology in the Cognitive Approach). Although parents act as primary reinforcers in the lives of their children there are other external forces at work which might influence gender identity. The process of acculturation might exert a powerful influence on gender roles, with boys and girls rejecting the strictures placed on them by their parents, so that collectivist cultures may eventually adopt the norms of more individualistic societies.

Are false-belief tasks the best way to determine theory of mind and, ultimately, autistic spectrum disorders (ASD)?
It is a fairly universal assumption (based on empirical evidence) that children and adults with ASD lack theory of mind, largely based on their failure at false-belief tasks. Some research in this field has highlighted the fact that not all children with ASD fail false-belief tasks and not all children with theory of mind pass false-belief tasks. False-belief task studies proliferate within developmental psychology and the assumption has always been that ASD and theory of mind are linked but this may not necessarily be the case. There may, in fact, be other reasons to account for why autistic children and adults fail false-belief tasks: they may find the task irrelevant; they may not wish to engage with the researcher; they may find the task too easy and 'switch off'; they may not understand the way that the question is worded. For a diagnosis of ASD to be given it is vital that a true understanding of what constitutes the autistic spectrum is absolutely understood by those offering the diagnosis. False-belief tasks may be an overly simplistic way of establishing this.

****

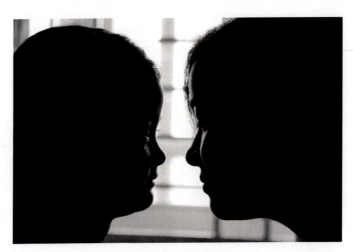

Developing an identity

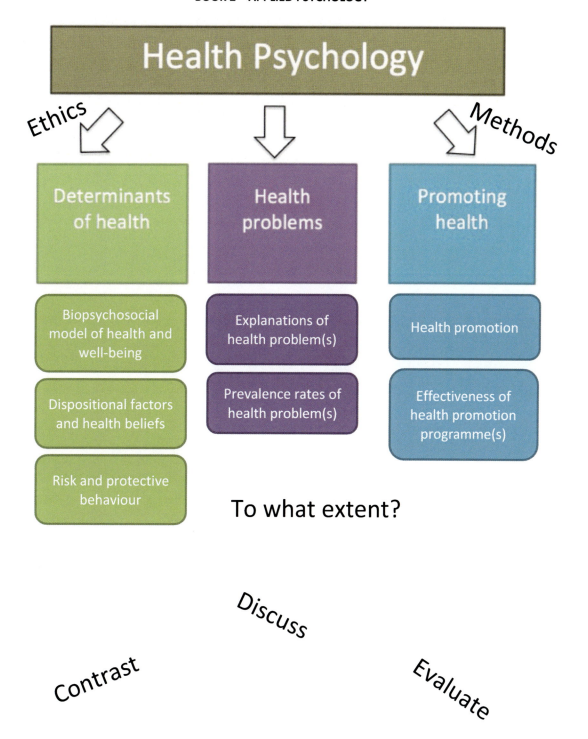

HEALTH PSYCHOLOGY

Topic 1: Determinants of health

Key Idea: Inheritance, behaviour and environment can pre-dispose us to good or bad health, as health is a combination of biological, psychological and social factors.

Content	Research	Use in Health Psychology	Links to
Biopsychosocial model of health and well-being	Classic **Engel (1977)**	Model of health and disease developed as an alternative to the then dominant biomedical model, that he viewed as reductionist and based on a faulty mind-body dualism. The biopsychosocial model is holistic, and explains health (and illness) as having biological, psychological and social dimensions.	**Abnormal Psychology:** normality vs. abnormality – disputes Szasz's claim that psychiatry should be taken out of medicine, but instead says it should be part of the biopsychosocial model.
	Critique/Extension **Marmot et al. (1991)** *Also for risk and protective factors – the role of socio-economic status, perceived job strain and relationships in stress.*	Carried out the 'Whitehall II study' (the Whitehall I study was conducted in 1967) into the social, biological and psychological aspects of stress, using a cohort of over 10,000 civil servants of different socio-economic status. Concluded that the accumulated burden of life stress coupled with limited protective psychosocial resources is associated with adverse psychological, biological, and quality of life outcomes.	
	Recent **Haslam et al. (2018)** *Also for risk and protective factors – the role of social support.*	Researched awareness of the importance of social factors for health — specifically, of the curative and protective role played by social support and social integration. Concluded that, while people were aware of biological and psychological factors in health, awareness of social factors is limited.	

Further resources

TED talk by Susan Pinker (April 2017). The secret to living longer may be your social life. https://tinyurl.com/y8q5j6ey

TED talk. Pinker - living longer

HEALTH PSYCHOLOGY

Topic 1: Determinants of health

Key Idea: Inheritance, behaviour, cognition and environment can pre-dispose us to good or bad health, as health is a combination of biological, psychological and social factors.

Content	Research	Use in Health Psychology	Links to
Dispositional factors and health beliefs	Classic **Rosenstock (1974)**	Described the development and structure of the health belief model (HBM) which explains how a person's perception of the possible seriousness of a potential health problem, and their susceptibility to it combine with a balance between the perceived benefits of taking action vs. barriers to taking action, to result in a person either acting to preserve their own health, or ignoring a health risk.	
	Critique/Extension **Davidson et al. (2010)** *Also for risk and protective factors.*	Examined whether higher levels of positive affect were associated with a lower risk of coronary heart disease (CHD) in a large prospective study with 10 years of follow-up. Found that indeed there was a significant negative correlation between positive affect and CHD.	
	Recent **Pänkäläinen et al. (2016)**	An 11-year prospective study on a regional sample of three cohorts, aged 52–56, 62–66, and 72–76 years, to investigate if there was a correlation between optimism, pessimism, and CHD mortality in a sample of Finnish participants. Found that pessimists had a higher occurrence of CHD, **but** failed to find any association with optimism and a decreased risk of coronary heart disease.	

Further resources

Connor, S. (20 Nov 2016). Is pessimism really bad for you? *The Guardian.*
https://tinyurl.com/y8q5j6ey

Dillner, L. (6 March, 2017). Can optimism make you live longer? *The Guardian.*
https://tinyurl.com/jn5oyqd

Is pessimism really bad for you?

HEALTH PSYCHOLOGY

Topic 1: Determinants of health

Key Idea: Inheritance, behaviour and environment can pre-dispose us to good or bad health, as health is a combination of biological, psychological and social factors.

Content	Research	Use in Health Psychology	Links to
Risk and protective factors	Classic **Marmot et al. (1991)** *Also for biopsychosocial model of health and well-being.*	Ongoing longitudinal prospective cohort study - researchers gathered data from all British civil servants between the ages of 35 and 55 who were working in the London offices between the years of 1985-1988. Over 30 years of data confirm the connection between psychosocial factors (socio-economic status, perceived job strain, relationships) and the development of disease.	
	Critique/Extension **Davidson et al. (2010)** *Also for dispositional factors and health beliefs.*	Examined whether higher levels of positive affect were associated with a lower risk of coronary heart disease (CHD) in a large prospective study with 10 years of follow-up. Found that indeed there was a significant negative correlation between positive affect and CHD.	
	Recent **Haslam et al. (2018)** *Also for biopsychosocial model of health and well-being.*	Researched awareness of the importance of social factors for health — specifically, of the curative and protective role played by social support and social integration. Concluded that, while people were aware of biological and psychological factors in health, awareness of social factors is limited.	

Further resources

Marmot, M. (19 March 2005). Social determinants of health inequalities. *Lancet, 365,* 1022 -1104. A comprehensive summary of cross-cultural differences in mortality worldwide. https://tinyurl.com/y5syo32z

Sample, I. (6 June 2018). Work stress raises risk of premature death in vulnerable men - study *The Guardian.* https://tinyurl.com/ydzarlqw

Social determinants of health inequalities

PSYCHOLOGY SORTED: KEY RESEARCH FOR STUDENTS AND TEACHERS
BOOK 2 – APPLIED PSYCHOLOGY

HEALTH PSYCHOLOGY

Topic 2: Health problems – stress as an example
Key Idea: Health problem(s) and their prevalence can be explained using biopsychosocial explanations.

Content	Research	Use in Health Psychology	Links to
Explanations of health problem(s)	Classic **Selye et al. (1936)**	General Adaptation Syndrome (GAS) as an explanation for the stress response, and an analysis of the alarm (fight or flight), resistance and exhaustion stages, with the exhaustion stage being responsible for long-term health problems. Links hypothalamic–pituitary–adrenocortical (HPA) system with stress and illness. (Biological).	**Biological Approach:** Hormones and behavior – the effect of cortisol on human behavior.
	Critique/Extension **Lazarus and Alfert (1964)**	Cognitive appraisal explanation of how appraisal of stressors may be experimentally manipulated, resulting in more or less stress experienced, as measured through galvanic skin response and self-report. (Interaction of cognitive and biological)	
	Recent **Fernald et al. (2008)**	Study into how the exhaustion stage can manifest in a blunted cortisol response in children after they experience repeated social stressors, like maternal depression and poverty. (Interaction of the social and the biological).	**Biological Approach:** Hormones and behavior – the effect of cortisol on human behavior.

Further resources (for health problems other than stress)

Qasim et al. (2018). On the origin of obesity: identifying the biological, environmental and cultural drivers of genetic risk among human populations. *Obesity Reviews, 19*, pp. 121–149.
https://tinyurl.com/y5mzt82t

Robinson, T.E. & Berridge, K.C. (1993). The neural basis of drug craving: an incentive-sensitization theory of addiction. *Brain Research Reviews, 18,* pp. 247-291.
https://tinyurl.com/y4hjj36d

TED talk by Sandra Aamodt (June 2013). Why dieting doesn't usually work.
https://tinyurl.com/qh392cd

TED talk. Aamodt - dieting

HEALTH PSYCHOLOGY

Topic 2: Health problems – stress as an example

Key Idea: Health problem(s) and their prevalence can be explained using biopsychosocial explanations.

Content	Research	Use in Health Psychology	Links to
Prevalence of health problem(s) [Note that there is no agreed published 'prevalence rate' for stress, as stress itself is not a disease as defined and classified by the DSM-5 or ICD-10 manuals].	Work **The European Agency for Safety and Health at Work (2009)**	Summary of the findings of a 2005 self-report survey among all member countries of the EU. Found that on average 22% of Europeans experience stress at work. However, this rate varies when considered through the lens of a specific country, gender, age, or occupation.	
	Age and gender **Otte et al. (2004)**	Meta-analysis of results from research databases between the years 1966 and 2003 to investigate age and gender-related differences in stress response to challenge (measured by cortisol levels). Prevalence of stress highest in older women.	
	Recent rise in prevalence **Mental Health Foundation (2018)**	Survey of over 4000 UK adults found that 74% reported feeling unable to cope with stress during the last year with women, those in poverty and younger people reporting over this average figure.	

Further resources (for health problems other than stress)

Monteiro, C.A. et al. (2018). Household availability of ultra-processed foods and obesity in nineteen European countries. *Public Health Nutrition, 21* (1), pp. 1-9. https://tinyurl.com/y3x2u5y8

Monteiro - obesity

WHO (2018). WHO global report on trends in prevalence of tobacco smoking 2000–2025 (2nd ed.) https://tinyurl.com/y5zrjnz3

WHO - tobacco smoking

HEALTH PSYCHOLOGY

Topic 3: Promoting health
Key Idea: Psychological theories can help inform health promotion.

Content	Research	Use in Health Psychology	Links to
Health Promotion	Classic **Quist-Paulsen et al. (2003)**	Looked at fear arousal as a method for encouraging the motivation to quit smoking. Found that those who had experienced negative, fear-inducing stimuli about smoking were more likely to quit than a control group.	
	Critique/Extension **Bandura (2004)**	Social cognitive theory of health promotion, wherein Bandura identified self-efficacy as the most important explanatory and predictive determinant in health promotion success. He equates this with the concept of 'perceived behavioural control' used in TPB. However, he explains how his model is social and how a socially-oriented agenda is needed for health promotion.	**Cognitive Approach:** Thinking and decision-making - 2. Theory of planned behaviour and theory of reasoned action.
	Recent **Conner et al. (2013)**	How sociocultural factors mitigate the cognitive theory of planned behavior when applied to health. Socio-economic status (SES) moderates the effectiveness of the theory of planned behaviour as an explanation for health behaviour, as the intention-health behaviour relationship is weaker in people from lower SES groups.	**Cognitive Approach:** Thinking and decision-making - 2. Theory of planned behaviour and theory of reasoned action.

Further resources
WHO health promotion page – full of information and infographics.
https://tinyurl.com/8yfpzvo

WHO health promotion page

PSYCHOLOGY SORTED: KEY RESEARCH FOR STUDENTS AND TEACHERS
BOOK 2 – APPLIED PSYCHOLOGY

HEALTH PSYCHOLOGY

Topic 3: Promoting health
Key Idea: Psychological theories can help inform health promotion.

Content	Research	Use in Health Psychology	Links to
Effectiveness of health promotion programmes	Classic **Witte & Allen (2000)**	Conducted a meta-analysis of studies into the effectiveness of fear messages as part of health promotion programmes. They found that providing a high-fear message was accompanied by a high-efficacy message, suggesting that that it was possible to change behaviour, then it was effective.	
	Critique/Extension **Colchero et al. (2016)**	An observational study into the result of the tax on sweetened drinks that was introduced in Mexico in Jan 2014 as part of a health promotion programme to reduce dental caries, obesity and Type 2 diabetes in the population. Found that the buying of sweetened drinks had reduced by 12% by Dec 2014.	
	Recent **Toft et al. (2018)**	Report of a 2012-2015 Danish community-based, multi-level intervention project ('supersetting') aimed at improving eating habits and physical activity in Danish families with young children. Found that involving multiple setting and multiple community stakeholders was more effective at promoting health than any individual approach.	

Further resources

Boseley, S. (2 Feb 2012). Mexico sugar tax lowers consumption for the second year running. *The Guardian.* When the individual fear approach is insufficient, then nationwide price policies can promote health. https://tinyurl.com/jmxqmm8

Lustig et al. (2 Feb 2012). The toxic truth about sugar. *Nature, Vol.282*, pp. 27-29. https://tinyurl.com/yyy6s6rc

Mexico sugar tax

HEALTH PSYCHOLOGY

TOPIC 1: DETERMINANTS OF HEALTH

Key Idea: Inheritance, behaviour and environment can pre-dispose us to good or bad health, as health is a combination of biological, psychological and social factors.

Content 1: Biopsychosocial model of health and well-being.

KEY STUDY 1.1: *Engel (1977). The need for a new medical model: a challenge for biomedicine.*

Brief Summary
Model of health and disease developed as an alternative to the then dominant biomedical model, that he viewed as reductionist and based on a faulty mind-body dualism. The biopsychosocial model is holistic, and explains health (and illness) as having biological, psychological and social dimensions.

Aim
To challenge the assumption that the biomedical model should be applied to the diagnosing and explanations of illnesses.

Procedure
A critical review of the biomedical model (BMM) in the light of other ways of approaching health and disease, with particular reference to the idea of the mind/body relationship (a psychosocial model).

Main comments and findings
- The BMM has at its core molecular biology and is thus unsuitable for measuring and commenting on mental illnesses and other conditions which may have social or psychological causes or explanations.

- Too much weight is given to the BMM due to its 'scientific' nature when in fact alternative models may be more appropriate when applied to specific illnesses. In this way the BMM is overly dogmatic (meaning that it attempts to force symptoms to fit biomedical criteria rather than attempting to find alternative explanations for them).

- The BMM focuses on a mind/body dualism, with the mind and body regarded as separate entities rather than there being a bi-directional relationship between them. Using this dualism, a clinician may diagnose diabetes as a 'body' disorder and schizophrenia as a 'mind' disorder, disregarding any relationship between body and mind in the experience and manifestation of each illness. A psychosocial model would consider each illness from all angles, incorporating the diverse range of factors that may contribute to the severity, duration and intensity of the illness.

- The BMM rests on reliable methods of data collection, including interviewing the patient but these are of little use if the clinician does not develop a sensitive and highly tuned understanding of the ways in which patients communicate their symptoms. Being aware of ambiguities in their reporting of symptoms, of how the patient may misuse or substitute medical terms is essential in the diagnostic process. The issue of culture is also important as there may be a culture clash between clinician and patient that could result in misdiagnosis or in the clinician assuming that the patient is a 'timewaster'.

- Clinicians should evaluate all the factors which could be contributing to the patient's illness, rather than focusing on biological factors alone. The psychosocial approach would shed light on the individual differences surrounding illness e.g. some people claim that they are ill whereas others may shrug off the same symptoms or put them down to simply being 'a fact of life'.

Conclusion

The BMM is the primary model for explaining disease but it has its shortcomings, mainly due to an over-reliance on reductionist biological explanations.

Evaluation of Engel (1977)

Strengths

- ✓ The review takes a much-needed critical approach to the BMM, which could result in alternative and more holistic models being adopted by the health community.
- ✓ The review was published in 1977 and it is clear to see that in some ways it is a visionary piece of research e.g. with the growing interest and investment in 'alternative' and holistic therapies within health such as reflexology, meditation, mindfulness and social support interventions.

Limitations

- X The article does not explain specifically *how* the psychosocial model could be instigated or utilised by clinicians.
- X The practicalities of employing the psychosocial model fully and comprehensively may be impaired due to lack of funding, lack of trained practitioners and a general mistrust of alternative methods in some sectors of the health industry which the article does not fully acknowledge.

Reference

Engel, G. L. (1977). The need for a new medical model: a challenge for biomedicine. Science, 196(4286), 129-136. Engel, G. L. (1977). The need for a new medical model: a challenge for biomedicine. *Science, 196*(4286), 129-136.

****

PSYCHOLOGY SORTED: KEY RESEARCH FOR STUDENTS AND TEACHERS
BOOK 2 – APPLIED PSYCHOLOGY

TOPIC 1: DETERMINANTS OF HEALTH

Content 1: Biopsychosocial model of health and well-being

KEY STUDY 1.2: *Marmot et al. (1991). Health inequalities among British civil servants: the Whitehall II study.*

Brief Summary
Carried out the 'Whitehall II study' (the Whitehall I study was conducted in 1967) into the social, biological and psychological aspects of stress, using a cohort of over 10,000 civil servants of different socio-economic status. Concluded that the accumulated burden of life stress coupled with limited protective psychosocial resources is associated with adverse psychological, biological, and quality of life outcomes.

Aim
To investigate the impact of a range of stressors on biological, psychological and sociocultural outcomes.

Participants
10,308 civil servants (6895 male; 3413 female; age range 35-55 years old) from the UK.

Procedure
The researchers used a longitudinal design as the research was conducted over 3 years. The research methods used included 7 questionnaires, each of which related to a different stressor in the participants' lives e.g. job control (stress experienced at work). This variable was also measured through independent assessments of the work environment by personnel managers, using job specifications and role responsibilities. The researchers kept records of stress-related illness and the participants were checked for signs of cardiovascular disease, e.g. chest pains. The researchers then conducted a correlational analysis to test the association between job control and stress-related illness. Biological measures were also used e.g. cholesterol levels (high levels can be linked to stress) as well as sociocultural measures such as environmental stressors such as neighbourhood, housing, loneliness, social support.

Results
The researchers found definite links between particular stressors e.g. low job control/feeling that one cannot cope at work with physiological conditions such as heart attack, cancer, strokes and gastrointestinal problems. In fact, these vulnerable participants were found to be four times as likely as less stressed participants to die from a stress-related illness.

Conclusion
There appears to be a link between low control over one's work and dangerous levels of stress (and with this the attendant illnesses).

Evaluation of Marmot et al. (1991)

Strengths
- ✓ Using a correlational analysis enabled the researchers to look for clear links between stressors and a range of physiological disorders.
- ✓ The findings of this research could be used to inform employers of how to protect their employees from extreme, illness-related levels to stress and it could help to identify proactive measures to prevent stress e.g. a supportive network in the workplace, giving employees more autonomy over their working life.

Limitations
- X It is possible that the participants succumbed to demand characteristics as the questionnaires were focused very much on stress as the key variable.
- X A correlation can only show associations rather than cause-and-effect so it cannot conclusively show what the source of the stress was in each participant's life.

Reference
Marmot, M. G., Stansfeld, S., Patel, C., North, F., Head, J., White, I., ... & Smith, G. D. (1991). Health inequalities among British civil servants: the Whitehall II study. *The Lancet, 337* (8754), pp.1387-1393.

****

TOPIC 1: DETERMINANTS OF HEALTH

Content 1: Biopsychosocial model of health and well-being

KEY STUDY 1.3: *Haslam et al. (2018). Social cure, what social cure? The propensity to underestimate the importance of social factors for health.*

Brief Summary
Researched awareness of the importance of social factors for health — specifically, of the curative and protective role played by social support and social integration. Concluded that, while people were aware of biological and psychological factors in health, awareness of social factors is limited.

Aim
To investigate the role played by social support and social integration on health.

Participants
502 participants who were recruited using internet crowd sourcing platforms (56% female; 44% male; age range 18-72 years old, and mean age of 36 years old). The participants came from a range of educational backgrounds, although 42% of them had a university degree at undergraduate level. The participants were from the USA and the UK.

Procedure
The participants completed questionnaires, using a range of Likert scales, on the following measures:

- **Perceived determinants of health:** the participants were asked to rank in importance a range of factors linked to health e.g. stopping smoking; the support of others. They were then asked to say how many years up to 20 each factor might add on to their life expectancy.

- **Anti-psychosocial health beliefs:** 12 items relating to beliefs about the importance that health professionals should attach to the psychosocial dimensions of health (e.g. "Talking about psychological issues is more trouble than it is worth").

- **Right-wing authoritarianism:** participants were asked to respond to statements such as, 'People should always comply with the decision of the majority.'

- **Social dominance orientation:** participants were asked to respond to statements such as 'Superior groups should dominate inferior groups.'

- **Belief in biological essentialism:** participants indicated their agreement to statements such as, 'Whether someone is one kind of person or another is determined by their biological make-up.'

- **Controlled variables:** participants were asked to indicate their age, gender, and highest level of education and to respond to questions about their current health status.

Results

The results showed that social factors for health are underestimated when compared to other factors such as biological and psychological factors. Particular groups of participants – those at the younger end of the age range; men; those participants from a lower educational background – continually placed social factors as a less important factor for health than other groups did.

Conclusion

Social factors appear to have been ignored and under-played as a factor governing health.

Evaluation of Haslam et al. (2018)

Strengths
- ✓ Using questionnaires with standardised questions and rating scales means that the study can be replicated easily.
- ✓ The participants came from a wide age range a variety of backgrounds which makes the findings more generalisable than a narrower demographic would be.

Limitations
- X Rating scales may be interpreted subjectively as one person's idea of what a number represents may not be the same as another person's idea of that same number.
- X Responses to rating scales cannot predict how participants will behave e.g. a participant may rank social support as being of low importance to health but they may then derive benefit from it in the future.

Reference

Haslam, S. A., McMahon, C., Cruwys, T., Haslam, C., Jetten, J., & Steffens, N. K. (2018). Social cure, what social cure? The propensity to underestimate the importance of social factors for health. *Social Science & Medicine, 198*, pp. 14-21.

PSYCHOLOGY SORTED: KEY RESEARCH FOR STUDENTS AND TEACHERS
BOOK 2 – APPLIED PSYCHOLOGY

TOPIC 1: DETERMINANTS OF HEALTH

Content 2: Dispositional factors and health beliefs

KEY STUDY 2.1: *Rosenstock (1974). Historical origins of the health belief model.*

Brief Summary
Described the development and structure of the health belief model (HBM) which explains how a person's perception of the possible seriousness of a potential health problem, and their susceptibility to it combine with a balance between the perceived benefits of taking action vs. barriers to taking action, to result in a person either acting to preserve their own health, or ignoring a health risk.

Aim
An explanation of the Health Belief Model.

The Model

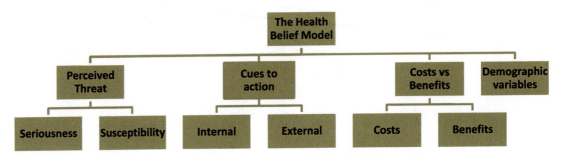

With the phenomenon of widespread media being available to large numbers of people in 1950s America, health researchers and medical professionals were increasingly puzzled as to why people continued to indulge in behaviours which were detrimental to their health e.g. not taking advantage of free tuberculosis screening.

Accordingly, the Health Belief model was suggested as a way of encapsulating the behavioural processes (cognitive and social) through which an individual goes to determine the type of action they will undertake in regard to their health. The model begins with the idea of perceived threat: *am I at risk of developing lung cancer if I continue to smoke?* The extent to which this threat is taken seriously will determine the action they take: *my father died of lung cancer and he was a heavy smoker so I will stop smoking.* If motivation is high (a strong internal factor) then it is likely the person will take affirmative action. External cues to action may involve seeing anti-smoking advertisements (which may encourage quitting smoking) or having friends who smoke (which may discourage quitting). A cost/benefit analysis is then undertaken to determine the future action: *cigarettes are expensive and unhealthy so I should stop, however I like smoking and I'll feel left out socially if I quit.* Demographic variables acknowledge that each health-related feeling or decision is unique to the individual – there is no, one, objective way of summing up how people feel about health matters or how they will respond. In other words, one size does not fit all and all health beliefs will be based on the individual: their personality, their background, their education, their personal history.

Evaluation of Rosenstock (1974)

Strengths
- ✓ The model is clear and easy to follow and it is flexible to some extent, as it does not assume that one person's decision-making will be the same as another's.
- ✓ By understanding some of the reasons why people do or do not follow health advice, medical professionals can implement specific strategies or interventions to help at-risk groups, such as smokers.

Limitations
- X The model cannot explain why someone may (for example) quit smoking for many years and then return to it.
- X A model is a rather simplistic way of viewing complex, unpredictable behaviour.

Reference
Rosenstock, I. M. (1974). Historical origins of the health belief model. *Health education monographs*, 2(4), pp.328-335.

Becker, M.H. (1974) The Health Belief Model and Personal Health Behavior. *Health Education Monographs, 2,* 324- 508.

****

TOPIC 1: DETERMINANTS OF HEALTH

Content 2: Dispositional factors and health beliefs

KEY STUDY 2.2: *Davidson et al. (2010). Don't worry, be happy: positive affect and reduced 10-year incident of coronary heart disease: the Canadian Nova Scotia Health Survey.*

Brief Summary
Examined whether higher levels of positive affect were associated with a lower risk of coronary heart disease (CHD) in a large prospective study with 10 years of follow-up. Found that indeed there was a significant negative correlation between positive affect and CHD.

Aim
To investigate the idea that good mood/happiness (positive affect) is linked to a decrease in coronary heart disease (CHD).

Participants
The researchers obtained their sample using the Medical Service Insurance register of Nova Scotia, Canada. This was a statistical random sample, designed to be representative of the population. The total sample consisted of 1739 adults (877 females; 862 males over the age of 18).

Procedure
Trained nurses were involved in the procedure, which had several stages:

- The first visit to the clinic involved the nurses taking the blood pressure of each participant, plus checking their risk factors for developing CHD: if they smoked, if they had diabetes, their age, etc.
- Then a range of psychological/affective measures was taken including their propensity for depression, anxiety and hostility.
- A 12-minute structured interview in which the participants were asked about stressful situations, what made them angry, stress at work, etc. The participants were being assessed as they were making their responses in the interview, for how upbeat and positive they seemed, their body language (e.g. smiling, open gestures) and whether their tone of voice was cheerful and animated.

Results
The results showed that, in the 10-year follow-up, the participants who had shown positive affect had a reduced risk of CHD, even when the scores for depression, anxiety and hostility had been taken into account.

Conclusion
The idea that it is 'mind over matter' and that a positive mental attitude can influence what happens to the body appears to be supported in this research.

Evaluation of Davidson et al. (2010)
Strengths
- ✓ This is the first of its type: a large-scale prospective study that clearly identifies a negative correlation between a cheerful, positive affect and coronary heart disease risk.
- ✓ The participants represented a cross-section of the population, making the results generalisable.

Limitations
- X There may have been an array of extraneous variables that produced CHD in some patients, such as genetic inheritance, lifestyle, or work stressors.
- X Measuring 'positive affect' as a contributing protective factor for CHD is overly vague and subjective.

Reference
Davidson, K. W., Mostofsky, E., & Whang, W. (2010). Don't worry, be happy: positive affect and reduced 10-year incident coronary heart disease: the Canadian Nova Scotia Health Survey. *European Heart Journal, 31*(9), pp. 1065-1070.

****

PSYCHOLOGY SORTED: KEY RESEARCH FOR STUDENTS AND TEACHERS
BOOK 2 – APPLIED PSYCHOLOGY

TOPIC 1: DETERMINANTS OF HEALTH

Content 2: Dispositional factors and health beliefs

KEY STUDY 2.3: *Pänkäläinen et al. (2016). Pessimism and risk of death from coronary heart disease among middle-aged and older Finns: an eleven-year follow-up study.*

Brief Summary
An 11-year prospective study on a regional sample of three cohorts, aged 52–56, 62–66, and 72–76 years, to investigate if there was a correlation between optimism, pessimism, and CHD mortality in a sample of Finnish participants. Found that pessimists had a higher occurrence of CHD, **but** failed to find any association with optimism and a decreased risk of coronary heart disease.

Aim
To investigate the connection between pessimism, optimism and mortality from CHD.

Participants
The participants were taken from the population registers of one region of Finland (the Lahti region). A stratified sample was obtained from a random sample, resulting in a sample of 2815 men and women born either between 1926-1930, 1936-1940 or 1946-1950.

Procedure
The participants were initially given questionnaires that asked about their socioeconomic status, health, lifestyle, if they smoked, their medication etc. Blood samples were taken, as was their blood pressure. They then filled in a questionnaire designed to measure their levels of optimism, pessimism and their hopes/expectations for the future. 11 years later there was a follow-up study in which the researchers compared their original data with the health status of the participants.

Results
The strongest finding was that pessimism is a stand-out risk factor for CHD mortality. Optimism did not have any mediating effect on the risk of developing CHD in these findings.

Conclusion
Pessimism may influence the onset of CHD but optimism may not, after all, be a protective factor.

Evaluation of Pänkäläinen et al. (2016)
Strengths
- ✓ The findings could be applied to medical settings: encouraging those at risk of CHD to re-train their thoughts away from pessimism may help to reduce the rates of CHD.
- ✓ The prospective design of the study – over 11 years between sessions – gave the researchers enough time to properly see the effect of optimism and pessimism on CHD mortality which increases the reliability of the findings.

Limitations

X   The participants may have given under-estimations of their smoking or lifestyle behaviours due to social desirability bias, which would lead to invalid data.

X   Pessimism and optimism are subjective constructs and questions pertaining to them may have been interpreted in a unique way by each participant.

Reference

Pänkäläinen, M., Kerola, T., Kampman, O., Kauppi, M., & Hintikka, J. (2016). Pessimism and risk of death from coronary heart disease among middle-aged and older Finns: an eleven-year follow-up study. *BMC Public Health, 16*(1), 1124, pp. 1-7.

****

TOPIC 1: DETERMINANTS OF HEALTH

Content 3: Risk and Protective Factors

KEY STUDY 3.1: *Marmot et al. (1991). Health inequalities among British civil servants: the Whitehall II study.*

See above, under **TOPIC 1: DETERMINANTS OF HEALTH,** *Content 1: Biopsychosocial model of health and well-being.* This study may also be used for examining risk and protective factors for stress.

****

TOPIC 1: DETERMINANTS OF HEALTH

Content 3: Risk and Protective Factors

KEY STUDY 3.2: *Davidson et al. (2010). Don't worry, be happy: positive affect and reduced 10-year incident of coronary heart disease: the Canadian Nova Scotia Health Survey.*

See above, under **TOPIC 1: DETERMINANTS OF HEALTH,** *Content 2: Dispositional factors and health beliefs.* This study may also be used for examining risk and protective factors for stress.

****

PSYCHOLOGY SORTED: KEY RESEARCH FOR STUDENTS AND TEACHERS
BOOK 2 – APPLIED PSYCHOLOGY

TOPIC 1: DETERMINANTS OF HEALTH

Content 3: Risk and Protective Factors

KEY STUDY 3.3: *Haslam et al. (2018). Social cure, what social cure? The propensity to underestimate the importance of social factors for health.*

See above, under **TOPIC 1: DETERMINANTS OF HEALTH,** Content 1: Biopsychosocial model of health and well-being. This study may also be used for examining risk and protective factors for stress.

****

TOPIC 1: DETERMINANTS OF HEALTH
Critical thinking points

Should self-report methods be used to assess healthy living?
In Haslam et al. (2108) participants who had been recruited online were given a series of questionnaires on topics involving health beliefs e.g. rank in importance a range of factors linked to health, level of right-wing authoritarianism, belief in biology as the ultimate basis for behaviour. Due to the socially sensitive nature of some of these questions – and bearing in mind that 'right-wing authoritarianism' is generally not a character trait that many people would like to be known by – it is more than possible that social desirability bias determined some of the responses to these questionnaires. When asked about healthy living and attitudes towards health most people will arguably overestimate and over-state their own adherence to healthy living regimes which calls into question the point of using self-report measures to collect data. For example, I may say that I abhor smoking and that I follow a 'clean eating' diet when in fact I get through 40 cigarettes a day and I am on first-name terms with my local supplier of junk food. What is said or stated on a questionnaire is not necessarily what is done by participants!

Does research on healthy living confuse things even further?
Taking in the news on a daily basis one could be forgiven for concluding that health professionals don't seem to be able to agree on anything when it comes to what is good/bad for people. There is contradictory research evidence on a range of factors e.g. 'drink one glass of red wine a day'/'all alcohol is harmful'. Health psychologists are also prone to such confusing claims, as seen in the results of Davidson et al. (2010) and Pänkäläinen et al (2016) with regards to the effect of mood/outlook on recovery from coronary heart disease. Davidson et al. concluded that it is 'mind over matter' i.e. a positive mental attitude which can influence what happens to the body, so if one were to take this advice one would aim to be cheerful and sunny of disposition throughout one's illness. Pänkäläinen et al., however, came to the conclusion that optimism may not, after all, be a protective factor against CHD as previously supposed. Does that mean that CHD patients should revel in feeling miserable and enjoy being pessimistic about their situation? Well, no, because this same study concluded that pessimism may influence the onset of CHD, meaning that neither optimism nor pessimism provide the best solution for dealing with illness. Until the latest research is published the jury is still out on this issue.

Acting on the findings of research into the determinants of health: a realisable goal or a fantasy?
Research by Marmot et al. (1991) found that the accumulated burden of life stress coupled with limited protective psychosocial resources is associated with adverse psychological, biological, and quality of life outcomes. The researchers suggest that employers need to enable their employees to find a work-life balance, to ensure that jobs are not overly stressful and/or mind-numbing, that deadline-meeting does not impose unnecessary anxiety on employees – but how realistic is this as a proposal? A lot of employers would respond that they don't have the time/money/energy or motivation to change the practices of their workplace and more than a few will simply not care about the mental well-being of their workers. Levels of stress at work only seem to be rising, with the global recession of 2008 still being felt in workplaces around the world and a tendency towards big business rather than the needs of the individual taking priority. Caring for one's employees may remain a pipe-dream for some employers whose intentions may be good but who find themselves simply unable to implement them.

****

Social desirability bias affects the validity of results from questionnaires

PSYCHOLOGY SORTED: KEY RESEARCH FOR STUDENTS AND TEACHERS
BOOK 2 – APPLIED PSYCHOLOGY

TOPIC 2: HEALTH PROBLEMS

Key Idea: Health problem(s) and their prevalence can be explained using biopsychosocial explanations.

Content 4: Explanation of health problem(s)

KEY STUDY 4.1: *Selye et al. (1936) A syndrome produced by diverse nocuous agents.*

Links to
- **Biological Approach:** Hormones and behavior – the effect of cortisol on human behaviour.

Brief Summary
General Adaptation Syndrome (GAS) as an explanation for the stress response, and an analysis of the alarm (fight or flight), resistance and exhaustion stages, with the exhaustion stage being responsible for long-term health problems. Links hypothalamic–pituitary–adrenocortical (HPA) system with stress and illness. (Biological).

Aim
To investigate the stress response in rats.

Participants
Selye used lab rats as his subjects.

Procedure
Selye and his fellow researchers exposed rats to a variety of stressful conditions:

- The rats were subjected to extreme cold.
- The rats were subjected to extreme heat.
- The rats were forced to engage in excessive physical exercises which put their muscles under extreme strain.
- The spinal cord of the rats was severed.
- The rats were injected with high doses of adrenaline.
- The rats were subjected to surgical procedures which caused them injury.

Results
The impact of the stressors on the rats had a range of short and long-term effects:

- Within the first 48 hours the rats' adrenal glands became enlarged (linked to the production of adrenaline in the fight-or-flight response), ulcers developed in their digestive system and their immune system became compromised. This phase was termed the 'alarm' phase by Selye.

- After this first phase the adrenal glands returned to their normal size and the immune system also re-balanced and normalised. This phase was termed the 'resistance' phase by Selye.

- With the continued stressors in place the adrenal glands in the rats once again became enlarged, the stress hormone cortisol was produced, the body's stores became depleted and the rats experienced collapse and eventually, death. Selye termed this phase the 'exhaustion' phase.

Conclusion
Continued, extreme stress may bring on a range of physical illnesses that have long-term effects on an individual.

Evaluation of Selye et al. (1936)
Strengths
- ✓ Selye's research on GAS has spawned a huge amount of research into the debilitating effects of stress which has contributed much to the understanding of both short and long-term effects of stress.
- ✓ Focusing on the biological effects of stress means that the effects are easier to measure than cognitive or emotional effects: it also means that drug or physical therapies could be developed to address and treat the symptoms of stress.

Limitations
- X The stress response in humans may be varied and may not necessarily follow the GAS pattern as determined by Selye.
- X There are some ethical concerns to address in the ways that the rats were treated.

Reference
Selye, H. (1936). A syndrome produced by diverse nocuous agents. *Nature, 138* (3479), p. 32.

****

TOPIC 2: HEALTH PROBLEMS

Content 4: Explanation of health problem(s)

KEY STUDY 4.2: *Lazarus & Alfert (1964). Short-circuiting of threat by experimentally altering cognitive appraisal.*

Brief Summary
Cognitive appraisal explanation of how appraisal of stressors may be experimentally manipulated, resulting in more or less stress experienced, as measured through galvanic skin response and self-report. (Interaction of cognitive and biological).

Aim
To investigate the effect of using appraisal on the biological stress response and to examine the role played by personality in stress management.

Participants
69 male undergraduate students from a university in California.

Procedure
The participants were first of all assessed as to their personality type. The participants were attached to electrodes in a chair and a heart monitor. The electrodes were used to measure their galvanic skin response to what they were shown. There were three conditions of the IV:

- **Silent condition:** the participants watched a 17-minute film of a graphic 'coming of age' ritual involving the use of incisions and subsequent blood.
- **Commentary during:** the participants watched the same film as above but there was a commentary soundtrack during the course of the film, explaining what was happening.
- **Commentary before:** the participants watched the same film as above but it was preceded by the commentary, explaining what they were *about* to see.

The participants were then given questionnaires that related to their mood, the degree of tension they felt and their feedback on what they'd seen.

Results
Participants in the 'commentary before' condition showed more resistance to the stress response, seen in their lower heart-rate and skin response than the participants in the other two conditions. Although not showing a significant effect, the participants who scored high on using denial to cope with stress also showed a lower heart rate than other participants.

Conclusion
Knowing what is about to happen during a stressful film-watching session and having it explained appears to lower the stress response. People who use denial to cope with their stress may also experience some reduction in the biological stress response.

Evaluation of Lazarus & Alfert (1964)
Strengths
- ✓ The use of the biological measures provides objective data which is free from bias.
- ✓ Using both biological and cognitive measures provides the findings with some degree of validity.

Limitations
- X The stress response emitted by the participants might have been as a result of factors other than those manipulated as part of the independent variable e.g. being in an unfamiliar situation, being attached to electrodes, squeamishness at the film's content.
- X It would be difficult to replicate the study today due to the ethical constraints placed on researchers.

Reference
Lazarus, R. S., & Alfert, E. (1964). Short-circuiting of threat by experimentally altering cognitive appraisal. *The Journal of Abnormal and Social Psychology, 69*(2), pp. 195-205.

****

TOPIC 2: HEALTH PROBLEMS

Content 4: Explanation of health problem(s)

KEY STUDY 4.3: *Fernald & Gunnar (2008). Salivary cortisol levels in children of low-income women with high depressive symptomatology.*

Links to:
- **Biological Approach:** Hormones and behaviour – the effect of cortisol on human behaviour.

Brief Summary
Study into how the exhaustion stage can manifest in a blunted cortisol response in children after they experience repeated social stressors, like maternal depression and poverty. (Interaction of the social and the biological).

Aim
To investigate the effect of continued stress on the cortisol levels of children with low-income, depressed mothers.

Participants
639 children aged between 2 and 6 years old (315 girls; 324 boys) from low-income areas of Mexico.

Procedure
The mothers of the children were interviewed in their homes, with each interview lasting one hour. The children were given cognitive tests to complete and their saliva was sampled three times during a 50-minute time-frame.

Results
The researchers found that the children of mothers who had high levels of depression produced very low levels of cortisol within the 50-minute testing session. This result is in direct contrast to previous studies in which have it that high child cortisol levels go hand in hand with high maternal depression.

Conclusion
Being exposed to extreme stressors early on in life (which include having a low-income, depressed mother) may lead to hypocortisolism (the production of very low levels of cortisol). This may be due to a blunted cortisol response in the face of an array of stressors.

Evaluation of Fernald et al. (2008)
Strengths
- ✓ The results are the first in this field of research to suggest that too much stress may, conversely, lead to *less* cortisol being produced which could then lead to further therapies and interventions for those affected.
- ✓ The children's cortisol levels were taken by the researchers on arrival then 25 minutes and 50 minutes later, enabling them to compare cortisol levels against the baseline measurement.

Limitations

✗ Some research has shown that post-natal depression in mothers is associated with altered levels of cortisol in their children so the hypocortisolism in the children may have been as a result of this.

✗ The researchers did not use a control group of children from higher-income families, which limits the generalisability of the findings.

Reference

Fernald, L. C., Burke, H. M., & Gunnar, M. R. (2008). Salivary cortisol levels in children of low-income women with high depressive symptomatology. *Development and Psychopathology, 20*(2), pp. 423-436.

****

TOPIC 2: HEALTH PROBLEMS

Content 5: Prevalence of health problem(s)

KEY STUDY 5.1: *The European Agency for Safety and Health at Work, European Communities, 2009.*

Brief Summary

Summary of the findings of a 2005 self-report survey among all member countries of the EU. Found that on average 22% of Europeans experience stress at work. However, this rate varies when considered through the lens of a specific country, gender, age, or occupation.

Aim

To examine the ways in which stress at work affects those in the EU.

Main comments and findings

- 22% of those working in EU countries reported feeling some level of stress at work. This is thought to cost around 20,000 million euros per year.

- The highest levels of stress were reported in Greece (55%); Slovenia (38%); Sweden (38%) and Latvia (37%). The lowest stress levels were reported in the UK (12%); Germany, Ireland and the Netherlands (16%).

- Having to work long hours (e.g. a 48-hour week) with tight deadlines and continual pressure at work were associated with high stress levels.

- The 45-54 age group appeared to be most affected by stress at work.

- Males (23%) reported feeling more stressed at work than females (20%).

- The highest levels of stress per occupation were reported by those working in the health and education sectors, with these workers also reporting higher incidences of physical abuse at work.

- People who were self-employed reported feeling greater amounts of stress than those who were employees.

Conclusion
Stress at work is experienced by many workers across the EU and may pose a real risk to health.

Evaluation of The European Agency for Safety and Health at Work (2009)
Strengths
✓ There appear to be very real health and economic risks with workplace stress so it is important that reviews such as this one are published in a bid to raise the issue and find solutions to the problem.
✓ Using all EU member countries is comprehensive in its scope and provides insightful comparisons across countries.

Limitations
X It is possible that some of the respondents to the survey did not properly know how to measure/assess their own stress levels which means that the data is lacking in rigour and precision.
X It is unlikely that some countries would be able to instigate any of the recommendations set out by the report e.g. working fewer hours, implementing anti-stress programmes at work due to lack of resources or available expertise.

Reference
The European Agency for Safety and Health at Work, European Communities, 2009.

****

TOPIC 2: HEALTH PROBLEMS

Content 5: Prevalence of health problem(s)

KEY STUDY 5.2: *Otte et al. (2005). A meta-analysis of cortisol response to challenge in human aging: importance of gender.*

Brief Summary
Meta-analysis of results from research databases between the years 1966 and 2003 to investigate age and gender-related differences in stress response to challenge (measured by cortisol levels). Prevalence of stress highest in older women.

Aim
To investigate the findings of research into the role of cortisol in age-related disorders e.g. Alzheimer's, diabetes, depression.

Main comments and findings

- The researchers used a total of 45 studies comprising 1295 participants in all (700 males; 538 females) with a mean age amongst the younger participants of 28 years old and amongst the older participants as 69 years old.

- Age was positively associated with cortisol response to challenge (challenge being illness, negative events, changing circumstances etc.) with older participants showing higher levels of cortisol than younger participants.

- Women showed a stronger cortisol response than men, particularly for older women, who had cortisol levels three times higher than their male counterparts.

- The onset of the menopause and the attendant decrease in oestrogen in women may contribute to increased levels of women in this group.

- Age-related diseases and conditions such as Alzheimer's are linked with high levels of cortisol.

Conclusion

Age-related cortisol levels may be affected by a variety of factors, with older women being more at risk than the other groups included in the sample

Evaluation of Otte et al. (2004)

Strengths

✓ The findings of this meta-analysis could be used to inform therapies and interventions for the most at-risk groups.
✓ By using a range of studies, the researchers were able to look for patterns in the data, enabling them to highlight the strongest trends in results.

Limitations

X It is not possible to use these findings to say what specifically causes high levels of cortisol in different groups as the data is correlational.
X The cortisol levels measured were based on single time-point readings and as cortisol levels fluctuate throughout the day it would have been more informative to have used studies where several measures were taken over time in order to gain a fuller picture of the actual levels of cortisol being secreted.

Reference

Otte, C., Hart, S., Neylan, T. C., Marmar, C. R., Yaffe, K., & Mohr, D. C. (2005). A meta-analysis of cortisol response to challenge in human aging: importance of gender. *Psychoneuroendocrinology, 30*(1), pp. 80-91.

****

PSYCHOLOGY SORTED: KEY RESEARCH FOR STUDENTS AND TEACHERS
BOOK 2 – APPLIED PSYCHOLOGY

TOPIC 2: HEALTH PROBLEMS

Content 5: Prevalence of health problem(s)

KEY STUDY 5.3: *Mental Health Foundation (May 2018). Stress: Are we coping?*

Brief Summary
Survey of over 4000 UK adults found that 74% reported feeling unable to cope with stress during the last year with women, those in poverty and younger people reporting over this average figure.

Aim
To investigate the levels and degree of depression in UK adults.

Main comments and findings

- This UK survey of 4169 adults found that 74% of those they surveyed have at some point felt so stressed that they felt overwhelmed or unable to cope.

- Over half a million had experienced work-related stress.

- Women (89%) tended to report more stress than men (76%). The most stressful factors for women were identified as personal finance (43%), health of family and friends (41%) and personal health (40%), These figures may in part be explained by traditional gender roles and the way women are socialised i.e. to be nurturing, to care for others.

- Some minority ethnic groups said that they had experienced more work-related stress (particularly Afro-Caribbean women), which has been linked to reported incidents of racism.

- An interesting finding was that people aged 55 and over report the least amount of stress: 29% of this age group reported not being stressed at all. 30% of those aged 55+ reported never feeling overwhelmed or unable to cope in the last year, compared to 7% of young adults (aged 18-24). This may be because it is increasingly difficult for young people to afford to pay for university fees, to find a job or to buy a house, whereas those in the 55+ group are less likely to face such problems.

- Those with existing mental disorders/conditions may be at greater risk of stress, as stress can precipitate symptoms and potentially result in relapse.

- Money worries, particularly those associated with personal debt, emerged as a well-recognised risk that was a key factor in the experience of stress. For people living in poverty, stress has been found to contribute to poorer mental health outcomes. High levels of debt and financial insecurity increase the likelihood of living in an unstable or poor-quality housing situation, experiencing job stress, having more adverse life events and less social support.

- Media and technology were also found to contribute to stress with 12% of those surveyed saying that feeling like the need to respond instantly to messages (e.g. replying to messages, social media etc.) was a stressor.

Conclusion
Stress is experienced by a high percentage of the population and it is particular at-risk groups (e.g. the young, the poor) who are at particular risk of succumbing to feeling extremely stressed.

Evaluation of Mental Health Foundation (2018)
Strengths
- ✓ The use of a large-scale survey using standardised questions is replicable, meaning that the same survey could be conducted using the same participants every few years to look for changes in the data.
- ✓ The results highlight which sectors of the population are most in need of intervention and strategies to reduce their stress, which could inform public health initiatives.

Limitations
- X Some of the findings point to issues that have long been recognised as problematic i.e. having no money is stressful, and yet very little appears to be done on a grand scale to really solve such problems.
- X The advice and guidance offered to help manage stress may simply be out of reach for some people e.g. 'find social support', 'access cognitive behaviour therapy' which makes the report somewhat lacking in usefulness.

Reference
Mental Health Foundation (May 2018). *Stress: Are we coping?* London: Mental Health Foundation

****

TOPIC 2: HEALTH PROBLEMS

Critical thinking points

Why are we bothering with research such as Selye's?
Selye et al.'s 1936 research is getting on for 90 years old and is rather distressing to read considering the torture-conditions the rats experienced. Is it not the case that we now live in more enlightened times, when unethical treatment of animals for research purposes is now seen as abhorrent and not always even necessary? The procedure used by Selye is upsetting to read and the findings which led to the development of General Adaptation Syndrome (GAS) as an explanation for the stress response could surely have come about via a different, less harmful route. Add to this the fact that one cannot generalise the findings of research using rats to the ways in which human beings experience stress, and the question remains - why go to such extreme lengths? And why not find research which can explain GAS in a more ethically considerate way and which is more applicable to human beings?

Isn't stress a cognitive construct rather than a biological condition?

Biological theories of stress such as GAS describe the biological response to a range of stressors, but they cannot account for what is going on inside the mind of someone who is experiencing stress. Surely stress is a phenomenon that 'lives' in the mind, with its attendant conditions of worry, anxiety and obsessive, destructive thoughts, all of which are psychological rather than physiological? Biological theories and models of stress do not address the psychological factors at work that determine what triggers stress for different people (e.g. I may relish the idea of performing in a play whereas for someone else this may bring with it a strong stress response). Lazarus & Alfert's (1964) research on the role of cognitive appraisal in the experience of a strong stressor highlights the role the cognition can play in mediating a biological response to stress.

Could research such as Otte et al. (2004) inadvertently contribute to stress?

Otte et al. (2004) found that age was positively associated with the stress hormone cortisol, as was being female, being a menopausal female and having age-related diseases such as Alzheimer's. While this may be true of Otte et al.'s results it is not necessarily a truth for everyone in the world: and by publishing findings such as these perhaps Otte could be accused of confirming stereotypical ideas of women and age. It could be argued that his findings may go some way towards perpetuating self-fulfilling prophecies which in turn could lead to negative health beliefs e.g. 'I'm getting older, I'm bound to feel stressed'; 'I'm menopausal, is that why I feel this way?' Instead of working through solutions and strategies to deal with these feelings it is possible that people may simply give in to them with an air of fatalism. Sometimes maybe a little knowledge can be a bad thing, particularly if it contributes to the condition that is being investigating in the first place.

****

Are the results of classic and unethical animal studies still valid?

PSYCHOLOGY SORTED: KEY RESEARCH FOR STUDENTS AND TEACHERS
BOOK 2 – APPLIED PSYCHOLOGY

TOPIC 3: PROMOTING HEALTH

Key Idea: Psychological theories can help inform health promotion.

Content 6: Health promotion

KEY STUDY 6.1: *Quist-Paulsen et al. (2003). Randomised controlled trial of smoking cessation intervention after admission for coronary heart disease.*

Brief Summary
Looked at fear arousal as a method for encouraging the motivation to quit smoking. Found that those who had experienced negative, fear-inducing stimuli about smoking were more likely to quit than a control group.

Aim
To investigate the effect of fear arousal on rates for quitting smoking.

Participants
240 smokers below the age of 76 who had been admitted to the cardiac ward of a hospital in Norway.

Procedure
There were two conditions of the independent variable: the 'fear arousal' (FA) condition consisting of 118 participants and a control condition consisting of 122 participants. Participants were assigned to condition via random allocation.

The FA condition was as follows: the researchers used nurses at the hospital to deliver the intervention. They gave the FA participants a booklet that informed them as to the benefits of quitting smoking, including graphs of mortality rates for smokers compared to non-smokers. These participants were told that the likelihood of them having another smoking-related heart attack was high (FA element of the intervention). They were also given information as to how to quit smoking and remain cigarette-free, advice about nicotine replacement therapy and how to deal with instances where they might relapse by providing them with action plans. These participants were also urged not to smoke while at hospital. They were directed towards using nicotine patches and if their partner also smoked, they were also asked to quit.

The control condition was as follows: the nurses recruited by the researchers offered twice-weekly group sessions to these participants, in which a range of topics was discussed including the importance of quitting smoking. They also watched a video and were given a booklet on heart disease including some advice on how to quit smoking.

The nurses then contacted the participants by phone at specified time points: two days, one week, three weeks, three months and finally five months after they had left hospital.

Results
After one year, 57% of the FA group had stopped smoking compared to 37% of the control group.

Conclusion
Fear arousal may be an effective way of motivating smokers who are in danger of having a further heart attack to quit smoking.

Evaluation of Quist-Paulsen et al. (2003)

Strengths
- ✓ The use of a sample of real smokers who had already experienced cardiac problems gives this research high ecological validity.
- ✓ The fact that the FA was only used in the intervention group could be used as compelling evidence for the validity of the claim that fear arousal makes the difference in quitting rates when applied to heavy smokers.

Limitations
- ✗ The intervention group was generally given much more attention and focused information from the nurses so it may be that it was a combination of factors that motivated the higher quitting rates rather than it simply being down to the FA aspect.
- ✗ The smokers in the control group did not experience the FA which the researchers linked to higher quitting rates and these participants subsequently showed a 20% lower incidence of quitting which is an ethical concern.

Reference
Quist-Paulsen, P., & Gallefoss, F. (2003). Randomised controlled trial of smoking cessation intervention after admission for coronary heart disease. *British Medical Journal, 327*(7426), p. 1254.

****

TOPIC 3: HEALTH PROMOTION

Content 6: Promoting Health

KEY STUDY 6.2: *Bandura (2004). Health promotion by social cognitive means.*

Links to:
- **Cognitive Approach:** Thinking and decision-making - theory of planned behaviour and theory of reasoned action.

Brief Summary
Social cognitive theory of health promotion, wherein Bandura identified self-efficacy as the most important explanatory and predictive determinant in health promotion success. He equates this with the concept of 'perceived behavioural control' used in the Theory of planned behaviour (TPB). However, he explains how his model is social and how a socially-oriented agenda is needed for health promotion.

Aim
To review social cognitive theory and disease prevention using social cognitive theory as the prism through which to view health behaviours.

Procedure
This is a review article which draws from Bandura's social cognitive theory (SCT).

Main comments and findings
The key concepts behind SCT are:

- The level of knowledge of the potential risks and behaviours of particular behaviours. e.g. smoking.

- The degree of self-efficacy that an individual has about that health behaviour. e.g. 'I can quit smoking.'

- The outcome expectations of that behaviour. e.g. 'I will feel better and spend less money.'

- The health goals that the individual sets for themselves. e.g. 'I want to be able to run 5K in 6 months' time.'

- How they will realise and achieve these goals e.g. 'I will join a gym and train 3 times a week.'

- The ways in what might aid or impede these goals. e.g. 'I live near a gym, but most of my friends smoke.'

Bandura states in his article that self-efficacy provides the foundation for change to occur in terms of health behaviours. In his article he states that, 'This focal belief is the foundation of human motivation and action. Unless people believe they can produce desired effects by their actions, they have little incentive to act or to persevere in the face of difficulties' (p146).

Bandura suggests that a key way to motivate people to change negative health behaviours is to motivate them to focus on their own self-interest in the matter -the goals and aspirations they value most highly. This idea is linked to the theories of reasoned action and of planned behaviour: attitudes towards the behaviour, the social norms surrounding the behaviour and the intentions that may determine the behaviour.

He claims that public health promotion campaigns are only really successful with people who have high self-efficacy. People with low self-efficacy, according to Bandura, are likely to ignore health advice and to take no action even if they know what the risks of their unhealthy lifestyle choices are. They are much more likely to perceive themselves to be vulnerable to disease. Bandura cites a study which found that people who had been exposed to a programme of high self-efficacy beliefs began to adopt more healthy eating habits and to take exercise.

The most effective way to promote healthy living is, in Bandura's view, to go beyond the individual level. He stresses the need for 'a more ambitious socially oriented agenda of research and practice', (p164) by making health promotion a concern of the whole community rather than just the individual concerned.

Conclusion
Health promotions should be able to target those with low self-efficacy who are at most risk due to their lifestyle choices. Such promotions should be at a community rather than an individual level.

Evaluation of Bandura (2004)
Strengths
- ✓ The idea of placing health promotion within wider social contexts emphasises the need for healthy behaviours to be viewed as a community issue rather than pointing the finger of blame at individuals for choices they may have made.
- ✓ Self-efficacy is a relatively straightforward concept to grasp which means that promoting it as a behaviour should involve little that is overly technical or specialist in nature.

Limitations
- ✗ There will be some communities who are not able to embrace a health promotion campaign due to issues with funding for example.
- ✗ Not everyone is able to develop high self-efficacy. People who have had a violent or abusive upbringing may feel worthless and have very low self-esteem which may be impermeable to change.

Reference
Bandura, A. (2004). Health promotion by social cognitive means. *Health Education & Behavior, 31*(2), pp. 143-164.

****

TOPIC 3: HEALTH PROMOTION

Content 6: Promoting health

KEY STUDY 6.3: *Conner et al. (2013). Moderating effect of socioeconomic status on the relationship between health cognitions and behaviors.*

Links to
- **Cognitive Approach:** Thinking and decision-making. - theory of planned behaviour and theory of reasoned action.

Background
Socio-economic status (SES) moderates the effectiveness of TPB as an explanation for health behaviour, as the intention-health behaviour relationship is weaker in people from lower SES groups.

Aim
To investigate correlations between SES and intention, self-efficacy and behaviour.

Participants
826 school-children aged 11-12 years at the start of the study from 20 schools in the North of England. Each school's SES was measured to give a guideline as to the background of each participant.

Method
This was a prospective study, conducted over the course of two years. The participants filled in questionnaires over the course of the two years at specific intervals. The questions, using rating scales, covered the following points:

- The intention to not smoke.
- Self-efficacy surrounding not smoking.
- Smoking behaviour itself in the specific time period.

Results
SES was a reliable predictor in whether the participants were more or less likely to smoke: as SES increased so the intention to smoke and actual smoking behaviour decreased. Lower SES participants did not show the same pattern, with their earlier intentions not to smoke unrelated to subsequent smoking behaviour.

Conclusion
Low SES may interfere with good health intentions and prevent individuals from making healthy choices.

Evaluation of Conner et al. (2013)
Strengths
- ✓ This study was one of three prospective studies carried out as part of this research, with the following two studies agreeing with this study's findings, showing good concurrent validity.
- ✓ Data from a sample of 826 participants at regular intervals over two years makes the findings robust and reliable.

Limitations
- ✗ The sample may be biased as a good portion of the initial sample of 1209 participants dropped out and it is likely that these participants were more likely to be smokers from the start, to have weaker intention to not smoke, weaker self-efficacy over not smoking and lower SES.
- ✗ The participants may have under or over-reported their intention to not smoke as well as their actual smoking behaviour due to social desirability bias.

Reference
Conner, M., McEachan, R., Jackson, C., McMillan, B., Woolridge, M., & Lawton, R. (2013). Moderating effect of socioeconomic status on the relationship between health cognitions and behaviors. *Annals of Behavioral Medicine, 46*(1), 19-30.

****

TOPIC 3: HEALTH PROMOTION

Content 7: Effectiveness of health promotion programmes

KEY STUDY 7.1: *Witte & Allen (2000). A meta-analysis of fear appeals: Implications for effective public health campaigns.*

Brief Summary
Conducted a meta-analysis of studies into the effectiveness of fear messages as part of health promotion programmes. They found that, providing a high-fear message was accompanied by a high-efficacy message, suggesting that that it was possible to change behaviour, then it was effective.

Aim
To review research on the effectiveness of fear-appeals with regards to changing or influencing people's health behaviour.

Procedure
This is a meta-analysis of the findings from a range of studies in the field.

Main comments and findings

- Most research on fear-appeals used in health psychology was conducted between 1953 and 1975, with three key factors being identified as independent variables used in such research. These factors are: fear (an emotional response); perceived threat (a cognitive response) and perceived efficacy (the belief of an individual as to how much control they have over their behaviour in terms of their ability to produce specific outcomes).

- It appears that there is a positive correlation between fear arousal and persuasiveness of the message: the stronger the fear component of the health message is, the more likely it is to persuade those it is targeting.

- Targeting self-efficacy in fear appeals produced a stronger relationship with persuasiveness of the message and the authors of this meta-analysis suggest that this should be used to inform future health campaigns and promotions.

- The researchers point out that there is a lot of variety within the findings they analysed, making the correlations fairly weak, even though they are positive, suggesting that there may be factors other than fear involved in the persuasiveness of a message and they suggest that future research should aim to discover what these factors are.

- Individual differences of age, gender or ethnicity appeared to have no influence on the outcome of fear appeals in health promotion campaigns.

- There appears to have been an improvement in the power and the quality of fear appeals used in health promotion over the years, possibly due to the message being handled more carefully and the nature of the message being refined, so that its purpose is more precise than in the earlier studies analysed. The use of gruesome imagery in some health promotion campaigns has been linked to a stronger persuasive message, probably due to the novel nature of the stimuli being more eye-catching and unexpected than other types of imagery.

Conclusion
A strong fear appeal when used in conjunction with self-efficacy messages may be the most persuasive means of changing or influencing health behaviours.

Evaluation of Witte & Allen (2000)
Strengths
- ✓ The use of a range of studies conducted over time enabled the researchers to establish reliability within the results.
- ✓ The findings have a direct applicability for use in media campaigns designed to focus on specific health behaviours.

Limitations
- ✗ As the authors point out the correlations are positive but weak, with unexplained factors that are also responsible for influencing health behaviours, which makes the findings less robust.
- ✗ It is unclear as to what type of fear appeal – if any - should be used to address specific negative health behaviours like drinking and driving, smoking or sexually-transmitted diseases.

Reference
Witte, K., & Allen, M. (2000). A meta-analysis of fear appeals: implications for effective public health campaigns. *Health Education & Behavior, 27*(5), pp.591-615.

****

TOPIC 3: PROMOTING HEALTH

Content 7: Effectiveness of health promotion programmes

KEY STUDY 7.2: *Colchero et al. (2016). Beverage purchases from stores in Mexico under the excise tax on sugar sweetened beverages: observational study.*

Brief Summary
An observational study into the result of the tax on sweetened drinks that was introduced in Mexico in Jan 2014 as part of a health promotion programme to reduce dental caries, obesity and Type 2 diabetes in the population. Found that the buying of sweetened drinks had reduced by 12% by Dec 2014.

Aim
To investigate the extent to which a government-imposed tax on sugary drinks in Mexico directly impacted the purchase of such drinks one year after the campaign was launched.

Participants
The researchers targeted 53 cities in Mexico, obtaining a sample of 62,535 households that yielded a total of 205, 112 samples of observed behaviour from January 2012 to December 2014.

Procedure
The researchers initially compiled a demographic profile for their sample: the socio-economic status of each person in each household, their sex, age, occupation. The researchers then used the records per household member of the number – how many bottles purchased – and the volume which comprised how many litres per bottle for each month of the study's duration. The drinks were categorised according to whether they were untaxed (plain water, fruit juice) or taxed (fizzy drinks such as non-diet cola and sweetened drinks).

Results
By December 2014 the purchases of taxed (sweetened fizzy) drinks had decreased by 12%, giving an average monthly decrease across the study's duration of 6%. Households with a low socioeconomic status showed the greatest decline in the purchase of the taxed drinks (17% by December 2014). More affluent households of middle socioeconomic status showed the highest increase in their purchase of taxed drinks.

Conclusion
Using a tax on sweetened drinks may produce a short-term decline in their consumption, particularly among less affluent households.

Evaluation of Colchero et al. (2016)
Strengths
- ✓ The use of such a large sample across time makes the findings highly robust and reliable.
- ✓ The study has good ecological validity as it measured real behaviour in real settings.

Limitations
- X The fact that the less affluent households showed the greatest decline in taxed drink purchases may simply be because they could not afford them as much as the more affluent households, making this campaign more about taxing the poor than imparting positive health strategies.
- X Similar research would have to be carried out in a range of different countries as these results are only generalisable to Mexicans living in cities in Mexico.

Reference
Colchero, M.A., Popkin, B.M., Rivera, J.A. & Ng, S.W. (2016). Beverage purchases from stores in Mexico under the excise tax on sugar-sweetened beverages: observational study. *British Medical Journal,352*, h6704.

****

TOPIC 3: PROMOTING HEALTH

Content 7: Effectiveness of health promotion programmes

KEY STUDY 7.3: *Toft et al. (2018). Project SoL—A Community-Based, Multi-Component Health Promotion Intervention to Improve Eating Habits and Physical Activity among Danish Families with Young Children. Part 1: intervention development and implementation.*

Brief Summary
Report of a 2012-2015 Danish community-based, multi-level intervention project (known as 'supersetting') aimed at improving eating habits and physical activity in Danish families with young children. Found that involving multiple setting and multiple community stakeholders was more effective at promoting health than any individual approach.

Aim
To promote healthy lifestyle habits: eating a healthy diet and taking part in regular physical activity to families in Denmark with children in the 3-8 years age range.

Participants
Families from the Bornholm district of Denmark with children aged 3-8 years old. Three adjoining districts comprised the control sample.

Procedure
The project was longitudinal in design, being carried out over the course of 4 years from 2012 to 2015. The intervention used as part of the campaign was multi-component, taking place in a variety of settings such as schools, childcare centres, supermarkets. The intervention took the form of a campaign to promote healthy eating of fruit and vegetables and fish, and to take part in physical activity. The idea was that the residents of Bornholm would gain a sense of ownership of the campaign and would therefore invest more time and energy into it and be motivated to fully realise the aims of the campaign.

Results
The result of the four-year campaign was that the multi-component approach (using a variety of settings in which to promote the message of healthy living) and which involved multiple stakeholders (people for whom the message was relevant and who had a vested interest in its success) was successful: using everyday contexts in which to communicate the message appears to have worked. This project also demonstrated that for such interventions to be successful there needs to be good collaboration between the groups involved in it, such as schools, childcare centres and local media.

Conclusion
A multi-component approach to health promotion, involving multiple stakeholders, may be the best way of implementing and sustaining changes to health behaviours.

Evaluation of Toft et al. (2018)

Strengths
- ✓ The longitudinal design means that progress and change over time could be assessed by the researchers.
- ✓ The campaign used a holistic approach to health promotion with its use of multiple channels to deliver the message and it took into consideration the real contexts of the stakeholders, ensuring that meaningful conclusions could be drawn from the findings.

Limitations
- X The breadth and scope of the research and the multiple agencies and parties involved means that it is possible that an array of extraneous variables might have clouded the findings.
- X It is not clear as to whether this approach was sustained in the Danish community it targeted: a follow-up study would be needed to ascertain the longevity of the health promotion.

Reference

Toft, U., Bloch, P., Reinbach, H. C., Winkler, L. L., Buch-Andersen, T., Aagaard-Hansen, J., ... & Glümer, C. (2018). Project SoL—A Community-Based, Multi-Component Health Promotion Intervention to Improve Eating Habits and Physical Activity among Danish Families with Young Children. Part 1: intervention development and implementation. *International journal of Environmental Research and Public Health*, *15*(6), p.1097.

****

TOPIC 3 PROMOTING HEALTH

Critical thinking points

Is it really acceptable – or productive - to use fear arousal as a means to promoting health?
The use of fear arousal as a tactic to encourage people to adopt healthier lifestyles or to stop an unhealthy habit may be likened to the 'short, sharp shock' approach of some correctional facilities. It may be deemed necessary to get smokers, for example, to confront the potentially harmful consequences of their behaviour but does the use of gruesome or graphic images/messages really, ultimately change long-term behaviour. And is it even ethical to do so? Horrific images related to the unhealthy behaviour certainly give people pause for thought and may result in them considering the damage that they are doing to themselves which may in turn lead to real changes for the better in their behaviour. The question is, though, how permanent are these changes? When the initial shock and revulsion wear off will the smoker forget the message and return to their bad habit? And is it acceptable to present vivid and shocking images to people in a bid to get them to change their behaviour? Cognitive dissonance theory suggests that fear messages may even be counter-productive, leading to a 'blocking out' of the message because it is too disturbing to think about, and a rationalisation of one's own behaviour.

Why can't people simply indulge in unhealthy behaviours – isn't this a matter of the right to choose one's bad habits?
The growing obesity epidemic in the West and the attendant strain it puts on health services has been met with government legislation carried out in order to attempt to stem the growing tide of

health-related problems within specific countries. Colchero et al. (2016) reported on the impact of a 'sugar tax' on sweet drinks in Mexico, implemented by the government to try to improve the state of the nation's health. Similar programmes may be put in place in countries where over-indulgence in unhealthy habits is seen to affect the health of children, the health service, productivity in the workplace etc. Messages such as, 'smoking is bad for you', 'too much sugar is bad for you' are continually communicated in the media and by governments so, logically, people should not smoke and they should reduce their sugar intake to a minimum. And yet this is not the case: some people continue to smoke and/or consume too much sugar, knowing the potential consequences of such habits. So – is this a matter of human rights, free will, the right to make bad health choices? Or do people need protecting from themselves and treated like wayward children who need to be taught the right thing to do? There is no easy answer to this: as anyone involved in the health system will tell you!

A longitudinal design is the only meaningful way of ascertaining the effect of health promotion programmes.
Toft et al. (2018) conducted their research over the course of four years, looking for the impact of a multi-component healthy lifestyle promotion amongst families in one region of Denmark. This study, and others like it, is perfectly suited to the use of a longitudinal design due to the nature of what is being measured - long-term effects of a sustained campaign aimed at promoting healthier habits. Although longitudinal research is time-consuming and expensive when compared to cross-sectional 'snapshot' research, it is the only way that researchers can check for progress/changes over time, with the starting behaviour providing the baseline from which to track the development of the target behaviours over the course of the months and years in which the campaign is run.

****

Exercise encouragement is also part of health promotion

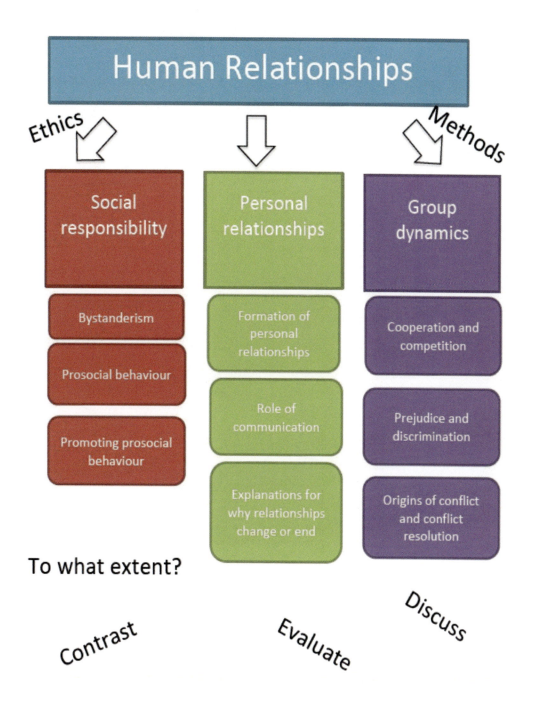

PSYCHOLOGY OF HUMAN RELATIONSHIPS

Topic 1: Social responsibility

Key Idea: We are all interdependent, but how we help each other is mediated biologically, cognitively and culturally.

Content	Research	Use in Human Relationships	Links to
Bystanderism	Classic **Latané & Darley (1968)**	Theory of the unresponsive bystander. Conducted an experiment to investigate diffusion of responsibility in a perceived emergency. Found that the more people there were assumed to be as witnesses, then the less likely a participant was to intervene in a perceived emergency.	
	Critique/Further **Piliavin et al. (1969)**	Arousal-cost-reward model: we want to help, but want to be sure that there is no risk to ourselves. Investigated bystanderism and how it may explain why some people tend to be given help more than others - they are seen as a 'deserving' victim rather than someone who has played a role in bringing about their own misfortune. Found that a victim who appears innocent is more likely to be helped than a victim who seems to have invited their fate, by being drunk, for example.	
	Recent **Schultz et al. (2014)**	Researchers explored if and how bystanders responded when presented with a cyber-bullying simulation. Found that dispositional factor (empathy) predicted most frequent intervention, but in majority of cases there was no intervention.	

Further resources

Weinman, S. (9 April 2016). 'Why we still look away: Kitty Genovese, James Bulger and the bystander effect.' *The Guardian.* https://tinyurl.com/yymxazm8

Whitson, S. (10 March 2013). 'Why kids choose not to intervene during bullying situations.' *Psychology Today.* https://tinyurl.com/y6hswae6

Bystanderism. Why we still look away

PSYCHOLOGY SORTED: KEY RESEARCH FOR STUDENTS AND TEACHERS
BOOK 2 – APPLIED PSYCHOLOGY

PSYCHOLOGY OF HUMAN RELATIONSHIPS

Topic 1: Social responsibility

Key Idea: We are all interdependent, but how we help each other is mediated biologically, cognitively and culturally.

Content	Research	Use in Human Relationships	Links to
Prosocial behaviour – biological explanations	Classic **Simmons et al. (1977)**	**Kin selection theory** as a biological explanation for altruism. Tested kin selection theory by investigating whether close relatives of a kidney patient would be more likely to offer themselves as kidney donors. Found that parents were more likely to donate a kidney to a child, than siblings were to donate one to a brother/sister.	
	Critique/Further **Axelrod & Hamilton (1981)**	**Reciprocal altruism** is based on the principles of evolutionary psychology and explains that altruistic acts are performed in order to gain some future benefit from the recipient. The researchers devised a computer-based model of chess games involving two players to test the idea behind the Prisoner's Dilemma and reciprocity. Found that that mutually advantageous behaviour may ultimately benefit individual more than purely self-serving acts.	
	Recent **Crockett et al. (2010)**	Biological explanation for prosocial behaviour. High levels of serotonin promote prosocial behaviour.	**Biological approach:** the brain and behaviour – neurotransmitters and their effect on behaviour.

Further resources

Crockett, M. (22 July 2012) Brain chemistry and moral decision-making. *Bioethics Bites.* https://tinyurl.com/yyovj5ej

Davis, N. (9 Oct 2017). 'Stereotype that women are kinder and less selfish is true, claim neuroscientists.' *The Guardian.* https://tinyurl.com/y9fkts37

PBS. The Human Spark – Kids are Naturally Altruistic. *Youtube.* https://tinyurl.com/yykzaj85

PBS. The Human Spark- kids and altruism

PSYCHOLOGY SORTED: KEY RESEARCH FOR STUDENTS AND TEACHERS
BOOK 2 – APPLIED PSYCHOLOGY

PSYCHOLOGY OF HUMAN RELATIONSHIPS

Topic 1: Social responsibility

Key Idea: We are all interdependent, but how we help each other is mediated biologically, cognitively and culturally.

Content	Research	Use in Human Relationships	Links to
Prosocial behaviour – cognitive (psychological) explanations	Classic **Cialdini & Schaller (1987)**	Negative state-relief model of altruism, which considers the extent to which personal discomfort at the sight of another's distress motivates altruistic acts.	
	Critique/Further **Batson et al. (1989)**	Tested Schaller and Cialdini's negative state-relief model, and found that people who felt sad were more likely to offer help than those who felt happy. This could be because they wanted to lessen their own distress by helping.	
	Recent **Barragan & Dweck (2014)**	This research showed that a very simple reciprocal activity elicited high degrees of altruism in 1- and 2-y-old children (as well as older children), whereas friendly but non-reciprocal activity did not. Showed that altruism could be learned by imitation, and contradicted the biological view that altruism is natural to very young children.	

Further resources

Hill, A. (6 May 2011). 'Boredom is good for you, study claims. Being bored can motivate people to engage in prosocial tasks and encourage more meaningful behaviour.' *The Guardian.* https://tinyurl.com/z2kyll8

Guardian - boredom is good for you

TED talk by Matthieu Ricard (Oct 2014). 'How to let altruism be your guide.' https://tinyurl.com/k3pfr4o

TED talk on altruism

PSYCHOLOGY SORTED: KEY RESEARCH FOR STUDENTS AND TEACHERS
BOOK 2 – APPLIED PSYCHOLOGY

PSYCHOLOGY OF HUMAN RELATIONSHIPS

Topic 1: Social responsibility

Key Idea: We are all interdependent, but how we help each other is mediated biologically, cognitively and culturally.

Content	Research	Use in Human Relationships	Links to
Prosocial behaviour – sociocultural explanations	Classic **Levine et al. (2001)**	Conducted a study to investigate prosocial behaviour as a function of collectivism/individualism. Found that there are cross-cultural differences in prosocial behaviour, but other variables may influence behaviour.	**Sociocultural approach:** Cultural origins of behaviour and cognition – cultural dimensions.
	Critique/Further **Aknin et al. (2013)**	Investigated the pleasure obtained from prosocial spending as universal. Found that the reward experienced from helping others may be deeply ingrained in human nature, as it emerged in diverse cultural and economic contexts.	
	Recent **Mitahara et al. (2018)**	The interdependence approach to prosocial behavior suggests that the extent to which an individual is dependent on interpersonal relationships increases the individual's altruism and subsequent prosocial behaviour. Compared Japanese females and New Zealand males and found that neither gender nor culture significantly affected the level of interdependence, but gender and culture differentially moderated empathetic altruism.	

Further resources

TED talk by Peter Singer (2013). 'The why and how of effective altruism.'
https://tinyurl.com/lw8wq9f

Wang, Y. et al. (2015). Cultural Differences in Donation Decision-Making. *PLoS ONE 10*(9), e0138219 https://tinyurl.com/y69ec9vx

TED talk. Why and how - altruism

PSYCHOLOGY OF HUMAN RELATIONSHIPS

Topic 1: Social responsibility

Key Idea: We are all interdependent, but how we help each other is mediated biologically, cognitively and culturally.

Content	Research	Use in Human Relationships	Links to
Promoting prosocial behaviour	Classic **Dickerson et al. 1992**	Investigated the extent to which a prior commitment to save water would be observed in subsequent behaviour. Found that a prior commitment to this prosocial behaviour resulted in a positive behaviour change.	
	Critique/Further **Barragan & Dweck (2014)**	Modelling pro-social behaviour can promote it. This research showed that a very simple reciprocal activity elicited high degrees of altruism in 1- and 2-y-old children (as well as older children), whereas friendly but non-reciprocal activity did not. Showed that altruism could be learnt, and contradicted the biological view that altruism is natural to very young children.	**Social cognitive theory:** Bandura's concept of modelling behaviour.
	Recent **Flook et al. (2015)**	To investigate the effect of a 12-week mindfulness-based 'kindness curriculum' on levels of prosocial behaviour in pre-school children. Found that the promotion of prosocial behaviour in young children has an immediate effect that seems to last over time.	

Further resources

Kidron, Y. & Fleischman, S. (April 2006). Research Matters/promoting Adolescents' Prosocial Behavior. *Educational Leadership, 63* (7), pp. 90-91.
https://tinyurl.com/y6ompsjl

Adolescents' prosocial behaviour

PSYCHOLOGY OF HUMAN RELATIONSHIPS

Topic 2: Personal relationships

Key Idea: Personal relationships may be explained through biological, cognitive and sociocultural approaches.

Content	Research	Use in Human Relationships	Links to
Formation of personal relationships – biological explanations	Classic **Singh (1993)**	Males choose female partners whose small (0.7) waist-to-hip ratio suggests fertility.	**Biological approach:** Genetics and behaviour – evolutionary explanations for behaviour.
	Critique/Further **Wedekind (1995)**	MHC (major histocompatability complex) is a group of genes that, while not pheromones, can be smelt in sweat, and if attraction to those with different MHC from our own is followed by mating (a big 'if'), this maximises the immune responses in offspring, making them stronger.	**Biological approach:** Pheromones and behaviour – subliminal attraction.
	Recent **Fisher et al. (2005)**	Used fMRI to investigate the brain systems involved in early-stage intense romantic love.	**Biological approach:** Neurotransmitters and their influence on human behaviour – dopamine and love. fMRI as a technique to study the brain.

Further resources

TED talk by Helen Fisher (2008). The brain in love. https://tinyurl.com/yx8n7cr4

Lyons, K. & Kimpton, P. (12 Feb 2016). How do I...fall in love? *The Guardian.* https://tinyurl.com/y6d54lt3

Psychology Today staff (1 Sep 2004). Cupid's Comeuppance. *Psychology Today.* https://tinyurl.com/yx8n7cr4

TED talk. Brain in love

Psychology Today - Cupid's Come-uppance

PSYCHOLOGY OF HUMAN RELATIONSHIPS

Topic 2: Personal relationships

Key Idea: Personal relationships may be explained through biological, cognitive and sociocultural approaches.

Content	Research	Use in Human Relationships	Links to
Formation of personal relationships – cognitive explanations	Classic **Walster (1966)**	Developed the matching hypothesis, suggesting that in making dating and mating choices people will be influenced by both the desirability of the potential match (what the individual wants) and their perception of the probability of obtaining the desired person (what an individual thinks they can get).	
	Critique/Further **Markey & Markey (2007)**	Tested the similarity-attraction hypothesis that people are attracted to those who share similar attitudes to their own. This research offers some support for the idea that we gravitate towards those who share similar views to our own. Also tested the complementarity model that argues that opposites attract. Found that only the model of similarity accurately explained the personalities to which participants tended to be attracted.	
	Recent **Taylor et al. (2011)**	Investigated the matching hypothesis by using real online dating behaviour. Found that the initiators tended to contact people on the site who were rated as more attractive than they were. People do not necessarily apply the matching hypothesis when it comes to dating decisions.	

Further resources

Cherry, K. (29 April 2018). 5 psychological theories of love: how psychologists describe and explain love. *Very Well Mind.* https://tinyurl.com/y24be5uf

Han, Y. & Lebowitz, S. (27 Sep 2016). 12 surprising psychological reasons someone might fall in love. *UK Business Insider.* https://tinyurl.com/yxqo99sh

Cherry. 5 psychological theories of love.

PSYCHOLOGY OF HUMAN RELATIONSHIPS

Topic 2: Personal relationships

Key Idea: Personal relationships may be explained through biological, cognitive and sociocultural approaches.

Content	Research	Use in Human Relationships	Links to
Formation of personal relationships – sociocultural explanations	Classic **Moreland & Beach (1992)**	Theory that mere exposure leads to familiarity and liking. They investigated the mere exposure effect on ratings of familiarity and attractiveness. The results showed only a weak support for a correlation with familiarity; however there was strong support for mere exposure influencing attraction.	
	Critique/Further **Peskin & Newell (2004)**	Investigated how both typicality and familiarity of female faces breed liking. Found that increasing exposure to faces increases their perceived attractiveness, regardless of how typical they are.	
	Recent **Regan et al. (2012)**	Compared the outcome of both love-based and arranged marriages in the USA. Found very little differences, and the overall experiences of love within the marriages appeared to be very similar.	

Further resources

Sardar, Z. (13 Sep 2008). First person. *The Guardian.* A personal view of arranged marriages. https://tinyurl.com/y27zrojg

Guardian. Arranged marriages.

TEDx talk by Ashvini Mashru. My arranged marriage: how I embraced the unknown. https://tinyurl.com/y5jz4obx

My arranged marriage

PSYCHOLOGY OF HUMAN RELATIONSHIPS

Topic 2: Personal relationships

Key Idea: Personal relationships may be explained through biological, cognitive and sociocultural approaches.

Content	Research	Use in Human Relationships	Links to
Role of communication	Classic **Tannen (1990)**	Communication differs according to gender: the researchers conducted a series of observations of couples involved in intimate relationships. The couples' conversations were recorded and then analysed to identify patterns of speech that showed differences in linguistic style	
	Critique/Further **Ahmad & Reid (2008)**	Culture affects communication: the researchers investigate the link between traditional marital expectations and listening styles in couples in arranged marriages.	
	Recent **Lavner et al. (2016)**	While it is assumed that good communication between spouses will positively affect their later judgments of their marriage, these researchers conducted a longitudinal study to see if good communication may be the **consequence** of being in a satisfactory marriage, rather than having any causal role in this.	

Further resources

Stosny, S. (23 Feb 2010). Marriage problems: how communication techniques can make them worse. *Psychology Today.* https://tinyurl.com/y5xtrfar

Stosny. Marriage problems

PSYCHOLOGY SORTED: KEY RESEARCH FOR STUDENTS AND TEACHERS
BOOK 2 – APPLIED PSYCHOLOGY

PSYCHOLOGY OF HUMAN RELATIONSHIPS

Topic 2: Personal relationships

Key Idea: Personal relationships may be explained through biological, cognitive and sociocultural approaches.

Content	Research	Use in Human Relationships	Links to
Explanations for why relationships change or end	Classic **Duck (2007)**	Proposed a stage theory of relationship breakdown that was predictable, with the partnership moving through four phases of gradual disconnection.	
	Critique/Further **Mitnick et al. (2009)**	Looked at the changes in the satisfaction levels (satisfaction with the relationship itself) of couples after they had become parents. Found that satisfaction levels decrease after having children.	
	Recent **Williamson et al. (2015)**	Investigated whether problems that led to divorce may exist at the beginning of the marriage (enduring dynamics model) or developed over time (emergent distress model). Results suggested an emergent distress model for wives.	

Further resources

Cosslett, R.L. (21 April 2018). 'It feels like having a limb cut off': the pain of friendship breakups. *The Guardian.* https://tinyurl.com/yaq3xjgp

Cosslett. Pain of friendship breakups

Wong, B. (4 May 2016). 8 relationship problems you just can't fix. *Huffington Post.* https://tinyurl.com/yxzwrhtm

Wong. 8 relationship problems

PSYCHOLOGY OF HUMAN RELATIONSHIPS

Topic 3: Group dynamics

Key Idea: How psychological theory can explain inter-group and intra-group relationships, including cooperation, competition, prejudice, discrimination and conflict.

Content	Research	Use in Human Relationships	Links to
Co-operation and competition	Classic **Sherif et al. (1961)**	Sherif proposed his **realistic conflict theory** in 1966, after this experiment and earlier ones. This 'Robber's Cave' field experiment investigated intergroup relations in the presence of competition for scarce resources. The results showed that 12 year-old boys at summer camp could be manipulated into conflict when groups were competing scarce resources, and then manipulated into cooperation when a shared superordinate goal is introduced.	**Sociocultural Approach: The individual and the group** -social identity theory.
	Critique/Further **Tauer & Harackiewicz (2004)**	Looked at the effect of cooperation and competition on intrinsic motivation. They found that a combination of cooperation and competition appears to result in the highest level of intrinsic motivation.	**Sociocultural Approach: The individual and the group** -social identity theory.
	Recent **Colpaert et al. (2015)**	Investigated the interaction between cooperation or competition and social comparison. They found that competitive settings moderated the impact of social comparison on self-evaluation.	**Sociocultural Approach: The individual and the group** -social identity theory.

Further resources

Coleman, P.T. (17 August 2017). What leads to cooperation and competition? *Psychology Today*. https://tinyurl.com/y6jtkfk4

TEDx talk by Mina Cikara (21 Oct 2015). When 'I' becomes 'we'. https://tinyurl.com/y6zxbxxe

Also links well to social identity theory.

Coleman. Cooperation and competition

PSYCHOLOGY OF HUMAN RELATIONSHIPS

Topic 3: Group dynamics

Key Idea: How psychological theory can explain inter-group and intra-group relationships, including cooperation, competition, prejudice, discrimination and conflict.

Content	Research	Use in Human Relationships	Links to
Prejudice and discrimination	Classic **Stephan et al (1998)**	Integrated threat theory: prejudice is the result of stereotyping, realistic threats (to jobs, for example), and symbolic threats.	**Sociocultural approach:** the individual and the group – social identity theory.
	Critique/Further **McLaren (2003)**	Conducted a study into 17 European countries and found that the symbolic threat – the belief that immigrants undermine national values were a stronger predictor of prejudice against immigrants than perceptions of realistic threat.	**Sociocultural approach:** the individual and the group – social identity theory.
	Recent **Lam & Seaton (2016)**	Social identity theory: used Tajfel's minimal groups paradigm (see below) to investigate the influence of intergroup competition on children's in-group and out-group attitudes.	**Sociocultural approach:** the individual and the group – social identity theory.

Further resources

TED talk by Paul Bloom (2014). Can prejudice ever be a good thing?
https://tinyurl.com/j98uotw

Bunting, M. (5 Sep 2007). A world of difference. *The Guardian*
https://tinyurl.com/y4eazztk

Evans, G. (2 March 2018). The unwelcome revival of 'race science'. *The Guardian.*
https://tinyurl.com/y9vkshsz

TED talk - prejudice

Guardian. Unwelcome revival of 'race science.'

PSYCHOLOGY OF HUMAN RELATIONSHIPS

Topic 3: Group dynamics

Key Idea: How psychological theory can explain inter-group and intra-group relationships, including cooperation, competition, prejudice, discrimination and conflict.

Content	Research	Use in Human Relationships	Links to
Origins of conflict and conflict resolution	Classic **Sherif et al. (1961)**	Sherif proposed his **realistic conflict theory** in 1966, after this experiment and earlier ones. This 'Robber's Cave' field experiment investigated intergroup relations in the presence of competition for scarce resources. The results showed that 12 year-old boys at summer camp could be manipulated into conflict when groups were competing scarce resources, and then manipulated into cooperation when a shared superordinate goal is introduced.	**Sociocultural Approach: The individual and the group** -social identity theory.
	Critique/Further **Tajfel et al. (1971)**	Minimal groups paradigm: he found that merely being put in a group is enough to instill loyalty to the group and some discrimination towards those outside the group. Can form the basis for later conflict. Unlike Sherif, Tajfel argued that even the perception of being in a group, with no competition for scarce resources, was enough to strengthen an in-group identity.	**Sociocultural approach:** the individual and the group – social identity theory.
	Recent **Hodson & Busseri (2012)**	Investigated the proposal that low cognitive ability is linked to right-wing views and that it is socially conservative ideology that mediates most of this effect. (i.e. it is the attraction to the right-wing authoritarianism that results in the prejudice, rather than just a direct route from low cognitive ability to prejudice and discrimination).	

Further resources

Crash Course Psychology no.39. Prejudice and Discrimination. *Youtube.* https://tinyurl.com/z45r6r4

PSYCHOLOGY SORTED: KEY RESEARCH FOR STUDENTS AND TEACHERS
BOOK 2 – APPLIED PSYCHOLOGY

PSYCHOLOGY OF HUMAN RELATIONSHIPS

TOPIC 1: SOCIAL RESPONSIBILITY

Key Idea: We are all interdependent, but how we help each other is mediated biologically, cognitively and culturally.

Content 1: Bystanderism

KEY STUDY 1.1: *Latané & Darley (1968). Group Inhibition of Bystander Intervention in Emergencies.*

Brief Summary
Theory of the unresponsive bystander. Conducted an experiment to investigate diffusion of responsibility in a perceived emergency. Found that the more people there were assumed to be as witnesses, then the less likely a participant was to intervene in a perceived emergency

Aim
To investigate the theory of the unresponsive bystander, with diffusion of responsibility as the key explanation for this behaviour.

Participants
72 students (59 female, 13 male) on an introductory psychology course from New York University. The researchers had contacted the participants to ask for their participation but the details of the research were not revealed to the participants in advance.

Procedure
Each participant was placed alone at a table with headphones and a microphone on it. The participant was then told that they would be taking part in a discussion of problems that college students faced and that due to the potentially sensitive nature of the topic they would be alone in the room, using the microphone and headphones to conduct the discussion. The participants were in the middle of listening to another person (a confederate) speaking when it became clear that the person on the other end of the intercom was having a seizure. The dependent variable was measured as the time it took the participant to seek assistance to help the person having the seizure.

The independent variable was designed as follows:

- The 'alone' condition: the participant believed that they alone were listening to the seizure.
- The 3-person group: the participant believed that one other person was listening in.
- The 6-person group: the participant believed that four other people were listening in.

Results

The following table shows what percentage of the participants reported the seizure per condition:

Condition	% of participants reporting the seizure
Alone	85
3-person group	62
6-person group	31

Conclusion

Diffusion of responsibility may to some extent explain the theory of the unresponsive bystander i.e. less help is likely to be given in an emergency if people believe that there are others present who can offer help.

Evaluation of Latané & Darley (1968)

Strengths

- ✓ This is a well-designed study with three distinct conditions of the independent variable; group size did seem to have an influence as to the speed and rate of helping so it supports the diffusion of responsibility hypothesis.
- ✓ The researchers reported that many of the participants were genuinely distressed at the sound of someone appearing to have a seizure. If true, this would give the study good external validity.

Limitations

- X It is possible that some of the participants may have guessed the aim of the study, which would make their responses invalid.
- X There are ethical considerations to the procedure as the participants were deceived as to the real nature of the seizures plus it is likely that they experienced some distress or shock when listening to the faked seizures down the phone.

Reference

Latané, B. & Darley, J.M. (1968). Group Inhibition of Bystander Intervention in Emergencies. *Journal of Personality & Social Psychology, 10* (3), pp. 215-221.

****

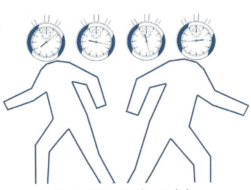

Bystanderism - too busy to help

PSYCHOLOGY SORTED: KEY RESEARCH FOR STUDENTS AND TEACHERS
BOOK 2 – APPLIED PSYCHOLOGY

TOPIC 1: SOCIAL RESPONSIBILITY

Content 1: Bystanderism

KEY STUDY 1.2: *Piliavin et al. (1969). Good Samaritanism: an underground phenomenon?*

Brief Summary
Arousal-cost-reward model: we want to help, but want to be sure that there is no risk to ourselves. Investigated bystanderism and how it may explain why some people tend to be given help more than others - they are seen as a 'deserving' victim rather than someone who has played a role in bringing about their own misfortune. Found that a victim who appears innocent is more likely to be helped than a victim who seems to have invited their fate, by being drunk, for example.

Aim
To conduct a field experiment to investigate the effect of several different variables on who responded to a passenger in need of help. The variables being measured included how quickly and how frequently help was given, the type of victim (drunk or ill) and the ethnicity of victim (black or white).

Participants
An opportunity sample of 4,450 passengers (55% white; 45% black) using the New York subway between Harlem and The Bronx between the hours of 11am and 3pm over the course of several months. The journey lasted 7.5 minutes without any stops at the intervening stations.

Procedure
4 confederates were used per trial: 2 females as observers, 1 white male aged 24 – 29 to model helping behaviour and 1 male victim aged 26 – 35 (either white or black, dressed identically; the 'drunk' victim smelled of alcohol and the 'ill' victim had a cane).

A total of 103 trials was conducted by alternating teams of researchers over the total course of the research's duration. The female confederates took seats and kept notes as unobtrusively as possible, while the male victim and male model stood near a pole in the centre of the train. After passing the first station (approximately 70 seconds) the victim collapsed. In the 'no help' condition; the model did nothing until the train slowed to a stop, and then helped the victim to his feet. In the 'helping' condition, the model came to the victim's assistance.

There were four different helping conditions used in both 'drunk' and 'cane' situations:
1. Critical area – early. The model stood in the critical area and waited until after the train passed the fourth station, and then helped the victim. (Approximately 70 secs after collapse.)
2. Critical area – late. The model stood in the critical area and waited until after the train passed the sixth station before helping the victim. (Approximately 150 secs after collapse.)
3. Adjacent area – early. The model stood a little further way, adjacent to the critical area and waited until after the train passed the fourth station, and then helped the victim
4. Adjacent area – late. The model stood in the adjacent area and waited until after the sixth station before helping.

Results
The table shows the help given dependent on victim condition and ethnicity:

Victim condition	% of help given
Ill (with cane)	95% (62 out of 65 trials)
Drunk (smelling of alcohol)	50% (19 out of 38 trials)
White (no model help) - Ill	100%
White (no model help) – Drunk	100%
Black (no model help) - Ill	100%
Black (no model help) - Drunk	73%

Spontaneous help before 70 secs had lapsed in the model trials was more likely in the 'ill' condition. The victims received help in 81/103 trials, and in 60% of these cases the help was received from more than one person. In fact, once the first person had moved to help, two or three others often followed quite quickly. Men were more likely to help than women (some of the women's comments were along the lines of 'It's a man's job to help'; 'I wouldn't know what to do'). Same-ethnicity helping was noted in the black/drunk condition more than in other conditions.

Conclusion
The diffusion of responsibility hypothesis was not supported by the results of this study, in fact the larger the group the more help was given. The results may be better explained using the negative-state relief model where help is given not purely for altruistic reasons but is instead prompted by the need to reduce feelings of anxiety and guilt in the presence of a victim.

Evaluation of Piliavin et al. (1969)
Strengths
- ✓ This was a highly organised, well-designed study that collected both quantitative and qualitative data, making it high in reliability due to the large sample and high in ecological validity due to the natural setting and unforced behaviour of the participants.
- ✓ The finding that diffusion of responsibility may not occur outside of lab settings was a hugely interesting finding and casts the topic of bystanderism in a new light.

Limitations
- X The study might have been affected by a range of extraneous variables that were impossible to control. e.g. participant mood on the day; some of the participants experiencing the procedure more than once. The number of participants in the carriage may have obscured the view of the emergency, meaning that some data may have been lost or misinterpreted by the observers.
- X The ethics of the study were compromised due to the lack of consent given, deception of participants, possible psychological harm and distress and the lack of right to withdraw. This means that it would not be possible to carry out the study today to check the findings with a modern population.

Reference:
Piliavin, I.M., Rodin, J.A. & Piliavin, J. (1969), Good Samaritanism: An underground phenomenon? *Journal of Personality & Social Psychology, (13),* pp 289-299.

****

TOPIC 1: SOCIAL RESPONSIBILITY

Content 1: Bystanderism

KEY STUDY 1.3: *Schultz et al. (2014). Cyber-bullying: An exploration of bystander behavior and motivation.*

Brief Summary
Researchers explored if and how bystanders responded when presented with a cyber-bullying simulation. Found that dispositional factor (empathy) predicted most frequent intervention, but in the majority of cases there was no intervention.

Aim
To investigate if and how bystanders respond when confronted with cyber-bullying.

Participants
149 university students from the USA, with a mean age of 20 years (age range 18-27 years), 69% female and 28% male (3% of the sample provided no data as to gender).

Procedure
The participants first filled in a questionnaire designed to test their level of empathy. They were then presented with an example of cyber-bullying posted on a fictitious student's Facebook page, involving exclusion from the group, insulting messages and the posting of private, embarrassing information about the student. The participants were then asked to imagine that they knew all of the fictitious people involved in the incident and they were asked which of the students they most identified with, what their role would be as part of the Facebook conversation, and then to explain their answers.

Results
91% of the participants agreed that the behaviour presented to them constituted cyber-bullying. 31% in the first testing phase and 47% in a second testing phase reported that they would intervene in a supportive way, backing up the student being bullied and/or standing up to the bullies. 9% of participants said that they would intervene offline, in a less direct way. 69% in the first test and 52% in the second test did not comment on the bullying. Participants who had scored high on the empathy questionnaire were more likely to identify with the victim of the bullying rather than with the bullies.

Conclusion
Having a naturally higher level of empathy may mean that an individual is more likely to identify with victims of bullying and therefore to intervene on their behalf.

Evaluation of Schultz et al. (2014)

Strengths
- ✓ The standardised nature of the procedure – both the initial empathy questionnaire and the subsequent cyber-bullying episode are replicable which increases the reliability of the findings.
- ✓ Using open-ended questions about the bullying episode means that the researchers could collect qualitative data which is rich and insightful, thus increasing the validity of the findings.

Limitations
- X It is quite likely that social desirability bias will have influenced the response of some participants, causing them to present their responses, downplaying any anti-social responses they might have experienced (e.g. feeling that they wanted to join in with the bullying).
- X The findings highlight that high empathy and intervention in bullying are linked but it is not clear *how* or *why* this is so.

Reference
Schultz, E., Heilman, R., & Hart, K. J. (2014). Cyber-bullying: An exploration of bystander behavior and motivation. *Cyberpsychology: Journal of Psychosocial Research on Cyberspace, 8*(4), article 3.

****

TOPIC 1: SOCIAL RESPONSIBILITY

Content 2: Prosocial behaviour: biological explanations.

KEY STUDY 2.1: *Simmons et al. (1977). Gift of Life: the social and psychological impact of organ transplantation.*

Brief Summary
Kin selection theory as a biological explanation for altruism. Tested kin selection theory by investigating whether close relatives of a kidney patient would be more likely to offer themselves as kidney donors. Found that parents were more likely to donate a kidney to a child, than siblings were to donate one to a brother/sister.

Aim
To test kin selection theory by investigating the extent to which close relatives of a kidney patient would be willing to offer themselves as kidney donors.

Participants
An opportunity sample of potential kidney donors (relatives of existing kidney patients) was obtained from the records of University of Minnesota hospitals.

Procedure
The participants were asked using questionnaires, whether or not they would be willing to donate one of their kidneys to their close relative, who was an existing patient receiving treatment for a kidney condition. The potential kidney recipients (the kidney patients) were asked to rate how

emotionally close they felt to all of their possible donors before the choice of a donor had been made.

Results
The following table shows the results for agreeing to donate a kidney and the degree of closeness felt by the kidney patients:

	Agree to donate kidney	Level of closeness felt by kidney patient
Parent	86%	
Sibling	47%	
Donor		63%
Non-donor		42%

Conclusion
Kin selection theory goes some way towards explaining prosocial behaviour from a biological/evolutionary perspective. There may, however, be sociocultural factors determining the decision to donate or not e.g. upbringing, culture, education.

Evaluation of Simmons et al. (1977)
Strengths
✓ The study used actual kidney patients who were awaiting kidney donation, which makes the ecological validity of the study high.
✓ The results support the idea of altruism as an evolutionary mechanism as it makes evolutionary sense for a parent to sacrifice their own fitness to ensure that their offspring survives.

Limitations
X The fact that 14% of the parents did *not* agree to donate a kidney to their son/daughter casts some doubt on the validity of the theory as if it held true then 100% of parents should automatically agree to donation. Sociocultural factors e.g. culture, religion, education level may account for the lack of 100% agreement to donate.
X There may have been other factors determining the decision to donate as the siblings who agreed to donate were more likely to be the same sex as the recipient, closer in age and probably with more in common with their sibling than with those who refused to donate and therefore kin selection theory has limited explanatory capacity.

Reference
Simmons, R.G.; Klein, S.D.; Simmons, R.L. (1977). *Gift of Life: the social and psychological impact of organ transplantation*. London, UK: Wiley.

****

TOPIC 1: SOCIAL RESPONSIBILITY

Content 2: Prosocial behaviour: biological explanations

KEY STUDY 2.2: *Axelrod* & Hamilton *(1981). The Emergence of Cooperation among Egoists.*

Brief Summary
Reciprocal altruism is based on the principles of evolutionary psychology and explains that altruistic acts are performed in order to gain some future benefit from the recipient. The researchers devised a computer-based model of chess games involving two players to test the idea behind the Prisoner's Dilemma and reciprocity. Found that that mutually advantageous behaviour may ultimately benefit individual more than purely self-serving acts.

Aim
To test Reciprocal Altruism using a conceptual game known as the Prisoner's Dilemma. The Prisoner's Dilemma revolves around the idea that two criminals are offered the same deal separately by the prosecutor: *give up your partner and say he committed the crime in which case you will go free and your buddy will get 3 years in prison.* If each man betrays the other then they both get 2 years in prison. If neither prisoner rats out the other one then they will each serve only one year. Reciprocal altruism would suggest that if both prisoners betray each other then they will both serve one more year in prison than if they said nothing, which is not good for either of them. But what if you betray your criminal buddy? He will serve 3 years in prison for the crime that *both* of you committed. So, when he gets out of prison he is likely to want his revenge. By saying nothing both prisoners are temporarily reducing their own fitness for long-term gain.

Procedure
The researchers devised a computer-based model of chess games involving two players to test the idea behind the Prisoner's Dilemma and reciprocity. The researchers analysed a range of strategies used in chess games that had been provided by economists, sociologists, political theorists and mathematicians. A second round of chess games was then analysed from 62 entries covering six countries. The submissions from this sample also came from computer enthusiasts, professors of biology, physics and computer science. Strategies employed in the chess games were analysed by the researchers.

Results
The most successful way of achieving the highest average score was to employ a simple strategy known as *tit for tat*. This strategy involves a reciprocal arrangement: players cooperate on the first move and then follow whatever move the preceding player makes. Subsequent games went on to highlight how well the *tit for tat* strategy was when compared to other less reciprocal strategies.

Conclusion
The *tit for tat* strategy reflects, to some extent, the Prisoner's Dilemma and illustrates that mutually advantageous behaviour may ultimately be more beneficial to an individual than pure self-serving acts.

Evaluation of Axelrod & Hamilton (1981)

Strengths
✓ The research is reliable as the procedure (a chess tournament with defined moves) is objective and replicable.
✓ The results support for the theory of reciprocal altruism – the *tit for tat* strategy continually scored highly and was used by players most frequently, thus emphasising its suitability for mutual gain.

Limitations
X The study did not investigate real behaviour in a naturalistic setting which makes it low in ecological validity.
X The sample of academic specialists is also not representative of the general population, making the study difficult to generalise.

Reference
Axelrod, R. (1981). The Emergence of Cooperation among Egoists. *American Political Science Review, Vol 75 (2)*; pp 306-318.

****

TOPIC 1: SOCIAL RESPONSIBILITY

Content 2: Prosocial behaviour: biological explanations

KEY STUDY 2.3: *Crockett et al. (2010). Serotonin selectively influences moral judgement and behaviour through effects on harm aversion.*

Links to
- **Neurotransmitters and their effect on behaviour:** Serotonin may be linked to prosocial (helpful and cooperative) behaviour.

Brief Summary
This study suggest that high levels of serotonin promote prosocial behaviour. Serotonin promotes control of violent impulses and prevents people from being provoked into violent actions.

Aim
To investigate how serotonin directly affects moral judgement by increasing the motivation of participants to help others and their aversion to personally harming others.

Participants
24 males from the Cambridge area of the UK with a mean age of 25.6 years. The participants were screened for psychiatric and neurological disorders before the study began.

Procedure
The participants were given either a drug used to treat depression, a drug used to treat ADHD and OCD or a placebo. The drugs were administered using a double-blind procedure.

The first part of the procedure involved participants being asked to make moral judgements about a series of hypothetical scenarios, for example:

- *Would you push someone in front of a train if it meant saving five other people?* This was the emotionally salient 'personal harm' condition.
- *Would you flick a switch so that a train hit one person instead of five?* This was the less emotionally salient 'impersonal harm' condition.

There was no time limit on how long the participants spent thinking about each scenario and making their decisions. The responses were measured according to how many times each participant judged that an action was 'acceptable'.

Results
- The emotionally salient personal harm condition (i.e. which involved participants imagining themselves harming someone else directly) produced the lowest number of 'acceptable' responses from all participants. In other words, participants could not agree to intervene personally to harm another person, even if it meant saving others.
- Participants who had been taking the anti-depressant citalopram (which works as a selective serotonin reuptake inhibitor) were far more likely to say that harmful actions were unacceptable compared to the other two groups. The moral judgements made by the ADHD medication group and the placebo group were roughly similar, showing no great differences.

Conclusion
Serotonin may induce prosocial behaviour and reduce acts of harm towards others.

Evaluation of Crockett et al. (2010)
Strengths
- ✓ The procedure involved a double-blind allocation of drugs and placebo, which increases the validity of the findings as it means that both researchers and participants did not know what drug was being taken, which should eliminate any bias. That is, neither participants nor researchers could act in accordance with expectations as to the effects of the drug.
- ✓ Using a biological approach to measure prosocial behaviour lends some objectivity and reliability to a topic that is notoriously difficult to test scientifically using a reliable measure.

Limitations
- X The small sample size of 24 males, divided between 3 drug conditions, means that the results are not statistically robust and cannot easily be generalised, and gender bias is also an issue.
- X There may be alternative explanations for the moral judgements made by the participants. They may have held religious principles, had individual differences in morality, personal experience related to specific scenarios, or displayed social desirability bias.

Reference
Crockett, M. J., Clark, L., Hauser, M. D., & Robbins, T. W. (2010). Serotonin selectively influences moral judgment and behavior through effects on harm aversion. *Proceedings of the National Academy of Sciences, 107*(40), pp.17433-17438.

****

TOPIC 1: SOCIAL RESPONSIBILITY

Content 3: Prosocial behaviour – cognitive (psychological) explanations.

KEY STUDY 3.1: *Cialdini & Schaller (1987). Empathy-based helping: is it selflessly or selfishly motivated?*

Brief Summary
Negative state-relief model of altruism, which considers the extent to which personal discomfort at the sight of another's distress motivates altruistic acts.

Aim
To investigate the role of the negative state-relief model in helping behaviour.

Participants
81 female psychology students from a university in the USA.

Procedure
The procedure was the same as the one used by Batson (1981) which went as follows: the participants were told that they would be working with another student, 'Elaine' in a study looking at how stress affects performance. Elaine was in fact a confederate who was working with the researchers. The participants were told that they had been randomly allocated to the position of observer; Elaine was to perform the tasks. They then observed Elaine over CCTV as she performed a memory task. Elaine was given electric shocks at random intervals, which were described as 'moderately uncomfortable'.

The researchers manipulated the participants' levels of empathy for Elaine by giving them either very similar or very different questionnaire responses (supposedly filled in by Elaine) from their own. Those participants in the similar condition believed that Elaine had filled in the questionnaire with responses almost identical to their own; this was done to make them feel a certain degree of empathy with Elaine compared to the dissimilar condition. Two different 'escape' conditions were also used in the study: the *difficult escape* condition consisted of participants being told that they had to stay and keep observing Elaine for the whole 10 trials; the *easy escape* condition involved the participants being able to leave after observing two trials. The participants were then given questionnaires which assessed their mood and emotional state. Finally, the participants were given the chance to swap places with Elaine and to take the shocks in her place.

Results
Participants in the high-empathy condition showed more empathic concern for Elaine and personal sadness than the low-empathy participants. The researchers thought that this was because personal sadness motivated the desire to help rather than a feeling of empathy for Elaine – which they explained using the negative-state relief model (the participants helped in order to improve their sad state by doing something good i.e. helping Elaine.

Conclusion
Help may be given to someone based on a potential helper's emotional state or on their need for social approval and fear of social disapproval.

Evaluation of Schaller & Cialdini (1987)
Strengths
- ✓ The findings of this study – that social desirability bias may stimulate helping – have been supported by other research in the field.
- ✓ The study used a standardised procedure which means that it can be replicated, increasing its reliability.

Limitations
- X There is the possibility that demand characteristics may have impaired the validity of the findings as this was a lab experiment using psychology students as participants.
- X There are some ethical concerns with the procedure: the participants were deceived as to the nature of the shocks and it is likely that some of them felt distressed at what they were seeing.

References
Batson, C. D., Bruce, D., Ackerman, P., Buckley, T., Birch, K. (1981). Is Empathic Emotion a source of Altruistic Motivation? *Journal of Personality and Social Psychology, 40* (20), pp. 290-302.

Cialdini, R. B., Schaller, M., Houlihan, D., Arps, K., Fultz, J., & Beaman, A. L. (1987). Empathy-based helping: Is it selflessly or selfishly motivated? *Journal of Personality and Social Psychology, 52*(4), p. 749-758.

****

TOPIC 1: SOCIAL RESPONSIBILITY

Content 3: Prosocial behaviour: cognitive (psychological explanations)

KEY STUDY 3.2: *Batson et al. (1989). Negative-state relief and the empathy-altruism hypothesis.*

Brief Summary
Tested Schaller and Cialdini's negative state-relief model, and found that people who felt sad were more likely to offer help than those who felt happy. This could be because they wanted to lessen their own distress by helping.

Aim
To further test the negative state-relief model of helping behaviour.

Participants
44 students (20 male; 24 female), who were enrolled on an introductory psychology course at the University of Kansas.

Procedure
The participants were randomly allocated to one of two conditions: half of them were told that they would be watching a video that would cause them 'moderate feelings of depression and sadness' (the *depression of mood* condition); the other half that they would be watching a video that would cause 'strong feelings of happiness and pleasure' (the *enhancement of mood* condition). The participants in the *depression of mood* condition were asked to recall for a few minutes an event from their past that made them feel sad; the participants in the *enhancement of mood* condition were simply asked to explain everyday activities such as driving or performing household chores. The experimenter left the room and a female confederate entered and asked the participants if they would be willing to give some time to help make phone calls related to blood donation, requiring their involvement in this helpful task up to a total of 10 calls.

Results
There were more offers of help from participants in the sad mood condition than in the positive mood condition.

Conclusion
The participants who had been induced to feel sad may have helped in a bid to feel better (self-reward), thereby supporting the negative state relief model, as they may have experienced self-reward from helping.

Evaluation of Batson et al. (1989)
Strengths
- ✓ The use of naïve participants means that the validity of the results is strong, as the participants were not told that it was their offer (or not) of help that was being measured. This therefore reduced the possibility of demand characteristics.
- ✓ The use of random allocation to condition and a single blind design (i.e. the confederate was not told to which condition each participant belonged) means that the research has a degree of objectivity that increases its reliability.

Limitations
- X Participant variables may have affected the validity: some people are simply more helpful than others; some of the participants may have reacted strongly or negatively to the female confederate for a range of reasons.
- X This study only provides evidence of a single instance of altruism, and therefore it is not possible to state conclusively that the participants would be likely to behave in a similar way in other contexts, which means the study lacks external validity.

Reference
Batson, C. D., Batson, J. G., Griffith, C. A., Barrientos, S., Brandt, J. R., Sprengelmeyer, P., Bayly, M. J. (1989). Negative-state relief and the empathy-altruism hypothesis. *Journal of Personality and Social Psychology, 56 (6),* pp 922-933.

****

TOPIC 1: SOCIAL RESPONSIBILITY

Content 3: Prosocial behaviour: cognitive (psychological) explanations

KEY STUDY 3.3: *Barragan & Dweck (2014). Rethinking natural altruism: simple reciprocal interactions trigger children's benevolence.*

Links to
- **Social cognitive theory:** Bandura's concept of modelling behaviour.

Brief Summary
Modelling pro-social behaviour can promote it. This research showed that a very simple reciprocal activity elicited high degrees of altruism in 1- and 2-year-old children (as well as older children), whereas friendly but non-reciprocal activity did not. Showed that altruism could be learned by imitation, and contradicted the biological view that altruism is natural to very young children.

Aim
To test the idea that altruism is stimulated by reciprocal activity, rather than being innate.

Participants
34 one and two-year-old children, 17 female and 17 male, from California, USA.

Procedure
The participants were randomly allocated to one of two conditions: reciprocal play or parallel play as follows:

- The **reciprocal play** condition: the experimenter and child sat together and played with toys taken from a single collection. They played together, taking turns, handing each other toys, sharing the play between them.
- The **parallel play** condition: the experimenter and child sat 3 feet from each other and played from two sets of toys (i.e. they were given one set of toys each). The experimenter followed a standardised schedule of looking at the child, smiling at them and making positive comments about the toys.

The next phase of the procedure involved the experimenter unambiguously signalling that they needed help to reach certain items, including a block and a pencil that were out of reach. Children were given 30 seconds to help on each trial, as the experimenter continued to reach toward the object(s).

Results
Children in the reciprocal play condition helped significantly more than children in the parallel play condition.

Conclusion
Engaging in reciprocal play may establish a norm of 'helping' that children learn quickly and this extends to them helping their playmate in other contexts. Thus altruism is learnt.

Evaluation of Barragan & Dweck (2014)
Strengths
- ✓ Using children of such a young age factors out the possibility that demand characteristics might have influenced their behaviour.
- ✓ The findings have good application to parenting and educational settings as it seems that prosocial behaviour can be learnt quite easily via something as simple as reciprocal play.

Limitations
- ✗ It is possible that the children in the reciprocal condition were just more prosocial than those in the parallel play condition. Replicating the study with a much larger and more diverse sample would be one way of establishing reliability of the results.
- ✗ This study does not reflect the variety of ways in which children learn prosocial behaviour, which means that it lacks external validity.

Reference
Barragan, R. C., & Dweck, C. S. (2014). Rethinking natural altruism: simple reciprocal interactions trigger children's benevolence. *Proceedings of the National Academy of Sciences, 111(48),* pp. 17071-17074.

****

TOPIC 1: SOCIAL RESPONSIBILITY

Content 4: Prosocial behaviour – sociocultural explanations.

KEY STUDY 4.1: *Levine et al. (2001). Cross-cultural differences in helping strangers.*

Links to
- **Sociocultural approach:** Cultural origins of behaviour and cognition – cultural dimensions.

Brief Summary
Conducted a study to investigate prosocial behaviour as a function of collectivism/individualism. Found that there are cross-cultural differences in prosocial behaviour, but other variables may influence behaviour.

Aim
To investigate prosocial behaviour using the cultural dimension of individualism/collectivism.

Procedure

23 major cities across the world were selected in which to carry out this large-scale field experiment. The cities chosen were classified as coming from either individualistic cultures (e.g. USA) or collectivist cultures (e.g. Malaysia). The researchers used psychologists and students from all over the world to help them collect their data. The sample consisted of people who were there at the time the behaviour was sampled from the 23 countries selected. Thus, the researchers used opportunity sampling.

The researchers (all male) set up three different scenarios in a variety of outdoor settings involving the following actions:
- A pedestrian drops a pen in the street without noticing.
- A pedestrian wearing a leg brace drops some magazines.
- A blind pedestrian with a cane waits at a traffic light for assistance crossing the street.

The researchers then proceeded to observe the rate and degree of help given in each of the above situations.

Results

Collectivist cultures yielded higher scores for helping behaviour, with Rio de Janeiro being the highest at 93% overall, followed by San Jose in Costa Rica, Lilongwe in Mali, Calcutta in India. Helping rates tended to be high in countries with low economic productivity where there is low purchasing power for each citizen. However, not all results obtained reflected this tendency: the one surprising finding here was that Vienna, a wealthy city in an individualistic culture, ranked fifth most helpful city. Another unexpected result was that Kuala Lumpur (the capital of Malaysia) ranked lowest out of all the 23 countries in terms of prosocial behaviour (40%). One of the related findings was that there was a positive correlation between slow pace of life (measured by walking speed) and pro-social behaviour.

Conclusion

There appear to be some cross-cultural differences in prosocial behaviour but these are not definitive and may not be down to culture alone. Pace of life and socio-economic status are also salient variables.

Evaluation of Levine et al. (2001)

Strengths
- ✓ **The huge scale of the research involving 23 countries and hundreds of participants means that** the results are generalizable across a range of cultures.
- ✓ The large data set of quantitative findings means that the results are robust and can withstand statistical analysis.

Limitations
- X Replicating this study would be extremely difficult which means that the reliability cannot be tested.
- X Using several different observers from different countries means that the researchers were not able to control the ways in which the data was recorded, plus each observer may have interpreted what they saw differently which would affect the validity of the findings.

Reference
Levine, R. V., Norenzayan, A., & Philbrick, K. (2001). Cross-cultural differences in helping strangers. *Journal of Cross-Cultural Psychology, 32*(5), pp. 543-560.

****

TOPIC 1: SOCIAL RESPONSIBILITY

Content 4: Prosocial behaviour: sociocultural explanations

KEY STUDY 4.2: *Aknin et al. (2013). Prosocial spending and well-being: cross-cultural evidence for a psychological universal.*

Brief Summary
Investigated the idea that the pleasure obtained from prosocial spending is universal. Found that the reward experienced from helping others may be deeply ingrained in human nature, as it emerged in diverse cultural and economic contexts.

Aim
To investigate the idea that human beings around the world derive emotional benefits from using their financial resources to help others (prosocial spending).

Participants
A total of 234,917 participants from 136 countries (1,321 per country) from a representative range of cities, towns and rural areas. The sample represents 95% of the adult (15 years+) population of the whole world. 51% of the participants were female; 49% were male, with a total mean age of 38 years.

Procedure
A correlational analysis of data was conducted based on interviews conducted with each participant (via a 30-minute phone interview in richer countries and a one-hour face-to-face interview in poorer countries). Participants were asked a yes/no response as to whether they had donated money to a charity in the past month and this was followed up with a question pertaining to their subjective well-being, where they were asked to 'Rate how satisfied you are with your life as a whole on an 11-point scale- (0, dissatisfied, to 10, satisfied).'

Results
Prosocial spending was positively correlated to higher reported feelings of subjective well-being around the world, whether the country was rich or poor.

Conclusion
Spending money on prosocial causes may be linked to a heightened mood and positive feelings of well-being.

Evaluation of Aknin et al. (2013)

Strengths
- ✓ The sample obtained for this study is almost unique in the field in terms of its representative nature: it can be generalised to almost anyone over the age of 15 from anywhere in the world.
- ✓ The researchers also found that the relationship between prosocial spending and subjective well-being was strong even when a range of demographic variables was taken into account, e.g. social support, perceived freedom, and perceived government corruption.

Limitations
- X Donating money to charity (prosocial spending) is something that is valued in all societies so it is possible that some participants may have exaggerated or lied about their prosocial spending (social desirability bias).
- X Although the link between prosocial spending and subjective well-being was strong, there was still variability between countries, which means that the researchers were not able to state conclusively that prosocial spending is a universal behaviour.

Reference
Aknin, L. B., Barrington-Leigh, C. P., Dunn, E. W., Helliwell, J. F., Burns, J., Biswas-Diener, R., ... & Norton, M. I. (2013). Prosocial spending and well-being: cross-cultural evidence for a psychological universal. *Journal of Personality and Social Psychology, 104*(4), pp. 635-652.

****

TOPIC 1: SOCIAL RESPONSIBILITY

Content 4: Prosocial behaviour: sociocultural explanations

KEY STUDY 4.3: *Mitahara et al. (2018). An interdependence approach to empathic concern for disability and accessibility: effects of gender, culture, and priming self-construal in Japan and New Zealand.*

Brief Summary
The interdependence approach to prosocial behavior suggests that the extent to which an individual is dependent on interpersonal relationships increases the individual's altruism and subsequent prosocial behaviour. Compared Japanese females and New Zealand males and found that neither gender nor culture significantly affected the level of interdependence, but gender and culture differentially moderated empathic altruism.

Aim
To investigate two possible factors influencing empathic concern related to disability (gender and ethnic culture) in specific helping scenarios in Japan and New Zealand.

Participants
129 Japanese participants (52 male; 77 female) and 104 New Zealand participants (48 male; 56 female) who were studying sports-related degrees at university in their home country.

Procedure
The participants first filled in a questionnaire based on cultural self-construal – how much they identified with their native culture and the extent to which it informed their self-image. The participants were then shown 60 photographs of real places and were asked to indicate their level of agreement using a 4-point scale as to how likely they would be to help someone with a specific disability, for example, blindness in a range of situations, such as when tree branches hang low over a footpath.

Results
Gender was not found to influence the degree of cultural self-construal expressed by the participants. However, gender did show a difference in New Zealand (but not Japan) with females in New Zealand showing more prosocial tendencies than males. Interestingly, Japanese males expressed a higher level of prosocial behaviour than Japanese females.

Conclusion
There are complex interactions between gender, culture, and prosocial behaviour.

Evaluation of Mitahara et al. (2018)
Strengths
- ✓ The findings are consistent with social stereotypes in Western cultures, whereby females are seen to be more caring than males. New Zealand female students were more willing to help people with impairments than were New Zealand male students.
- ✓ The researchers used the same materials for all participants, making this study replicable with a range of participants from different cultures.

Limitations
- X It is possible that some of the participants may have responded to what they felt was their *expected* response (e.g. to show concern or to be a responsible citizen) rather than risk expressing their true feelings, thus exhibiting a social desirability effect.
- X The participants were shown a range of photographs and asked to rate their willingness to help. This procedure lacks ecological validity and cannot predict how they might actually respond if the situations were real.

Reference
Mitahara, M., Sawae, Y., Wilson, R., Briggs, H., Ishida, J., Doihata, K., & Sugiyama, A. (2018). An interdependence approach to empathic concern for disability and accessibility: effects of gender, culture, and priming self-construal in Japan and New Zealand. *Journal of Pacific Rim Psychology, 12*, pp.1-10.

****

TOPIC 1: SOCIAL RESPONSIBILITY

Content 5: Promoting prosocial behaviour

KEY STUDY 5.1: *Dickerson et al. (1992). Using Cognitive Dissonance to Encourage Water Conservation.*

Brief Summary
Investigated the extent to which a prior commitment to save water would be observed in subsequent behaviour. Found that a prior commitment to this prosocial behaviour resulted in a positive behaviour change.

Aim
To investigate the extent to which a prior commitment to use less water would be observed in subsequent behaviour.

Participants
80 female students from a college in Santa Cruz, California (USA) who were swimmers. The method used was opportunity sampling.

Procedure
The procedure was conducted as follows – each of the following numbered bullet points describes each of the four conditions of the independent variable:

1. **Questionnaire only:** a female confederate approached the participants individually as they were on their way from the swimming pool to the showers. They were given a questionnaire about how much water they used while showering (their water consumption).

2. **Poster only:** the participants were asked to sign a poster that said: *'Please conserve water. Take shorter showers'*. The confederate also drew the participants' attention to water-conservation posters that had been put up around the campus.

3. **Both:** the participants answered the questionnaire and then signed the poster.

4. **Neither:** the control condition – no manipulation on the part of the researchers.

A second female confederate then occupied one of the shower cubicles in the shower block and she timed the length of each participant's shower once they had finished speaking to the first confederate.

Results
The results were as follows:

Condition	Mean time (in seconds) of showering
1	248.3
2	241.05
3	220.5
4	301.8

The participants in condition 3 who had made the prior commitment of signing the poster **and** answering the questionnaire on their use of water spent less time showering than participants in all of the other conditions.

Conclusion
Making a prior commitment (to using less water) seems to influence the related behaviour (using less water while showering).

Evaluation of Dickerson et al. (1992)
Strengths
- ✓ The manipulation of the IV using four conditions means that the researchers were able to impose some degree of control over the procedure which is not always easy in field experiments.
- ✓ This is a field experiment using naïve participants (they would not have been aware of the IV or of the confederate timing their showers) which makes it high in ecological validity.

Limitations
- ✗ There are some ethical concerns over the procedure: the students were not aware that their showering time was being timed and it could be argued that their privacy was breached due to the intimate way in which the dependent variable was measured.
- ✗ Only one confederate timed the length of the showers: she may have easily missed the start or the end of the showering sessions, so a second confederate should have been used for the sake of reliability.

Reference
Dickerson, C. A., Thibodeau, R., Aronson, E. and Miller, D. (1992), Using Cognitive Dissonance to Encourage Water Conservation. *Journal of Applied Social Psychology, 22*, pp. 841–854.

****

TOPIC 1: SOCIAL RESPONSIBILITY

Content 5: Promoting prosocial behaviour

KEY STUDY 5.2: *Flook et al. (2015). Promoting prosocial behavior and self-regulatory skills in preschool children through a mindfulness-based kindness curriculum.*

Links to
- **Social cognitive theory:** Bandura's concept of modelling behaviour.

Brief Summary
To investigate the effect of a 12-week mindfulness-based 'kindness curriculum' on levels of prosocial behaviour in pre-school children. Found that the promotion of prosocial behaviour in young children has an immediate effect that seems to last over time.

Aim
To investigate the effect of a 12-week mindfulness-based kindness curriculum on levels of prosocial behaviour in pre-school children.

Participants
68 pre-school children from a Midwestern city in the USA (mean age of 4.67 years), 59% white, and the remainder comprising a range of ethnic minority groups e.g. 6% African American; 12% Hispanic. Almost 40% of the sample was described as 'socioeconomically disadvantaged'.

Procedure
The children were randomly allocated to one of the following three conditions:

1. A mindfulness-based 'kindness curriculum' which took play twice a week over 12 weeks, for 20-30 minutes per session. This involved training on how to practice mindfulness by focusing on the moment and enhancing children's prosocial behaviour through empathy and sharing.
2. A group that was waiting to participate in the kindness curriculum.
3. A control group.

The teachers then observed the children over the 12 weeks and rated all of them using measures such as 'sharing', 'delay of gratification' and cognitive tasks involving decision-making.

Results
The children in condition 1, the kindness curriculum, condition, were rated as showing definite improvement in social skills and interaction with others, in their learning as a whole and in their emotional intelligence e.g. thinking about other people, and regulating their own emotions. The control group showed the highest levels of selfish behaviour. The children in condition 1 who started the experiment with low levels of social skills and cognitive functioning showed the highest rates of improvement overall.

Conclusion
Promoting prosocial behaviour in pre-school children has an immediate effect that seems to last over time, and even those on the waiting list showed some improvement in social skills, presumably in anticipation of the curriculum.

Evaluation of Flook et al. (2015)
Strengths
- ✓ The study was carried out in real time and in a real setting, which means that ecological validity of the results is high.
- ✓ The age of the children means that it is unlikely that they guessed the aim of the research, thereby avoiding demand characteristics, and increasing the internal validity.

Limitations
- ✓ The behavioural variables (empathy and sharing) are difficult to measure precisely and may be subject to interpretation, which would affect the reliability of the findings.
- ✓ It is possible that the teachers who were rating the children's behaviour might have used confirmation bias in their appraisal of the children's behaviour, possibly over or under estimating the prosocial behaviour based on their prior knowledge of the children.

Reference
Flook L., Goldberg S. B., Pinger, L., Davidson R. J. (2015). Promoting prosocial behavior and self-regulatory skills in preschool children through a mindfulness-based kindness curriculum. *Developmental Psychology (51)*, pp. 44–51.

****

TOPIC 1: SOCIAL RESPONSIBILITY

Content 5: Promoting prosocial behaviour

KEY STUDY 5.3: *Barragan & Dweck (2014). Rethinking natural altruism: simple reciprocal interactions trigger children's benevolence.*

See above, under **TOPIC 1: SOCIAL RESPONSIBILITY,** *Content 3: Prosocial behaviour: cognitive (psychological) explanations.* This study may also be used for discussing promoting social behaviour.

****

TOPIC 1: SOCIAL RESPONSIBILITY

Critical thinking points

Do kin selection theory and reciprocal altruism really support a biological theory of altruism?
Considering the findings of Simmons et al. (1977) there could well have been a variety of non-biological factors which influenced the response of the participant, such as closeness to the patient; mood at the time of being asked; their own state of health, etc. Bearing in mind the decision-making process involved in such a choice it is difficult to conclude that Kin Selection theory is the only factor at work in such a situation as decision-making is purely cognitive. Reciprocal altruism purports to be a biological theory but there is very little, if any, evidence of biological processes at work. The idea that evolutionary mechanisms have evolved to ensure that species protect each other and, by doing so, themselves, is something that is extremely difficult to find evidence for at the biological level. Axelrod & Hamilton (1981) used a chess tournament as a construct to test Reciprocal Altruism which – again – uses higher-order cognitive processes so that the idea of evolutionary mechanisms governing the behaviour is inferential rather than evidential.

Cognitive research into altruism is problematic due to the difficulty of operationalising the key variables.
Both the empathy-altruism hypothesis and the negative state relief model rely on researchers being able to operationalise the variables of empathy and sadness respectively. These variables - which are key to the aims of Batson (1989) and Schaller & Cialdini (1987) - are highly subjective and open to interpretation, making it difficult to exert control in the same way as is possible in a lab experiment. One person's response to another person in need (e.g. 'Elaine' in Schaller & Cialdini, 1987) will depend on a range of factors: whether she is similar to someone the participant knows; their mood on the day; their attitudes, beliefs, opinions; their upbringing and family history; their cultural/religious background. One way of improving the validity of this research might be to include a range of measures involving both quantitative and qualitative data (triangulation) as each measure would act as a check on the other and so would enable the researcher to be confident that they were actually measuring the variables of interest.

Do the results of research into promoting prosocial behaviour reveal anything about long-term changes in behaviour?
The study on promoting awareness of water consumption by Dickerson et al. (1992) seems to show good support for prior commitment as an influential factor in promoting prosocial behaviour but as this was a snapshot study there is no way of knowing whether or not this water-awareness was long-term or if it only had an effect on the day. For the promotion of prosocial behaviour to be truly effective the message needs to be ongoing and consistent, but a problem is that people may experience 'compassion fatigue', a kind of weariness that comes over people when they are fed too much of the same guilt-inducing information for too long. Being constantly reminded to use less water or donate to a charity might actually backfire on itself: people either stop taking proper notice of the message or they become immune to its power. Another problem is that diffusion of responsibility might occur, with people assuming that because a message (such as to 'conserve water') is everywhere, then most people must be following the instruction which means that they don't really have to because their actions won't impact too much on the situation. Flook et al. (2015) conducted longitudinal research, which is a better way of demonstrating change over time

but as the kindness curriculum was only operational for 12 weeks the further long-term effects remain unknown.

****

TOPIC 2: PERSONAL RELATIONSHIPS

Key Idea: Personal relationships may be explained through biological, cognitive and sociocultural approaches.

Content 6: Formation of personal relationships – biological explanations.

KEY STUDY 6.1: *Singh (1993). Adaptive significance of female physical attractiveness: role of waist-to-hip ratio.*

Links to
- **Biological approach:** Genetics and behaviour – evolutionary explanations for behaviour.

Brief Summary
Males choose female partners whose small (0.7) waist-to-hip ratio suggests fertility.

Aim
To investigate the role played by the waist-hip-ratio (WHR) in determining how attractive a woman is rated by a man.

Participants
106 male university students aged 18-22 years old. 74 of the sample were white; 34 were Hispanic.

Procedure
The participants were shown 12 line drawings of an identical female who differed only in regard to her WHR and her weight (underweight, normal or overweight). The participants then had to rank all 12 figures in order of most to least attractive. They were then asked to choose their top and bottom 3 figures using categories such as sexiness, healthiness and childbearing potential.

Results
Figures with the lowest WHR and of a 'normal' body weight were found to be the most attractive and the healthiest. The highest WHR across the categories was found to be least attractive, with the overweight women being ranked as the least attractive of all categories. The 'normal' body weight was preferred to the 'underweight' category by 30% difference in ranking scores.

Conclusion
Men appear to prefer a woman's body shape to show a low WHR as long as she is generally deemed to be 'normal'. This may be linked to an evolutionary preference for healthy mates who also exude powerful attraction signals.

Evaluation of Singh (1993)

Strengths
- ✓ The use of a replicable procedure in controlled conditions and quantitative data make this a reliable study.
- ✓ The findings of this study have some practical application as they indicate that men do not prefer thinner women: this information could be used to inform a range of services from the fashion industry to advertising, as well as contributing to health service providers, e.g. eating disorder clinics.

Limitations
- X The findings do not explain why some men prefer large women, older women, thin women, disabled women. Nor do they explain homosexuality or lesbianism.
- X There is the possibility that the participants were affected by demand characteristics which could be manifest in some of them responding in the way they felt they 'should' respond (i.e. conforming to society's ideal) rather than how they really felt about preferred female shape.

Reference
Singh, D. (1993). Adaptive significance of female physical attractiveness: role of waist-to-hip ratio. *Journal of Personality and Social Psychology, 65*(2), pp. 293-307.

****

TOPIC 2: PERSONAL RELATIONSHIPS

Content 6: Formation of personal relationships: biological explanations

KEY STUDY 6.2: *Wedekind et al. (1995) MHC-dependent mate preferences in humans.*

Links to
- **Biological approach:** Pheromones and behaviour – subliminal attraction.

Brief Summary
MHC (major histocompatability complex) is a group of genes that, while possibly not pheromones, can be smelt in sweat, and if attraction to those with different MHC than our own is followed by mating (a big 'if'), this maximises the immune responses in offspring, making them stronger.

Aim
To investigate whether females prefer male odours from males with a different MHC from their own.

Participants
49 female students and 44 male students; both groups with a mean age of 25 years. All of the students were from the University of Bern, Switzerland.

Procedure
Experiment, where the male participants were given a plain, cotton T-shirt and were told to wear it for 48 hours, aiming to keep 'odour-neutral', i.e. no deodorant, perfume-free soap, to eat specific foods, avoid sex, alcohol and smoking. The females were then asked to give a rating for six T-shirts which had been specifically chosen, as three of them had been worn by males with a similar MHC to them and the other three by males with a very different MHC from them. The females had to smell the T-shirts by via a triangular hole cut into a cardboard box in which the T-shirt had been placed. Each T-shirt was assessed by the females according to how intense and how pleasant they found their smell. The researchers provided a control in the form of an unworn T-shirt and all smelling was done blind.

Results
The researchers found that women whose MHC was different to the male's MHC found his body odour to be more pleasant than did women with a similar MHC to the male's. However, the finding, was the opposite if the woman was taking an oral contraceptive pill: these women were more attracted to males who had an MHC similar to their own.

Conclusion
Women are normally attracted to males with a different MHC than their own, but the contraceptive pill may interfere with natural mate choice based on MHC dissimilarity.

Evaluation of Wedekind et al. (1995)
Strengths
- ✓ This was a well-controlled study: as well as the males' behaviour being subject to controls, the females also used a nasal spray for two weeks prior to the study to enhance their sensitivity to smell.
- ✓ Whether or not MHC genes are pheromones, they act in a similar way to how pheromones act in animals: the results seem to support the idea that humans are naturally drawn to members of the opposite sex who have a different immune system from their own, thereby increasing the chances of stronger offspring and limiting the chances of inbreeding.

Limitations
- X Forming a conclusion based on body odour preference is tenuous at best: there may be an array of variables that could have influenced the women's preference that have nothing to do with MHC.
- X The males in the task may not have all kept to the demands put upon them by researchers. For example, some may have not been able to deny themselves sex or alcohol. As this was an aspect of the procedure that the researchers could not control, it limits the reliability of the findings.

Reference
Wedekind, C., Seebeck, T., Bettens, F., & Paepke, A. J. (June, 1995). MHC-dependent mate preferences in humans. *Proceedings of the Royal Society, London: Biology, 260* (1359), pp. 245-249.

****

TOPIC 2: PERSONAL RELATIONSHIPS

Content 6: Formation of personal relationships: biological explanations

KEY STUDY 6.3: *Fisher et al. (2005). Reward, motivation, and emotion systems associated with early-stage intense romantic love.*

Links to
- **Biological Approach:** Neurotransmitters and their influence on human behaviour – dopamine and love. fMRI as a technique to study the brain.

Brief Summary
An approach to explaining attraction which focuses on the workings of those neurotransmitters, the chemical messengers in the brain, which are responsible for emotional responses to a range of stimuli.

Aim
To investigate the brain systems involved in early-stage intense romantic love.

Participants
10 females and 7 males, who were students at New York State University via a self-selecting sampling method, aged from 18-26 years old (mean age 20). All participants reported being 'in love' (a range of 1-17 months with a mean of 7 months).

Procedure
Participants were placed in an fMRI scanner and shown a photograph of their loved one followed by a distraction task and then a 'neutral' photograph of an acquaintance with whom they had a non-emotional relationship.

Results

Brain area	Associated with specific neurotransmitter	Associated behaviour
Right ventral tegmental areas (midbrain)	Dopamine	Reward and motivation
Right caudate nucleus (midbrain)	Dopamine	Reward and motivation

Conclusion
The results suggest that people in the early, intense stages of romantic love access the areas of the brain most associated with motivation and reward, giving rise to the idea that people become 'addicted to love'. Fisher et al (2005) suggest that dopaminergic reward pathways contribute to the 'general arousal' component of romantic love and that romantic love is primarily a motivation system, rather than an emotion, making it a biological process rather than a cognitive one.

Evaluation of Fisher et al. (2005)

Strengths
- ✓ This is a highly controlled clinical method of obtaining data and Fisher and her colleagues checked objectivity at every stage of the procedure. This standardised procedure means that the study is replicable, which increases its reliability.
- ✓ Identification of the reward centre of the brain as being active during the fMRI gives support to the idea that human beings may have evolved a brain system which ensures that they become 'hooked' on an individual, which increases the possibility of them reproducing. This gives Fisher et al.'s theory of love being addictive some validity.

Limitations
- X The small sample size of 17 participants means that the results are not very meaningful and may not be robust in terms of statistical analysis. The size of the sample also limits generalisability of the findings.
- X It is overly reductionist to use brain scans to determine how romantic love is experienced: there may be a range of other factors involved, such as similarity, same upbringing, shared ideals, cultural influences.

Reference
Fisher, H., Aron, A., Mashek, D. J., Strong, G., Li, H., & Brown, L. L. (2005). Reward, motivation, and emotion systems associated with early-stage intense romantic love. *Journal of neurophysiology*, *94*(1), pp. 327-337.

****

TOPIC 2: PERSONAL RELATIONSHIPS

Content 7: Formation of personal relationships – cognitive explanations.

KEY STUDY 7.1: *Walster (1966). Importance of physical attractiveness in dating behavior.*

Brief Summary
Developed the matching hypothesis, suggesting that in making dating and mating choices people will be influenced by both the desirability of the potential match (what the individual wants) and their perception of the probability of obtaining the desired person (what an individual thinks they can get). This is a cognitive study.

Aim
To investigate the matching hypothesis via a field experiment.

Participants
376 female and 376 male undergraduate students who had tickets to attend a 'Welcome' dance on a Friday night during the first week of the semester at the University of Minnesota, USA.

Procedure
The researchers had set up the 'Welcome' dance but the participants were not aware of this (they believed that it was part of the first week of welcome events at the university). The participants had been asked to submit details of their personality and interests, with a view to being matched with someone similar. As the participants went through the process of buying tickets for the dance and filling in the personal details they were actually being rated on an 8-point scale by confederates according to how attractive they were. Two days after filling in this questionnaire each participant was randomly assigned a date (although they did not know that the selection was done randomly) and told to meet them at the dance. At the end of the evening each participant filled in a questionnaire about their date including questions such as how much they liked their date, if they found them attractive, if they had arranged another date, etc. 4-6 months after the dance there was a follow-up data collection in which all participants were asked whether or not they had dated (and if so were still dating) their partner from the dance.

Results
The participants rated as the most attractive had high expectations of their date (that he/she should also be highly attractive as well as likeable and considerate). The more attractive a man was, the less attractive he judged his female partner to be. The researchers did not find support for their hypothesis that people will only date those of a similar level of attraction: the best predictor of someone being asked out on a date is how attractive that person is, regardless of the level of attraction of the person asking them. Participants expressed a greater liking for attractive dates than for the less attractive dates.

Conclusion
People may ignore their own level of attractiveness when asking someone out for a date and it is likely that more attractive people will be asked for more dates than 'average' types.

Evaluation of Walster (1966)
Strengths
- ✓ Ecological validity is high due to the real life setting of the research – participants did not know they were in a study.
- ✓ The findings regarding the appeal of attractive people could be used in a variety of contexts from advertising to politics to charity work.

Limitations
- ✓ Rating an individual according to their level of attractiveness is highly subjective. Also, there was only rater per participant in this study and the raters only had a couple of seconds to make their assessment of each participant's attractiveness.
- ✓ Rating other people according to how attractive they are – without their knowledge that this is happening – raises ethical concerns, particularly as one of the categories in which the raters had to place people was 'ugly'.

Reference
Walster, E., Aronson, V., Abrahams, D., & Rottman, L. (1966). Importance of physical attractiveness in dating behavior. *Journal of Personality and Social Psychology, 4*(5), pp. 508-516.

****

TOPIC 2: PERSONAL RELATIONSHIPS

Content 7: Formation of personal relationships - cognitive explanations

KEY STUDY 7.2: *Markey & Markey (2007). Romantic ideals, romantic obtainment and relationship experience: the complementarity of interpersonal traits among romantic partners.*

Brief Summary
Tested the similarity-attraction hypothesis that people are attracted to those who share similar attitudes to their own. This research offers some support for the idea that we gravitate towards those who share similar views to our own. Also tested the complementarity model that argues that opposites attract. Found that only the model of similarity accurately explained the personalities to which participants tended to be attracted.

Aim
To test the similarity-attraction hypothesis: the idea that similarity breeds attraction.

Participants
169 participants comprising 103 female and 66 male US undergraduates obtained via self-selection (an advertisement asking for single people who were looking for a romantic partner).

Procedure
The participants filled in a series of questionnaires covering the following topics:

- **Personality:** each participant rated their own personality using a list of 64 predetermined adjectives.
- **Filler questionnaires:** these were used to disguise the actual purpose of the research and included questions that were not relevant to the topic being investigated.
- **Personality of ideal romantic partner:** this questionnaire was similar to the personality questionnaire but it focused on what the participant was looking for in a partner.

Results
The participants consistently chose their romantic ideal as being someone with a personality very similar to their own: the traits they listed to describe themselves were also seen in the traits they chose to describe their ideal romantic partner. Warm individuals were hoping to meet others who were warm, while people who were dominant were attracted to others who were dominant.

Conclusion
People may be attracted to others who display similar personality traits to themselves.

Evaluation of Markey & Markey (2007)
Strengths
✓ The nature of the standardised questions means that this study can be replicated easily; quantitative data can be compared and analysed easily as well.

✓ The use of the filler questionnaires means that demand characteristics should have been reduced as the aim of the research would be less obvious to the participants.

Limitations
X The participants may have succumbed to social desirability bias and presented an idealised version of themselves and their potential partner which would affect the validity of the findings.
X Quantitative data does not provide detail as to *why* certain choices are made on a questionnaire, which means that the study lacks explanatory power.

Reference
Markey, P. M. & Markey, C. N. (2007). Romantic ideals, romantic obtainment and relationship experience: The complementarity of interpersonal traits among romantic partners. *Journal of Social and Personal Relationships, 24* (4), pp. 517-533.

****

TOPIC 2: PERSONAL RELATIONSHIPS

Content 7: Formation of personal relationships - cognitive explanations

KEY STUDY 7.3: *Taylor et al. (2011). 'Out of my league': a real-world test of the matching hypothesis.*

Brief Summary
Investigated the matching hypothesis by using real online dating behaviour. Found that the initiators tended to contact people on the site who were rated as more attractive than they were. People do not necessarily apply the matching hypothesis when it comes to dating decisions.

Aim
To investigate the matching hypothesis by using real online dating behaviour.

Participants
The researchers selected 60 heterosexual male and 60 heterosexual female profiles from an online dating site at random. These 120 participants were identified as 'initiators', meaning that they initiated contact with other users of the site.

Procedure
The researchers used the actual online activity of the participants who used the dating site. Records were kept to show who responded ('reciprocating contacts') and did not respond ('non-reciprocating contacts') to other people's profile on the site. They collected a maximum of six of the initiators' profile photographs as well as the reciprocating and non-reciprocating profile photographs. A total of 966 photographs was amassed by the researchers – 527 female and 439 male. The researchers used their own contacts who were not involved in the research process to rate the photos. The ratings were based on a 7-point scale of attractiveness (-3 to +3). Each photo was rated by at least 14 and at most 43 judges. Calculations were based on the mean attractiveness rating given to each initiator, to each of their contacts and separate attractiveness means for each

initiator's reciprocating and non-reciprocating contacts.

Results
The results did not support the matching hypothesis: the initiator's physical attractiveness showed no correlation with the mean physical attractiveness of all the people they contacted on the site. What the researchers found was that the initiators tended to contact people on the site who were rated as more attractive than they were.

Conclusion
The matching hypothesis cannot account for real-life decisions determining attraction.

Evaluation of Taylor et al. (2011)
Strengths
- ✓ The use of real online dating activity means that the results of this study are high in ecological validity. The participants could not possibly have been influenced by demand characteristics due to the nature of the procedure.
- ✓ The use of correlational analysis means that it is easy to compare quantitative data and to look for associations between variables.

Limitations
- ✗ The sample only included heterosexual people so it cannot be generalised to homosexuals.
- ✗ People tend to present themselves in a somewhat edited way on dating sites: they may make aspirational dating choices or present the best version of themselves online in a way that is not possible in real-life.

Reference
Taylor, L..S., Fiore, A. T., Mendelsohn, G. A., & Cheshire, C. (2011). 'Out of my league': A real-world test of the matching hypothesis. *Personality and Social Psychology Bulletin, 37*(7), pp. 942-954.

****

TOPIC 2: PERSONAL RELATIONSHIPS

Content 8: Formation of personal relationships – sociocultural explanations

KEY STUDY 8.1: *Moreland & Beach (1992). Exposure effects in the classroom: the development of affinity among students.*

Brief Summary
Theory that mere exposure leads to familiarity and liking. They investigated the mere exposure effect on ratings of familiarity and attractiveness. The results showed only weak support for a correlation with familiarity; however, there was strong support for mere exposure influencing attraction.

Aim
To investigate the mere exposure effect on ratings of familiarity and attractiveness.

Participants
130 male and female students from a university in the USA. They were naïve participants as their involvement in the study depended on which classes they were taking at the time the study was conducted; they did not know that they were taking part in the study.

Procedure
The researchers set up a real-life, real-time field experiment using a longitudinal design. The researchers enlisted the help of four female confederates of college age who were rated as physically similar to each other. They were instructed to attend college classes with the participants but not to interact with them; in other words, be 'merely' present. They attended classes either 0 times, 5 times, 10 times or 15 times (each confederate was allocated only one of these conditions), and this formed the independent variable of the study. After the experimental phase was over the participants were then asked to look at photographs of each of the four women and rate them on specific variables, including how familiar and how attractive they were.

Results
The results did not provide strong support for the idea of familiarity influencing attraction. There was strong support for mere exposure influencing attraction - the woman who had been seen the most times by participants was rated as being more attractive and better liked than the females who had been seen less often.

Conclusion
The mere exposure effect may produce preference for a familiar face because it stimulates a feeling that the person is 'one of us'.

Evaluation of Moreland & Beach (1992)
Strengths
- ✓ The use of naïve participants and a real-life, real-time environment makes the study high in ecological validity.
- ✓ The implementation of four conditions of the independent variable means that the researchers had some degree of control over the procedure, which is not easy to achieve in a naturalistic situation.

Limitations
- X The fact that this was a field experiment means that there may have been an array of extraneous variables that could have confounded the results and which the researchers were powerless to control, such as the subjective judgements made of each confederate by the participants.
- X Replicating the study would be possible but the researchers could not be confident that they would obtain the same results given a different sample and conditions: this reduces the reliability of the findings.

Reference
Moreland, R. L., & Beach, S. R. (1992). Exposure effects in the classroom: the development of affinity among students. *Journal of Experimental Social Psychology, 28,* pp. 255–276.

****

TOPIC 2: PERSONAL RELATIONSHIPS

Content 8: Formation of personal relationships - sociocultural explanations

KEY STUDY 8.2: *Peskin & Newell (2004). Familiarity breeds attraction: effects of exposure on the attractiveness of typical and distinctive faces.*

Brief Summary
Investigated how both typicality and familiarity of female faces breed liking. Found that increasing exposure to faces increases their perceived attractiveness, regardless of how typical they are.

Aim
To investigate whether or not typicality and familiarity of female faces are factors affecting liking.

Participants
The researchers used three separate groups to investigate three different aspects affecting liking: attractiveness was rated by 10 female and 21 male students from Trinity College, Dublin, Ireland (21-43 years old); distinctiveness was rated by 25 female and 12 male students also from Dublin (15-25 years old); familiarity was rated by 21 female and 9 male students also from Dublin (17-37 years old).

Procedure
The stimulus comprised 84 monochrome photographs of unfamiliar female faces taken from US high-school yearbooks.

The procedure for each group went as follows:

1. **Attractiveness-rating:** Participants were asked to rate each face on a 1-7 scale for how attractive they thought it was.

2. **Distinctiveness-rating:** Participants were asked to rate each face according to how eye-catching, unusual or distinctive it was using a 1-7 scale.

3. **Familiarity-rating:** Participants were asked to rate each face on a 1-7 scale for how familiar looking they thought it was. The researchers told the participants that the faces were 10-year-old photographs of current Trinity College students so as to lend some credibility to this aspect of the procedure.

Results
The more familiar the rating of the faces by participants, the more attractive they were judged to be, showing a positive correlation between attractiveness and familiarity. Faces judged to be 'distinctive' (i.e. unusual) were judged to be less attractive.

Conclusion
People appear to be attracted to faces that are deemed 'average' or non-distinctive and familiar.

Evaluation of Peskin & Newell (2004)
Strengths
- ✓ The use of three separate categories to judge the faces meant the researchers were able to look for correlations between the key variables.
- ✓ Using rating scales to measure the dependent variable means that the results were easy to analyse statistically which increases reliability.

Limitations
- X Some of the key variables being measured are subjective and rely on individual judgement. For example, 'distinctiveness' may be interpreted differently by each participant.
- X Obtaining a sample from the same university in Ireland means that the results are not generalisable beyond this demographic.

Reference
Peskin, M., & Newell, F. N. (2004). Familiarity breeds attraction: effects of exposure on the attractiveness of typical and distinctive faces. *Perception, 33*(2), 147-157.

****

TOPIC 2: PERSONAL RELATIONSHIPS

Content 8: Formation of personal relationships - sociocultural explanations

KEY STUDY 8.3: *Regan et al. (2012). Relationship outcomes in Indian-American love-based and arranged marriages.*

Brief Summary
Compared the outcome of both love-based and arranged marriages in the USA. Found very little differences, and the overall experiences of love within the marriages appeared to be very similar.

Aim
To look for differences in feelings towards arranged or love-based marriages in an immigrant community.

Participants
58 Indian adults (34 female; 24 male) aged 23-55 years old who were living in a city in the USA. The participants were married (though none of their spouses were included in the sample) and the

average length of marriage was 9.7 years. 28 of the participants reported that they had had an arranged marriage; 30 reported that their marriage was love-based (i.e. self-chosen).

Procedure
Participants completed rating scales designed to measure companionate love (e.g. how much they cared about their spouse); passionate love (e.g. how much 'in love' they were with their spouse) and relationship satisfaction and commitment (e.g. how much they wanted to stay with their partner).

Results
There was no difference found between arranged marriages and love marriages: both types of marriages produced responses from those in them that were high in love, commitment and satisfaction. Men across both groups reported higher amounts of commitment, passionate love and companionate love than the women did.

Conclusion
There may be little difference in how married Indian people view their marriage – whether it is arranged or love-based.

Evaluation of Regan et al. (2012)
Strengths
✓ The use of rating scales to measure the variables is replicable and could be used to test for reliability.
✓ The findings go some way towards challenging the idea that arranged marriages are not as loving or satisfying for those involved in them as love-based marriages.

Limitations
X The use of such a small sample means that the results lack statistical power: a larger sample might have yielded some evidence of differences between the marriage types.
X All of the participants lived in the USA and had married there which means that they may already have been of a similar mind-set compared to Indians living in India, particularly in more rural areas.

Reference
Regan, P. C., Lakhanpal, S., & Anguiano, C. (2012). Relationship outcomes in Indian-American love-based and arranged marriages. *Psychological Reports*, *110*(3), pp. 915-924.

****

PSYCHOLOGY SORTED: KEY RESEARCH FOR STUDENTS AND TEACHERS
BOOK 2 – APPLIED PSYCHOLOGY

TOPIC 2: PERSONAL RELATIONSHIPS

Content 9: Role of communication

KEY STUDY 9.1: *Tannen, D. (1990). You Just Don't Understand: Women and Men in Conversation.*

Brief Summary
Communication differs according to gender: the researchers conducted a series of observations of couples involved in intimate relationships. The couple's conversations were recorded and then analysed to identify patterns of speech that showed differences in linguistic style.

Aim
To look for differences in the language used by male-female couples in intimate relationships.

Participants and Procedure
Tannen carried out a series of recorded observations of couples who were involved in intimate relationships. These conversations were analysed to identify patterns of speech that showed differences in linguistic style.

Results
Tannen identified a range of gender differences in language, some of which are as follows:

- Men interrupt more than women and they expect to be interrupted themselves. Women use a much more reciprocal style of conversation with turn-taking and conversational rules applying.

- Men use conversation to establish their status and independence; women use conversation to establish intimacy and connectedness between people.

- A man doesn't always like it when a woman is empathetic towards him (e.g. *"Yes, I've felt like that too"*) as they feel that she is 'intruding' upon his feelings, rendering them 'just like hers' and therefore not special or unique to him. Women may be baffled by this response as they may have offered the empathy in order to make the man feel less alone in his feelings; it has been done to show understanding, to communicate that negative feelings are permissible and that we all feel bad sometimes.

- Women do not appreciate men coming up with practical solutions to their distress or low mood, whereas a man may be oriented towards finding something he can *do* to help his female partner practically. Women prefer men to listen to them when they are upset or unhappy about something: a man trying to find a pragmatic solution to the problem may make the woman think that he has missed the point, which is that she needs him to listen and empathise (as a woman would do), rather than immediately try to find a way of solving the problem.

- When women say 'sorry' they tend to use it as a way to express empathy (e.g. *'I'm so sorry you feel bad/that this happened to you')* whereas men hear 'sorry' as an apology, which is a sign of weakness and so they may avoid saying it.

- Women tend to use more language tags (really? uh-huh, right, no kidding?). These serve as support to the main speaker, encouraging them in what they are saying and indicating that the communication lines are still open. Tannen calls this *overlapping speech*.

- Women tend to be more inclusive, asking the other person's opinion more than men do.

Conclusion
Men and women use language differently and for different purposes.

Evaluation of Tannen (1990)
Strengths
✓ The use of rich qualitative data gives this research depth and insight, with high internal validity.
✓ The findings could be applied to therapeutic settings such as marriage counselling.

Limitations
✗ It is possible that some of the participants may have succumbed to the observer effect, giving responses that were self-conscious or contrived in some way.
✗ The findings are very generalised and cannot account for individual differences in language between males and females.

Reference
Tannen, D. (1990). *You Just Don't Understand: Women and Men in Conversation,* USA: Harper Collins.

****

TOPIC 2: PERSONAL RELATIONSHIPS

Content 9: Role of communication

KEY STUDY 9.2: *Ahmad, S., & Reid, D. W. (2008). Relationship Satisfaction among South Asian Canadians: The Role of 'Complementary-Equality' and Listening to Understand.*

Brief Summary
Culture affects communication: the researchers investigate the link between traditional marital expectations and listening styles in couples in arranged marriages.

Aim
To see if there is a link between traditional marital expectations and listening styles in arranged marriage couples.

Participants
114 Indo-Pakistani married couples who were in arranged marriages, living in a large city in Canada. The participants were 19-67 years old (mean age 36); 51 males and 63 female. The couples had been married from 6 months to 35 years (mean 12.5 years).

Procedure
Participants completed the Marital Satisfaction Scale which measured variables including

- **Listening styles** - did their spouse pay full attention to them when they were talking?
- **How traditional** each participant's attitude towards marriage was in terms of roles within the marriage. For example, how they felt about women going out to work.
- **How satisfied** they were with the marriage (e.g. did they feel they were getting out of the marriage what they put into it?)

Results
The more traditional the marriage was then the less satisfaction was reported. This was also linked to communication, with lower levels of active listening being linked to a traditional attitude/expectation towards marriage. There was an interaction between traditional beliefs, listening style and marital satisfaction: in other words the less someone listens to their partner then the lower marital satisfaction is.

Conclusion
Perceptions of equality and communication styles can predict how satisfied a couple is with their arranged marriage. Communication seems to play a key role in the maintenance of arranged marriages along with traditional beliefs about marriage roles.

Evaluation of Ahmad & Reid (2008)
Strengths
- ✓ The measure used is replicable, meaning that both external and internal reliability can be checked (via the test-retest method and split-half method respectively) to look for consistency over time and within the measure itself.
- ✓ There is a wide age range represented in the sample which makes the results generalisable within that demographic.

Limitations
- X The statements rated on the Marital Satisfaction Scale may not adequately sum up or express exactly how the participant felt about their partner which would affect the validity of the findings.
- X Responding to a scale is limited in terms of the insight it can shed on highly subjective and complex variables such as were measured in this study.

Reference
Ahmad, S., & Reid, D. W. (2008). Relationship Satisfaction among South Asian Canadians: The Role of 'Complementary-Equality' and Listening to Understand. *Interpersona, 2*(2), pp. 131-150.

****

TOPIC 2: PERSONAL RELATIONSHIPS

Content 9: Role of communication

KEY STUDY 9.3: *Lavner et al. (2016). Does couples' communication predict marital satisfaction, or does marital satisfaction predict communication?*

Brief Summary
While it is assumed that good communication between spouses will positively affect their later judgments of their marriage, these researchers conducted a longitudinal study to see if good communication may be the **consequence** of being in a satisfactory marriage, rather than having any causal role in this.

Aim
To investigate whether good communication is at the heart of positive marriages or if it is a result of the marriage being positive.

Participants
431 married couples from a district of Los Angeles, USA (which was reflected in the ethnicity of the sample: 76% Hispanic; 12% African American; 12% Caucasian). The mean age for men was 28 years old and for women 26 years old. The mean duration for the marriages was 4.8 months at the intial contact from the researchers.

Procedure
This was a longitudinal study, with participants involved in a variety of self-reports: a questionnaire and videoed discussions between both partners which covered a range of topics from problem-solving to social support with roles in the second discussion being reversed during the third interview session (i.e. one partner was asked to talk about what they would like to change about themselves and the other partner was asked to respond to this in whatever way they wished). All aspects of the procedure were repeated at 9-month intervals up to the point of the couples being at least 36 months into the marriage. The interactions between the couples were observed by the researchers.

Results
The couples who were more satisfied with their marriage displayed more positive, less negative, and more effective communication. Satisfaction with the marriage was a good way of predicting good communication between the couples.

Conclusion
A satisfying marriage does appear to affect communication – for the better.

Evaluation of Lavner et al. (2016)
Strengths
- ✓ The measures used in this study were well controlled with clear behavioural categories being identified by the researchers.

✓ The use of a longitudinal design means that the researchers could track progress over time, comparing one couples' behaviour at one time-point with previous and future behaviours in their analysis.

Limitations
✗ The researchers point out that the links between communication and relationship satisfaction *'are not particularly strong or consistent over time'* which means that the findings are not wholly reliable.
✗ It is possible that the observer effect might have affected the participants, causing them to behave in self-conscious, contrived ways while being observed.

Reference
Lavner, J. A., Karney, B. R., & Bradbury, T. N. (2016). Does couples' communication predict marital satisfaction, or does marital satisfaction predict communication? *Journal of Marriage and Family, 78*(3), pp. 680-694.

****

TOPIC 2: PERSONAL RELATIONSHIPS

Content 10: Explanations for why relationships change or end

KEY STUDY 10.1: *Duck (2007). Human relationships.*

Brief Summary
Proposed a stage theory of relationship breakdown that was predictable, with the partnership moving through four phases of gradual disconnection.

Aim
To suggest that relationships break down and ultimately fail in a universal four-stage process.

Outline of the theory
Duck proposed that relationship breakdown followed a set pattern with one phase logically following on from the one before it. The four stages of relationship breakdown according to his model are as follows:

1. **Intra-Psychic** phase: this involves one of the partners in the relationship looking 'inwards', spending a lot of time dwelling on the relationship, wondering what he/she is getting from the relationship, evaluating the worth of the relationship and whether or not they should seek freedom from the relationship.

2. **Dyadic** phase: A dyad refers to the pairing of the two individuals that make up the couple involved in the relationship. In this phase both partners go over their relationship, talking and possibly arguing about the nature of it. Feelings such as resentment, anger, frustration and distress may emerge from either or both parties: deep-seated but so far unexpressed feelings

may be given voice to and this may be hurtful and/or brutally frank. At this point the couple will decide to either split up or to continue trying to make the relationship work.

3. **Social** phase: If the Dyadic phase has resulted in no positive outcome then the couple 'go public', with news of their imminent break-up being delivered to friends and family. What happens next is dependent upon the social networks, friendship groups and loyalties each partner has: some couples find that they are deserted by one set of friends; some friends may support the break-up while others are upset and want to help repair the relationship.

4. **Grave Dressing** phase: This phase is marked by each partner trying to survive the fallout of the breakup by presenting their version of it to others (the 'break-up story'). It is likely that each partner will attempt to minimise their fault in the breakup, emphasising the shortcomings of their partner instead.

Conclusion
Relationship breakdown may be charted by a continuous sequence of distinct phases, all of which lead to an inevitable parting of the ways.

Evaluation of Duck (2007)
Strengths
- ✓ Duck's model could be said to follow some kind of logical sequence: relationship breakdown does often follow this pattern of introspection followed by action between then outside of the couple.
- ✓ The model could be applied to relationship counselling - for a couple could use it to identify the stage they are at in terms of the breakdown and aim to avoid the next phase in their own relationship.

Limitations
- X Not all examples of relationship breakdown necessarily follow this sequential pattern, which renders the model of little practical use.
- X The model is culture-biased as it does not account for cultures in which this sequence of relationship breakdown may be possible or expected e.g. some cultures would not welcome the Social phase.

Reference
Duck, S. (2007). *Human Relationships*. Sage, London.

****

TOPIC 2: PERSONAL RELATIONSHIPS

Content 10: Explanations for why relationships change or end

KEY STUDY 10.2: *Mitnick et al. (2009). Changes in relationship satisfaction across the transition to parenthood: a meta-analysis.*

Brief Summary
Looked at the changes in the satisfaction levels (satisfaction with the relationship itself) of couples after they had become parents. Found that satisfaction levels decrease after having children.

Aim
To investigate changes in satisfaction levels of couples after becoming parents compared to couples who have not had children.

Participants
The method used was a meta-analysis comprising samples from the data of 37 US-based longitudinal studies tracking first-time parents from pregnancy up to the child being about a year old. 4 longitudinal studies of childless couples were used for comparison. A total of almost 6,000 individual samples were included in the study.

Procedure
A meta-analysis was conducted using research articles of couples with and without children dating from as far back as 1887 up to and including 2006. The researchers identified key words which formed the basis of the research e.g. 'transition', 'parenthood', 'relationship satisfaction'. The researchers also obtained unpublished research from key researchers in the field of relationships to add to their findings. The studies included in the meta-analysis were generally self-report questionnaires and surveys which used rating scales to measure the level of satisfaction expressed by the participants.

Results
There was a significant decline in relationship satisfaction for the couples who had children compared to the childless couples: particularly in the first couple of years after the first child had been born. There was a good deal of variability in this particular finding, with some couples recording large decreases in satisfaction compared to slight increases in some cases.

Conclusion
Becoming first-time parents may affect the satisfaction levels of a relationship, with a mostly negative impact on the relationship.

Evaluation of Mitnick et al. (2009)
Strengths
- ✓ A meta-analysis is less prone to bias as researchers using secondary data have fewer opportunities to confound the results.

✓ This meta-analysis used a variety of statistical measures, which is an objective and consistent way of conducting the procedure that increases the reliability of the findings.

Limitations
✗ There is a lack of ecological validity in the results as the rather cold and detached statistical measures cannot reveal why and how this lack of satisfaction occurs, or even its precise nature, only that it does.
✗ One of the issues with this study is that it measured satisfaction up to only around one year after the birth of the child, which means that long-term effects of becoming a parent have not been addressed.

Reference
Mitnick, D. M., Heyman, R. E., & Slep, A. M. S. (2009). Changes in relationship satisfaction across the transition to parenthood: a meta-analysis. *Journal of Family Psychology,* 23, pp 848–852.

****

TOPIC 2: PERSONAL RELATIONSHIPS

Content 10: Explanations for why relationships change or end

KEY STUDY 10.3: *Williamson et al. (2016). Are problems that contribute to divorce present at the start of marriage, or do they emerge over time?*

Brief Summary
Investigated whether problems that led to divorce may exist at the beginning of the marriage (enduring dynamics model) or developed over time (emergent distress model). Results suggested an emergent distress model for wives.

Aim
To investigate whether divorce is the result of early problems in the marriage or if it is a product of trouble over time.

Participants
431 married couples narrowing to 40 divorced individuals over time, from a district of Los Angeles, USA which was identified by the researchers as 'low-income'. The average duration of marriage before breakup was 2.6 years and couples had been divorced/separated for 1.6 years on average. Women's mean age was 30 years by the end of the study and for men it was 30.7 years. 57% of participants were Hispanic with the rest of the sample being 27% African American and 16% Caucasian.

Procedure
It was a longitudinal study, with participants interviewed separately by researchers and this interview being repeated after 9 months, 18 months, and 27 months.

Results
Women were more attuned to what was going wrong with the marriage (what the researchers term 'emergent distress'): they saw problems that led to divorce increasing over time. Men, on the other hand, were less attuned to problems overall and may have been unaware that there was anything wrong with the marriage.

Conclusion
Women may take a leading role in the identification of problems in a marriage and therefore may take the lead in initiating divorce proceedings.

Evaluation of Williamson et al. (2015)
Strengths
- ✓ The measures used in this study are replicable, as they take the form of a standardised list of items, making it easy to test for external reliability.
- ✓ The use of a longitudinal design means that the researchers could identify trends amongst the participants over time, linking interview responses by individuals to instances of divorce.

Limitations
- ✗ The sample consisted of couples who divorced early on in their marriage so the results cannot be generalised to couples who divorce later in marriage.
- ✗ This is a small sample so the results are not robust, meaning that they cannot withstand close statistical analysis.

Reference
Williamson, H. C., Nguyen, T. P., Bradbury, T. N., & Karney, B. R. (2016). Are problems that contribute to divorce present at the start of marriage, or do they emerge over time? *Journal of Social and Personal Relationships, 33*(8), pp.1120-1134.

****

TOPIC 2: PERSONAL RELATIONSHIPS

Critical thinking points

Can evolutionary psychology explain the complexity of attraction?
*Singh (1993) seems to suggest that, yes it can, with its emphasis on the instinctive drives that spur on men to look for women with that 'magic' waist-hip ratio, signalling youthfulness and fertility. But surely there is more to relationships than this study suggests, or are **all** men programmed to find a specific waist-hip measurement as being the ultimate marker of an attractive woman? Relationships do not fall into such easy formulae, and anecdotal (everyday) evidence abounds to challenge and refute Singh's findings. Some men may prefer much rounder/thinner/muscular/older women than is proposed by evolutionary psychology and we have evolved far beyond a basic level of attraction which uses only one defining feature to characterise it.*

By emphasising so-called gender differences in language are researchers contributing to misrepresentation of men and women?
Emphasising stereotypical ideas about male-female communication styles, such as women being better listeners and men dominating conversations, may not serve either gender particularly well and may, ultimately, be divisive. Tannen (1990) reports clear distinctions in the conversations she obtained from male and female couples but this may simply be a case of confirmation bias: she may have looked for examples of gendered language that confirmed her pre-existing ideas as to male/female conversational style. We increasingly live in an age when self-identity via gender is being challenged – particularly by young people – with gender becoming a fluid, ever-changing construct that cannot necessarily be pinned down easily. It may be better to talk about idiolect – a person's individual style of speech – rather than about gendered language. An idiolect may contain both male and female 'types' of speech and it may change frequently depending on contexts like age, time and place. Taking a dichotomous male/female approach to language seems reductive and old-fashioned in the 21st century.

Is the course of a relationship breakdown too subjective to measure?
One of the main problems in relationship research is that the variables being investigated are essentially personal and bound up in the unique experience of each individual and couple. Duck's (2007) phase model is a generalised account of how relationships fall apart but it is oddly specific as to the sequence of supposedly universal stages in which this happens. However, actual relationship breakdown may not necessarily begin with the intra-psychic phase and some breakdowns may jump a phase, making the model too 'one-size-fits-all' rather than being a flexible tool. Mitnick et al.'s (2009) meta-analysis attempted to bring a quantitative measure to the issue of relationship satisfaction that involves the assumption that satisfaction ratings mean the same thing to each participant separately when the opposite is probably more likely, with one person's rating of '7' representing another's '6' or even a '9'. The very term 'satisfaction' may mean different things to different people and when a large-scale study is used, drawing from many different items of research, then the objectivity of the process is severely compromised as an array of individual differences may intrude.

****

TOPIC 3: GROUP DYNAMICS

Key Idea: How psychological theory can explain inter-group and intra-group relationships, including cooperation, competition, prejudice, discrimination and conflict.

Content 1: Co-operation and competition.

KEY STUDY 11.1: *Sherif et al. (1961). Intergroup conflict and cooperation: The Robbers' Cave experiment (Vol. 10).*

Links to:
- **Sociocultural approach:** the individual and the group – social identity theory.

Brief Summary
Sherif proposed realistic conflict theory in 1966 after this experiment and earlier ones. Known as the 'Robber's Cave' field experiment, this study investigated intergroup relations in the presence of competition for scarce resources. The results showed that 12-year-old boys at summer camp could be manipulated into conflict when groups were competing for scarce resources, and then manipulated into cooperation when a shared superordinate goal was introduced.

Aim
To investigate intergroup relations in the presence of competition for scarce resources (leading to conflict) and then cooperation induced through a common goal.

Participants
An opportunity sample of 22 boys aged around 12 years old who happened to be attending the Robber's Cave summer camp in Oklahoma, USA during the period of the research. The boys were from white, middle-class, Protestant, two-parent families. They did not know each other before the onset of the study.

Procedure
The boys were randomly assigned to one of two groups, but they were not told of the existence of the other group. The camp was run by the experimenters, (although the boys were not aware that this was the case). The two groups of boys were initially kept apart from each other and were encouraged to form strong in-group bonds and a clear group identity. Once the two groups had formed strong group identities the researchers introduced the idea of competition between them as the boys were made aware that another group existed at the camp. In fact, the boys had been asking for competitions to be put in place even before the experimenters introduced the 4-6-day competition phase. A series of competitive games and tasks followed, with the winning team receiving a trophy and individual prizes and the losers getting nothing.

Results
The boys very quickly formed strong group identities, for example creating group names: the Eagles for one group and the Rattlers for the other group. Each group created a flag to denote their

identity and each group showed strong out-group prejudice, treating the other group with disrespect, hostility and negativity. The experimenters then attempted to unite the groups by getting them involved in activities such as watching a film or engaging in 'getting to know you' games but this was unsuccessful: the boys still held strong to their 'Eagles' or 'Rattlers' identities. At this point the experimenters created some 'problems' (e.g. a water tank that needed fixing, money for a movie that night, a truck that was stuck) which would inconvenience the whole camp and which presented an issue that went beyond in-group and out-group concerns. Sherif stated that these tasks represented superordinate goals, put in place to create a common motive and to trigger intergroup cooperation. This is exactly what happened: the boys came together to solve the problems and intergroup relations improved to the point that the two separate groups forged a new group identity and cast aside intergroup rivalries and prejudice. In short, where there was once conflict and competition there now existed co-operation between the groups.

Conclusion
Intergroup conflict created through competition may be resolved by the introduction of a superordinate goal that is shared by both groups, showing that both competition and co-operation can be manipulated.

Evaluation of Sherif et al. (1961)
Strengths
- ✓ The issue of demand characteristics would not have arisen as the boys were unaware that they were taking part in a study, enhancing the validity of the
- ✓ This study is high in ecological validity as it took place in a real camp, using the day-to-day activities and tasks that the participants would have considered a natural part of camp life.

Limitations
- X Researcher bias may have affected the findings: the researchers involved in the process may have influenced the boys to behave in ways which were in line with their hypothesis.
- X The study lacks temporal validity, as it is possible that social changes over the last 60 years might produce different results if the study were to be carried out today.
- X This study is unethical, as there was no informed consent, a stressful situation and a high level of deception.

Reference
Sherif, M., Harvey, O. J., White, B. J., Hood, W., & Sherif, C. (1961). *Intergroup conflict and cooperation: The Robbers' Cave experiment* (Vol. 10 pp. 150-198). Norman, OK: University of Oklahoma Institute of Intergroup Relations.

****

TOPIC 3: GROUP DYNAMICS

Content 11: Co-operation and competition

KEY STUDY 11.2: *Tauer & Harackiewicz (2004). The Effects of Cooperation and Competition on Intrinsic Motivation and Performance.*

Links to:
- **Sociocultural Approach:** The individual and the group - social identity theory.

Brief Summary
Looked at the effect of cooperation and competition on intrinsic motivation. They found that a combination of cooperation and competition appears to result in the highest level of intrinsic motivation.

Aim
To investigate the effects of cooperation and competition on intrinsic motivation and performance in sport.

Participants
36 boys from grades 7-9 (mean age 12 years) who were attending a basketball day camp in the USA.

Procedure
The researchers used a matched pairs design, randomly allocating the boys according to their ability in basketball (the key variable which was used to determine the matched pairs design). Each participant had been pre-tested on their ability at throwing and scoring baskets. There were three conditions of the independent variable:

- **The pure cooperation condition** – the paired participants' pre-test scores were combined and they were told that that they had to beat this score by one point by working together.

- **The pure competition condition** – this was a straightforward case where one boy was pitted against the other to see who could score the most baskets.

- **The intergroup competition condition** – one pair of boys was put in competition against another pair of boys so that the pairs had to work together to win against another pair.

The dependent variable was the number of free throws each participant made and their responses to a questionnaire about how much they had enjoyed the activity (from 1 – 10 with 10 indicating most enjoyment).

Results
The intergroup competition condition resulted in the highest levels of task performance and self-reported task enjoyment. There was no real difference in performance and enjoyment found between pure cooperation and pure competition.

Conclusion
Cooperation and competition combined appears to result in optimum performance and intrinsic motivation for the task.

Evaluation of Tauer & Harackiewicz (2004)
Strengths
- ✓ Using a matched pairs design helps to reduce participant variability between the groups.
- ✓ The study has high ecological validity due to the real-life setting and nature of the tasks set by the researchers.

Limitations
- X The sample consisted of American males in grades 7-9 which limits the generalisability of the findings.
- X There could have been an array of extraneous variables that interfered with the study due to the uncontrolled nature of the procedure and the real-life setting.

Reference
Tauer, John M., Harackiewicz, Judith M. (June 2004). The Effects of Cooperation and Competition on Intrinsic Motivation and Performance. *Journal of Personality and Social Psychology, Vol 86*(6), pp. 849-861.

****

TOPIC 3: GROUP DYNAMICS

Content 11: Co-operation and competition

KEY STUDY 11.3: *Colpaert et al. (2015). A mindset of competition versus cooperation moderates the impact of social comparison on self-evaluation.*

Links to:
- **Sociocultural Approach:** The individual and the group - social identity theory.

Brief Summary
Investigated the interaction between cooperation or competition and social comparison. They found that competitive settings moderated the impact of social comparison on self-evaluation.

Aim
To investigate the ways in which social comparison may affect cooperation and competition.

Participants
198 students from a university in France: 165 female and 33 male, with a mean age of 20 years old.

Procedure
Participants were positioned in front of a computer and told that seven other participants would be taking part at the same time as they were. There were four conditions of the IV:

- Upward comparison (comparing oneself to a superior other)
- Downward comparison (comparing oneself to an inferior other)
- Competition mindset
- Co-operation mindset

The competition mindset participants were told that they would perform two tasks in which they would be in competition with one person in the room. The co-operation mindset participants were told that they would complete the tasks while co-operating with one person in the room.

Competition mindset participants read that their answers to the task would be compared to their 'opponent'. The co-operation mindset participants were told that their answers would be pooled with their 'team-mate'. The participants were then told that they had to complete a short questionnaire they received by e-mail about their opponent/team-mate.

At this point, the experimenter gave each participant a questionnaire where they read the pretend self-description of their opponent/teammate. In the upward comparison condition, the pretend person was depicted as being very successful in school and university, loved to read, had good social skills, and had many friends. In the downward comparison condition, the pretend person was depicted as having difficulties at school, did not like to read, was rather lonely, and had only a few friends. Participants then used 7-point scales (1 = not at all and 7 = very) to rate whether they felt they were successful in college, bright, competent, balanced, promising, and successful in life. Participants were then asked to use a rating scale (1-7) to express the extent to which they thought their opponent/teammate resembled them.

Results
Participants in the cooperative mindset condition evaluated themselves more positively in upward than in downward comparison. That is, when participants believed they had been a team-mate of a superior person their own self-esteem increased.

Conclusion
A competitive/cooperative mindset moderates the impact of social comparison on self-evaluation, with a cooperative mindset producing more positive self-evaluation when using upward comparison.

Evaluation of Colpaert et al. (2015)

Strengths
- ✓ The use of a 2 x 2 design of the independent variable means that the researchers were able to assess the effect of a range of variables (competition/cooperation; upward/downward comparison; self-evaluation).
- ✓ The study used a range of measures, each of which checks the other measures used which increases the internal validity.

Limitations
- X The sample consisted of French students, with five times as many females as males, which limits the generalisability of the findings.
- X It is possible that response bias could have affected the validity of the findings e.g. participants in the upward comparison condition might have felt that they were intended to give a high self-evaluation based on the information they'd been given.

Reference
Colpaert, L., Muller, D., Fayant, M. P., & Butera, F. (2015). A mindset of competition versus cooperation moderates the impact of social comparison on self-evaluation. *Frontiers in Psychology, 6* (1337), n.p.

****

TOPIC 3: GROUP DYNAMICS

Content 12: Prejudice and Discrimination.

KEY STUDY 12.1: *Stephan et al. (1998). Prejudice toward immigrants to Spain and Israel: An integrated threat theory analysis.*

Links to:
- **Sociocultural Approach:** The individual and the group -social identity theory.

Brief Summary
Integrated threat theory: prejudice is the result of stereotyping, realistic threats (to jobs, for example), and symbolic threats.

Aim
To investigate the specific attitudes that combine to produce prejudice towards outgroups such as immigrants.

Participants
228 students from a university in Israel (129 female and 99 male, aged 18-45 years old) and 96 students from a university in Spain (58 female and 38 male, aged 18-48 years old). 79-85% of the participants were aged 21-30 years old.

Procedure
The participants were given questionnaires using rating scales and asked to give a rang of responses focused on immigrant groups from Morocco, Russia and Ethiopia using the following measures:

- **Prejudicial Attitudes:** how each participant felt about the different immigrant groups e.g. dislike, hatred, acceptance, superiority etc.
- **Realistic Threat:** the extent to which the immigrant groups were thought to be responsible for taking natives' jobs, committing crime, using social services etc.
- **Symbolic Threat:** the extent to which the immigrants' values, beliefs, religions etc. were thought to be different, harmful, invasive etc.
- **Intergroup Anxiety:** how the participants felt about interacting with the immigrant groups.
- **Stereotype Index:** the extent to which the immigrant groups were viewed using stereotypical ideas.

Results
The results strongly supported the theory of integrated threat theory, with intergroup anxiety and stereotyping being the strongest predictors of prejudice.

Conclusion
Stereotyping and fear of intergroup interaction may combine to form prejudice towards outgroups such as immigrants.

Evaluation of Stephan et al. (1998)
Strengths
- ✓ The use of standardised rating scales means that the procedure is replicable which increases the reliability of the findings.
- ✓ Using participants from two very different countries means that the researchers were able to look for patterns across both groups and to ascertain that prejudice is not confined to one particular country or social group.

Limitations
- X The responses of the participants might have been affected by social desirability bias, lying or misinterpretation of the questions, which would affect the validity of the findings.
- X The study lacks explanatory power as it only consists of rating scale questions and quantitative data so the reasons behind the responses is unclear.

Reference
Stephan, W. G., Ybarra, O., Martinez, C. M., Schwarzwald, J., & Tur-Kaspa, M. (1998). Prejudice toward immigrants to Spain and Israel: An integrated threat theory analysis. *Journal of Cross-Cultural Psychology, 29*(4), pp. 559-576.

****

TOPIC 3: GROUP DYNAMICS

Content 12: Prejudice and discrimination

KEY STUDY 12.2: *McLaren (2003). Anti-immigrant prejudice in Europe: contact, threat perception, and preferences for the exclusion of migrants.*

Links to:
- **Sociocultural Approach:** The individual and the group - social identity theory.

Brief Summary
Conducted a study into 17 European countries and found that the symbolic threat – the belief that immigrants undermine national values were a stronger predictor of prejudice against immigrants than perceptions of realistic threat, such as that of immigrants taking jobs.

Aim
To give an overview of the theories of contact, group conflict, and symbolic prejudice to explain attitudes towards immigrants in Western Europe.

Procedure
The researchers conducted a review of research in the field.

Main comments and findings
The research highlights two key theories that are relevant to this research: the contact hypothesis and perceived threat. The contact hypothesis revolves the idea that harmony between two very different groups such as a host culture (e.g. French people who identify fully as 'French') and immigrants (e.g. those who have settled in France from countries such as Morocco) can be achieved by contact with each other. This contact should be mutually meaningful, ideally it should involve working towards a mutual goal and both cultures should feel that they are of equal status. Perceived threat occurs when the dominant group – the host culture – rightly or wrongly feels that the incoming group – the immigrants – pose a real and present danger to their way of life both practically (e.g. taking jobs) or symbolically (e.g. bringing in cultural behaviours which are alien to the host culture).

- **The contact hypothesis:** research using this theory has tended to conclude that it is necessary for opposing groups e.g. host culture and immigrants to interact frequently in order to forge positive and meaningful relationships and to reach mutual understanding of each other. Having minorities as friends is associated with less prejudice in Western Europe and the more intimate the friendship the less prejudice occurs. Because some prejudice is based on symbolic threat then if a situation provides an opportunity to see that the beliefs of those of the host culture and immigrants are similar, then prejudice should be reduced.

- **Perceived threat:** the researchers divide this idea into realistic group conflict and symbolic threat. The focus of this realistic group threat/conflict is that members of the host culture may come to feel that certain resources belong to them, and when those resources are threatened by a minority group such as immigrants, members of the host culture are likely to react with hostility. It is also expected that fear of competition over resources is only likely if there are many immigrants with whom to compete – this is more likely to result in the host culture rejecting the immigrants. This is less likely if there is only a small minority of immigrants, because the realistic threat of scarce resources is reduced. Symbolic threat revolves around the idea that certain cultural symbols of the dominant host group must be protected and are at risk of being 'polluted' by the immigrant group or of disappearing completely. Immigrants to Europe today are often perceived as culturally different from the dominant host culture and negative or uninformed media coverage of them may affect the ways in which they are perceived.

Conclusion
The research reviewed shows strong evidence in support of the contact hypothesis. Having friendships with members of minority groups produces lower levels of prejudice and negative feelings towards those minority groups.

Evaluation of McLaren (2003)
Strengths
- ✓ The researchers amassed a good amount of quantitative data which makes the results robust and reliable.
- ✓ The findings have good applicability and usefulness, as immigration to Western Europe has become a political and humanitarian issue this century and it is incumbent upon all of those concerned to make the process a positive and a peaceful one.

Limitations
- X The researchers point out the problem of causality regarding the contact hypothesis: cross-sectional studies cannot determine the issue of cause-and-effect, nor can experimental studies manipulate intimate contact between people.
- X Participants in contact hypothesis research may *state* positive attitudes towards minority groups but this may not necessarily reflect their true feelings.

Reference
McLaren, L. M. (2003). Anti-immigrant prejudice in Europe: Contact, threat perception, and preferences for the exclusion of migrants. *Social forces, 81*(3), pp.909-936.

****

TOPIC 3: GROUP DYNAMICS

Content 12: Prejudice and discrimination

KEY STUDY 12.3: *Lam & Seaton (2016). In-group/Out-group Attitudes and Group Evaluations: the role of competition in British classroom settings.*

Links to:
- **Sociocultural Approach:** The individual and the group -social identity theory.

Brief Summary
Social identity theory: used Tajfel's minimal groups paradigm (see below) to investigate the influence of intergroup competition on children's in-group and out-group attitudes.

Aim
To investigate the influence of intergroup competition on children's in-group and out-group attitudes.

Participants
112 children: 65 girls and 47 boys aged 6 to 10 years old from a primary school in East London. The sample reflected the ethnic mix of the school, with a quarter having South Asian heritage, and with Black African/Caribbean being the second largest demographic.

Procedure
The children were given either a green or a yellow tie to wear as part of their school uniform over a period of two weeks. There were two conditions of the IV:

- **The experimental condition:** the children were encouraged to see the colours they had been randomly allocated as 'team' colours and they were reminded frequently that there would be a competition and that the members of the winning team would win a prize.
- **The control condition:** the children were not encouraged to think in terms of them being part of two different teams and no reference was made to the two teams competing.

The last day of the two-week period involved the children taking part in spelling and numeracy tests, competing as teams. The children were then interviewed about their attitudes towards their own team and the other team; they also completed rating scale questionnaires designed to measure in-group and out-group attitudes.

Results
Children in the experimental condition (competition encouraged) showed the strongest in-group bias, with positive distinctiveness for the in-group being shown more in the rating scales and interviews. The younger children in this group gave lower ratings for the out-group than the control condition children did. Children of all ages in the experimental group attributed fewer positive traits to members of the out-group compared to the in-group.

Conclusion
In-group bias can develop when a strong sense of group identity and a competitive element are introduced through social categorisation using the minimal groups paradigm.

Evaluation of Lam & Seaton (2016)
Strengths
- ✓ The study was carried out in real time, in a real setting, involving everyday tasks that the children would find familiar, which gives it high ecological validity.
- ✓ The use of both questionnaire and interview measures mean that both quantitative and qualitative data were gathered (triangulation of method and data) which would have enabled the researchers to check both measures for agreement, thus increasing the internal validity of the study.

Limitations
- X Replicating this study would be difficult due to the unique setting of the school, the children, the staff involved and other variables which could not be standardised.
- X The sample can only be generalised to inner-city children from London from a low to lower-middle income bracket which limits the results somewhat.

Reference
Lam, V. L., & Seaton, J., (2016). In-group/Out-group Attitudes and Group Evaluations: The Role of Competition in British Classroom Settings. Child Development Research, vol. 2016, Article ID 8649132, 10 pages.

****

TOPIC 3: GROUP DYNAMICS

Content 13: Origins of conflict and conflict resolution.

KEY STUDY 13.1: *Sherif et al. (1961). Intergroup conflict and cooperation: The Robbers' Cave experiment (Vol. 10).*

See above, under **TOPIC 3: GROUP DYNAMICS,** *Content 11: Prosocial behaviour: cooperation and competition.* This study may also be used for origins of conflict and conflict resolution.

****

TOPIC 3: GROUP DYNAMICS

Content 13: Origins of conflict and conflict resolution.

KEY STUDY 13.2: *Tajfel et al. (1971). Social categorization and intergroup behaviour.*

Links to
- **Sociocultural approach:** the individual and the group – social identity theory.

Background
Minimal groups paradigm: he found that merely being put in a group is enough to instill loyalty to the group and some discrimination towards those outside the group. Can form the basis for later conflict. Unlike Sherif, Tajfel argued that even the perception of being in a group, with no competition for scarce resources, was enough to strengthen an in-group identity.

Aim
To investigate how social categorisation affects intergroup behaviour.

Participants
48 males aged 14-15 from the same state school in Bristol, UK. The boys were randomly allocated to 3 groups consisting of 16 boys per group.

Procedure
Once they had been randomly assigned to a group the boys were shown slides of paintings by the artists Klee and Kandinsky and told that their preference for one of these two artists would form the basis of the group they would be assigned to. The boys were not told which of the other boys were members of their group and there was no face-to-face contact with other group members once they had made their choice. The boys were then shown, individually, to a cubicle and asked to conduct the following task: assign money (virtual, not real) to members of either the boy's ingroup (based on the preference for the artist previously stated) or outgroup (preference for the other artist). The boys did not know the identity of each boy, only a code number which identified whether they were ingroup or outgroup. The trials were set up in a randomised design by the researchers and tested the boys on a range of measures including whether they would opt for maximum joint profit, maximum ingroup profit, maximum difference between ingroup and outgroup.

Results
The boys made decisions which highlighted preference for the ingroup and some discrimination towards the outgroup. They tended to favour the ingroup members with higher reward and to work in a way which maximised the difference between ingroup and outgroup, often at the expense of possible maximum joint profit. This was based solely on the mere idea of the other group rather than on any actual interaction between ingroup and outgroup members, even when the difference between the groups was minimal i.e. preference for one artist over another.

Conclusion
Ingroup favouritism can be manipulated via the minimal groups paradigm in which participants use social categorisation to make decisions.

Evaluation of Tajfel et al. (1971)
Strengths
- ✓ This is a replicable experiment which uses a standardised procedure and quantitative data which should ensure reliability.
- ✓ The boys were kept apart from each other with no face-to-face interaction allowed and anonymity preserved which means that they were responding to the *idea* of ingroups and outgroups without having any actual contact with group members which limits possible sources of bias.

Limitations
- X The findings can only be generalised to boys aged 14-15 from Bristol.
- X The task used is highly artificial and does not reflect how people may respond to social categorisation in everyday life, therefore it lacks external validity.

Reference
Tajfel, H., Billig, M. G., Bundy, R. P., & Flament, C. (1971). Social categorization and intergroup behaviour. *European Journal of Social Psychology*, 1(2), pp. 149-178.

****

TOPIC 3: GROUP DYNAMICS

Content 3: Origins of conflict and conflict resolution

KEY STUDY 3.3: *Hodson & Busseri (2012). Bright minds and dark attitudes: lower cognitive ability predicts greater prejudice through right-wing ideology and low intergroup contact.*

Brief Summary
Investigated the proposal that low cognitive ability is linked to right-wing views and that it is socially conservative ideology that mediates most of this effect. They were interested in whether it was the attraction of right-wing authoritarianism that resulted in the prejudice, rather than just a direct route from low cognitive ability to prejudice and discrimination.

Aim
To investigate a possible correlation between low cognitive ability, preference for right-wing authoritarianism and prejudice and discrimination.

Procedure
The researchers conducted a meta-analysis using data from two samples from the UK which measured intelligence in childhood and conservative ideology and racism in adulthood. The

researchers compiled data from over 7,500 men and 8,000 women who had been born in either 1958 or 1970. The meta-analysis was focused on the following variables:

- Cognitive ability in childhood (i.e. the level of intelligence each participant had shown as a child).
- Social Conservatism as an adult (i.e. the extent to which each participant believed in maintaining the status quo of society, government and traditional values such as marriage, the law etc.)
- Racism (I.e. the extent to which each participant expressed views such as their own race being superior to other races or cultures).
- Parental socioeconomic status: the level of affluence/wealth of each participant's parents.
- Personal socioeconomic status: each participant's own level of wealth/affluence.
- Education level in childhood and adulthood: how far each participant's education went e.g. to high school, university etc.

Results
The researchers found that the lower a participant's cognitive ability in childhood had been, the higher was their tendency to express right-wing authoritarian views and racist ideologies, and vice-versa. This was a significant negative correlation and it held true for males and for females, regardless of socioeconomic status.

Conclusion
Cognitive ability in childhood appears to be linked to the socially conservative and authoritarian views in adulthood through which prejudice and discrimination can flourish.

Evaluation of Hodson & Busseri (2012)
Strengths
- ✓ By using a meta-analysis, the researchers had access to a huge amount of research, enabling them to make meaningful conclusions based on robust data.
- ✓ The findings of this research have great applicability in a world that is becoming increasingly conservative and bound by authoritarian views.

Limitations
- ✗ The sample used in the meta-analysis is not cross-cultural which makes the findings unrepresentative of a range of cultures and countries.
- ✗ The main finding ignores other variables by focusing only on IQ, which could contribute to the forming of right-wing authoritarian views. Clearly some highly intelligent people are attracted to right-wing authoritarianism, and are racist?

Reference
Hodson, G., & Busseri, M. A. (2012). Bright minds and dark attitudes: lower cognitive ability predicts greater prejudice through right-wing ideology and low intergroup contact. *Psychological Science, 23*(2), pp. 187-195.

****

TOPIC 3: GROUP DYNAMICS

Critical thinking points

Do studies on competition really demonstrate the ways in which competition is manifest in everyday life?
In Sherif's (1961) Robber's Cave study the children involved in competitive rivalries between groups quickly formed strong group identities and group loyalty which was only broken by the imposing of a super-ordinate goal by the researchers. It could be argued that this study is a good example of the ways in which intergroup rivalries develop and persist but this idea should be approached with some caution. For a start, the participants were young boys away from home on a summer camp: it would be natural for them to expect that team games and a strong competitive spirit would be part and parcel of such an experience. Considering this, it could be that the boys were competitive within the context of the summer camp experience, possibly exaggerating the extent of their competitiveness to fit in with the atmosphere manipulated by the researchers. It does not tell us how the boys might be competitive in other contexts or if their feelings of competitiveness were partly the result of conforming to the group norm. Due to the limited sample used in the study the findings cannot highlight how adults, in more mundane contexts, develop competitive group rivalries or the extent to which competitiveness is avoided in order to protect group cohesion.

Does research into prejudice and ingroup bias tell us anything new?
Lam & Seaton (2016) used the idea of creating distinctive differences between children via a real-time longitudinal study which demonstrated that competitiveness breeds ingroup favouritism and a lower rating of the outgroup. Do these findings, though, tell us anything that we don't already know? We already know that children will form strong in-group allegiances and a disinclination to reward the out-group when given permission to do so by adult? Knowing this is one thing but it would be more interesting to investigate **why** this occurs, particularly in a world where social media is a highly influential gatekeeper for even very young children.

One person's prejudice is another person's ideology.
One major problem when investigating the roots of/effects of prejudice is that there is no agreed version of what prejudice is across a range of contexts. Person A may find Person B's views highly offensive and evidence of prejudice but Person B may argue that their views are an essential part of their religion/culture/value set/belief system/ideology. If Person B follows an ideology in which people with blue eyes are considered inferior to others then Person A may accuse them of prejudice. Person B may then respond by saying that Person A considers billionaires to be evil psychopaths so isn't that prejudice too? Whose prejudice is the 'wrong' sort of prejudice and who is to be the judge of what is, objectively, right and wrong in terms of attitudes?

****

For further psychology resources and ideas for using the content in this book, see our blog at https://psychologysorted.blog/. Details of *Book 1 - Core approaches* can also be found there.

PSYCHOLOGY SORTED: KEY RESEARCH FOR STUDENTS AND TEACHERS
BOOK 2 – APPLIED PSYCHOLOGY

BIBLIOGRAPHY AND INDEX

Name	Pages
Ahmad, S., & Reid, D. W. (2008). Relationship Satisfaction among South Asian Canadians: The Role of 'Complementary-Equality' and Listening to Understand. *Interpersona, 2*(2), pp. 131-150.	208, 251-252.
Ainsworth, M. D. S., & Bell, S. M. (1970). Attachment, exploration, and separation: illustrated by the behaviour of one-year-olds in a strange situation. *Child Development*, pp.49-67.	104, 136-137.
Aknin, L. B., Barrington-Leigh, C. P., Dunn, E. W., Helliwell, J. F., Burns, J., Biswas-Diener, R., ... & Norton, M. I. (2013). Prosocial spending and well-being: cross-cultural evidence for a psychological universal. *Journal of Personality and Social Psychology, 104*(4), pp. 635-652.	203, 229-230.
Auerbach, R. P., Bigda-Peyton, J. S., Eberhart, N. K., Webb, C. A., & Ho, M. H. R. (2011). Conceptualizing the prospective relationship between social support, stress, and depressive symptoms among adolescents. *Journal of Abnormal Child Psychology, 39*(4), 475-487.	9, 50-51.
Axelrod, R. & Hamilton, (1981). The Emergence of Cooperation among Egoists. *American Political Science Review, Vol 75 (2)*; pp 306-318.	201, 220-221.
Bandura, A. (2004). Health promotion by social cognitive means. *Health Education & Behavior, 31*(2), pp. 143-164.	163, 188-190.
Baron-Cohen, S., Leslie, A. M., & Frith, U. (1985). Does the autistic child have a 'theory of mind'? *Cognition, 21*(1), pp. 37-46.	107, 150-152.
Barragan, R. C., & Dweck, C. S. (2014). Rethinking natural altruism: simple reciprocal interactions trigger children's benevolence. *Proceedings of the National Academy of Sciences, 111(48),* pp. 17071-17074.	202, 204, 226-227, 235.
Batson, C. D., Batson, J. G., Griffith, C. A., Barrientos, S., Brandt, J. R., Sprengelmeyer, P., Bayly, M. J. (1989). Negative-state relief and the empathy-altruism hypothesis. *Journal of Personality and Social Psychology, 56 (6),* pp 922-933.	202, 224-226.

PSYCHOLOGY SORTED: KEY RESEARCH FOR STUDENTS AND TEACHERS
BOOK 2 – APPLIED PSYCHOLOGY

Name	Pages
Batson, C. D., Bruce, D., Ackerman, P., Buckley, T., Birch, K. (1981). Is Empathic Emotion a source of Altruistic Motivation? *Journal of Personality and Social Psychology, 40* (20), pp. 290-302.	224.
Beck, A. T. (2005). The current state of cognitive therapy. A 40-year retrospective. *Archives of General Psychiatry, 62,* pp.953-959.	14, 77-78.
Beck, A.T. & Haigh, E.A.P. (2014). Advances in Cognitive Theory and Therapy: The Generic Cognitive Model. *Annual Review of Clinical Psychology, 10* (1), pp.1–24.	8, 10, 43-45, 57.
Becker, M.H. (1974) The Health Belief Model and Personal Health Behavior. *Health Education Monographs, 2,* 324- 508.	171.
Bem, S. L. (1981). Gender schema theory: A cognitive account of sex typing. *Psychological Review, 88*(4), pp. 354-364.	105, 145-146.
Bertakis, K.D., Helms, J., Callahan, E.J., Rahman, A., Leigh, P. & Robbins, J.A. (2001). Patient Gender Differences in the Diagnosis of Depression in Primary Care. *Journal of Women's Health & Gender-Based Medicine, 10*(7), pp. 689-698.	5, 29-31.
Boggio, P.S., Rocha, M., Oliveira, M.O....et al. (2010). Noninvasive brain stimulation with high-frequency and low-intensity repetitive transcranial magnetic stimulation treatment for post-traumatic stress disorder. *Journal of Clinical Psychology, 71*(8), pp. 992-999.	16, 84-85.
Bowlby, J. (1988). *A Secure Base. Parent-Child Attachment and Healthy Human Development.* New York: Basic Books.	104, 138-139.
Boyden, J. (2003). Children under fire: challenging assumptions about children's resilience. *Children Youth and Environments, 13*(1), pp. 1-29.	102, 129-130.
Brown, G.W. & Harris, T.O. (1978). *Social Origins of Depression: A Study of Psychiatric Disorder in Women.* London: Tavistock Publications.	9, 48-49.
Bryant, R. A., Gallagher, H. C., Gibbs, L., Pattison, P., MacDougall, C., Harms, L., ... & Richardson, J. (2017). Mental health and social networks after disaster. *American Journal of Psychiatry, 174*(3), pp.277-285.	9, 11, 51-53, 64.
Caspi, A., Sugden, K., Moffitt, T. E., Taylor, A., Craig, I. W., Harrington, H., ... & Poulton, R. (2003). Influence of life stress on depression: moderation by a polymorphism in the 5-HTT gene. *Science, 301*(5631), pp. 386-389.	8, 39-40.

PSYCHOLOGY SORTED: KEY RESEARCH FOR STUDENTS AND TEACHERS
BOOK 2 – APPLIED PSYCHOLOGY

Name	Pages
Chugani, H. T. (1998). A critical period of brain development: studies of cerebral glucose utilization with PET. *Preventive Medicine, 27*(2), pp. 184-188.	98, 108-109.
Cialdini, R. B., Schaller, M., Houlihan, D., Arps, K., Fultz, J., & Beaman, A. L. (1987). Empathy-based helping: Is it selflessly or selfishly motivated? *Journal of Personality and Social Psychology, 52*(4), p. 749-758.	202, 223-224.
Colchero, M.A., Popkin, B.M., Rivera, J.A. & Ng, S.W. (2016). Beverage purchases from stores in Mexico under the excise tax on sugar-sweetened beverages: observational study. *British Medical Journal, 352*, h6704.	164, 193-194.
Colpaert, L., Muller, D., Fayant, M. P., & Butera, F. (2015). A mindset of competition versus cooperation moderates the impact of social comparison on self-evaluation. *Frontiers in Psychology, 6* (1337), n.p.	210, 263-265.
Conner, D. B., & Cross, D. R. (2003). Longitudinal analysis of the presence, efficacy and stability of maternal scaffolding during informal problem-solving interactions. *British Journal of Developmental Psychology, 21*(3), pp. 315-334.	99, 118-119.
Conner, M., McEachan, R., Jackson, C., McMillan, B., Woolridge, M., & Lawton, R. (2013). Moderating effect of socioeconomic status on the relationship between health cognitions and behaviors. *Annals of Behavioral Medicine, 46*(1), 19-30.	163, 190-191.
Cowell, J. M., Samek, A., List, J., & Decety, J. (2015). The curious relation between theory of mind and sharing in preschool age children. *PLoS One, 10*(2), e0117947.	107, 153-155.
Crockett, M. J., Clark, L., Hauser, M. D., & Robbins, T. W. (2010). Serotonin selectively influences moral judgment and behavior through effects on harm aversion. *Proceedings of the National Academy of Sciences, 107*(40), pp.17433-17438.	201, 221-223.
Davidson, K. W., Mostofsky, E., & Whang, W. (2010). Don't worry, be happy: positive affect and reduced 10-year incident coronary heart disease: the Canadian Nova Scotia Health Survey. *European Heart Journal, 31*(9), pp. 1065-1070.	159, 160, 171-172, 174.
Davidson, J., Baldwin, D., Stein, D.J., Kuper, E., Benattia, I., Ahmed, S., Pedersen, R. & Musgung, J. (2006). Treatment of Post-traumatic Stress disorder with venlafaxine extended release. A 6-month randomized controlled trial. *Archives of General Psychiatry (63)*, pp. 1158-1165.	16, 82-83.

PSYCHOLOGY SORTED: KEY RESEARCH FOR STUDENTS AND TEACHERS
BOOK 2 – APPLIED PSYCHOLOGY

Name	Pages
Davidson, J.R.T., Rothbaum, B.O., van der Kolk, B.A., Siles, C.R. & Farfel, G.M. (2001). Multicenter, double-blind comparison of sertraline and placebo in the treatment of Post-traumatic Stress disorder. *Archives of General Psychiatry, 58*, pp. 485-492.	16, 81-82.
Dickerson, C. A., Thibodeau, R., Aronson, E. and Miller, D. (1992), Using Cognitive Dissonance to Encourage Water Conservation. *Journal of Applied Social Psychology, 22*, pp. 841–854.	204, 232-233.
Duck, S. (2007). *Human Relationships*. Sage, London.	209, 254-255.
Elias, C.J. & Berk, L.E. (2002). Self-regulation in young children: is there a role for sociodramatic play? *Early Childhood Research Quarterly 17*, pp. 216–238.	101, 123-124.
El Leithy, S., Brown, G. P., & Robbins, I. (2006). Counterfactual thinking and posttraumatic stress reactions. *Journal of Abnormal Psychology, 115*(3), pp.629-635.	10, 58-59.
Engel, G. L. (1977). The need for a new medical model: a challenge for biomedicine. Science, 196(4286), 129-136. Engel, G. L. (1977). The need for a new medical model: a challenge for biomedicine. *Science, 196*(4286), 129-136.	158, 1 65-166.
Fernald, L. C., Burke, H. M., & Gunnar, M. R. (2008). Salivary cortisol levels in children of low-income women with high depressive symptomatology. *Development and Psychopathology, 20*(2), pp. 423-436.	161, 180-181
Fiorelli, J. A. & Russ, S. (2012). Pretend play, coping, and subjective well-being in children: A follow-up study. *Journal of Play, 5*(1), pp. 81-103	101, 124-125.
Fisher, H., Aron, A., Mashek, D. J., Strong, G., Li, H., & Brown, L. L. (2005). Reward, motivation, and emotion systems associated with early-stage intense romantic love. *Journal of Neurophysiology, 94*(1), pp. 327-337.	205, 240-241.
Flook L., Goldberg S. B., Pinger, L., Davidson R. J. (2015). Promoting prosocial behavior and self-regulatory skills in preschool children through a mindfulness-based kindness curriculum. *Developmental Psychology (51)*, pp. 44–51.	204, 234-235.
Foa, E.B., Hembree, E.A., Cahill, S.P., Rauch, S.A.M., Riggs, D.S & Feeny, N.C. (2005). Randomized trial of prolonged exposure for post-traumatic stress disorder with and without cognitive restructuring: outcome at academic and community clinics for post-traumatic stress disorder. *Journal of Consulting and Clinical Psychology, 73*(5), pp. 953-964.	16, 85-86.

PSYCHOLOGY SORTED: KEY RESEARCH FOR STUDENTS AND TEACHERS
BOOK 2 – APPLIED PSYCHOLOGY

Name	Pages
Geracioti Jr, T. D., Baker, D. G., Ekhator, N. N., West, S. A., Hill, K. K., Bruce, A. B., … & Kasckow, J. W. (2001). CSF norepinephrine concentrations in posttraumatic stress disorder. *American Journal of Psychiatry*, *158*(8), pp.1227-1230.	10, 53-54.
Gotgay, G., Giedd, J., Lusk, L., Hayashi, K., Greenstein, D., Vaituzis, A., Nugent III, T., Herman, D., Clasen, L., Toga, A., Rapoport, J., Thompson, P. (2004). Dynamic Mapping of Human Cortical Development During Childhood Through Early Adulthood. *Proceedings of the National Academy of Sciences*, *101*(21), pp. 8174-8179.	98, 110-11.
Gross, J. T., Stern, J. A., Brett, B. E., & Cassidy, J. (2017). The multifaceted nature of prosocial behavior in children: Links with attachment theory and research. *Social Development*, *26*(4), pp. 661-678.	104, 141-142.
Haeffel, G. J., & Hames, J. L. (2014). Cognitive vulnerability to depression can be contagious. *Clinical Psychological Science*, *2*(1), pp.75-85.	8, 47-48.
Halpern, H. P., & Perry-Jenkins, M. (2016). Parents' gender ideology and gendered behavior as predictors of children's gender-role attitudes: A longitudinal exploration. *Sex Roles*, *74*(11-12), pp. 527-542.	106, 149-150.
Hankin, B. L., & Abramson, L. Y. (2001). Development of gender differences in depression: An elaborated cognitive vulnerability–transactional stress theory. *Psychological bulletin*, *127*(6), pp.773-796.	9, 13, 45-46, 66..
Haroz, E.E., Ritchey, M., Bass, J.K., Kohrt, B.A., Augustinavicius, J., Michalopoulos, L., Burkey, M.D. & Bolton, P. (2017). How is depression experienced around the world? A systematic review of qualitative literature. *Social Science & Medicine*, *183*, pp. 151-162.	5-8, 26-27, 31, 35, 37.
Haslam, S. A., McMahon, C., Cruwys, T., Haslam, C., Jetten, J., & Steffens, N. K. (2018). Social cure, what social cure? The propensity to underestimate the importance of social factors for health. *Social Science & Medicine*, *198*, pp. 14-21.	158, 160, 168-169, 175.
Hinton, D.E., Chhean, D., Pich, V., Safren, S., Hofmann, S.G. & Pollack, M.H. (2005). A randomized controlled trial of cognitive-behavior therapy for Cambodian refugees with treatment-resistant PTSD and panic attacks: a cross-over design. *Journal of Traumatic Stress*, *18* (6), pp. 617–629.	19, 91-92.
Hodge, D.R. & Nadir, A. (2008). Moving toward culturally competent practice with Muslims: modifying cognitive therapy with Islamic tenets. *Social Work, 53*, pp. 31-41	19, 93-94.

PSYCHOLOGY SORTED: KEY RESEARCH FOR STUDENTS AND TEACHERS
BOOK 2 – APPLIED PSYCHOLOGY

Name	Pages
Hodson, G., & Busseri, M. A. (2012). Bright minds and dark attitudes: lower cognitive ability predicts greater prejudice through right-wing ideology and low intergroup contact. *Psychological Science, 23*(2), pp. 187-195.	212, 272-273.
Imperato-McGinley, J., Guerrero, L., Gautier, T., & Peterson, R. E. (1974). Steroid 5α-reductase deficiency in man: an inherited form of male pseudohermaphroditism. *Science, 186*(4170), pp. 1213-1215.	105, 144-145.
Jahoda, M. (1958). *Joint commission on mental health and illness monograph series: Vol. 1. Current concepts of positive mental health.* New York, NY, US: Basic Books.	4, 20-21.
Jenkins-Hall, K. & Sacco, W.P. (1991). Effect of Client Race and Depression on Evaluations by White Therapists. *Journal of Social and Clinical Psychology, 10*(3), pp. 322-333.	6, 28-29.
Kar, B. R., Rao, S. L., & Chandramouli, B. A. (2008). Cognitive development in children with chronic protein energy malnutrition. *Behavioral and Brain Functions, 4* (1), p.1	103, 133-134.
Keller, M.B., McCullough, J.P. & Klein, D.N. (2000). A comparison of Nefazodone, the Cognitive Behavioral-Analysis System of Psychotherapy, and their combination for the treatment of chronic depression. *The New England Journal of Medicine, Vol 342,* p. 1462.	16, 78-79.
Kilpatrick, D. G., Ruggiero, K. J., Acierno, R., Saunders, B. E., Resnick, H. S., & Best, C. L. (2003). Violence and risk of PTSD, major depression, substance abuse/dependence, and comorbidity: results from the National Survey of Adolescents. *Journal of Consulting and Clinical Psychology, 71*(4), pp.692-700.	12, 14, 63-64, 69.
King, A.P., Erickson, T.M., Giardino, N.D....et al. (2013). A pilot study of group Mindfulness-Based Cognitive Therapy (MBCT) for combat veterans with Post-traumatic Stress Disorder (PTSD). *Depression and Anxiety, (30)*7, pp. 638-645.	18, 88-89.
Kirsch, I., Deacon, B. J., Huedo-Medina, T. B., Scoboria, A., Moore, T. J., & Johnson, B. T. (2008). Initial severity and antidepressant benefits: a meta-analysis of data submitted to the Food and Drug Administration. *PLoS medicine, 5*(2), e45.	15, 74-75.
Klaassens, E. R., Giltay, E. J., Cuijpers, P., van Veen, T., & Zitman, F. G. (2012). Adulthood trauma and HPA-axis functioning in healthy subjects and PTSD patients: a meta-analysis. *Psychoneuroendocrinology, 37*(3), pp.317-331.	11, 54-55.

PSYCHOLOGY SORTED: KEY RESEARCH FOR STUDENTS AND TEACHERS
BOOK 2 – APPLIED PSYCHOLOGY

Name	Pages
Krafft, K. C., & Berk, L. E. (1998). Private speech in two preschools: Significance of open-ended activities and make-believe play for verbal self-regulation. *Early Childhood Research Quarterly*, *13*(4), pp. 637-658.	
Kroenke, K., West, S.I., Swindle, R., Gilseman, A., Eckert, G.J., Dolor, R., Stang, P....& Weinberger, M. (2001). Similar Effectiveness of Paroxetene, Fluoxetene, and Sertralene in Primary Care. *JAMA, 286* (23), pp.2947-2955.	15, 73-74.
Kuyken, W., Warren, F.C., Taylor, R.S.....et al. (2016). Efficacy of Mindfulness-Based Cognitive Therapy in Prevention of Depressive Relapse. An Individual Patient Data Meta-analysis from Randomized Trials. *JAMA Psychiatry, 73*(6), pp. 565-574.	16, 80-81.
Lam, V. L., & Seaton, J., (2016). In-group/Out-group Attitudes and Group Evaluations: The Role of Competition in British Classroom Settings. *Child Development Research*, vol. 2016, Article ID 8649132, 10 pages.	211, 269-270.
Langer, E. J., & Abelson, R. P. (1974). A patient by any other name... Clinician group difference in labeling bias. *Journal of Consulting and Clinical Psychology*, *42*(1), p.4.	7, 33-34.
Latané, B. & Darley, J.M. (1968). Group Inhibition of Bystander Intervention in Emergencies. *Journal of Personality & Social Psychology*, *10* (3), pp. 215-221.	200, 213-214.
Lavner, J. A., Karney, B. R., & Bradbury, T. N. (2016). Does couples' communication predict marital satisfaction, or does marital satisfaction predict communication? *Journal of Marriage and Family*, *78*(3), pp. 680-694.	208, 253-254.
Lazarus, R. S., & Alfert, E. (1964). Short-circuiting of threat by experimentally altering cognitive appraisal. *The Journal of Abnormal and Social Psychology*, *69*(2), pp. 195-205.	161, 178-179.
Levav, I.L., Kohn, R., Golding, J. M. & Weissman, M.M. (1997). Vulnerability of Jews to affective disorders, *American Journal of Psychiatry*, *154* (7), pp.941-947.	13, 65-66.
Levine, R. V., Norenzayan, A., & Philbrick, K. (2001). Cross-cultural differences in helping strangers. *Journal of Cross-Cultural Psychology*, *32*(5), pp. 543-560.	203, 227-229.
Luby, J., Belden, A., Botteron, K., Marrus, N., Harms, M. P., Babb, C., ... & Barch, D. (2013). The effects of poverty on childhood brain development: the mediating effect of caregiving and stressful life events. *JAMA pediatrics*, *167*(12), pp. 1135-1142.	98, 103, 111-112, 134.

PSYCHOLOGY SORTED: KEY RESEARCH FOR STUDENTS AND TEACHERS
BOOK 2 – APPLIED PSYCHOLOGY

Name	Pages
Markey, P. M. & Markey, C. N. (2007). Romantic ideals, romantic obtainment and relationship experience: The complementarity of interpersonal traits among romantic partners. *Journal of Social and Personal Relationships, 24* (4), pp. 517-533.	206, 243-244.
Marmot, M. G., Stansfeld, S., Patel, C., North, F., Head, J., White, I., ... & Smith, G. D. (1991). Health inequalities among British civil servants: the Whitehall II study. *The Lancet, 337* (8754), pp.1387-1393.	158, 160, 167-168, 174.
McLaren, L. M. (2003). Anti-immigrant prejudice in Europe: Contact, threat perception, and preferences for the exclusion of migrants. *Social forces, 81*(3), pp.909-936.	211, 267-268.
Mental Health Foundation (May 2018). *Stress: Are we coping?* London: Mental Health Foundation	162, 184-185.
Mitahara, M., Sawae, Y., Wilson, R., Briggs, H., Ishida, J., Doihata, K., & Sugiyama, A. (2018). An interdependence approach to empathic concern for disability and accessibility: effects of gender, culture, and priming self-construal in Japan and New Zealand. *Journal of Pacific Rim Psychology, 12*, pp.1-10.	203, 230-231.
Mitnick, D. M., Heyman, R. E., & Slep, A. M. S. (2009). Changes in relationship satisfaction across the transition to parenthood: a meta-analysis. *Journal of Family Psychology, 23,* pp. 848–852.	209, 256-257.
Mojtabai, R. (2011). Bereavement-Related Depressive Episodes: characteristics, 3-year course, and implications for the DSM-5. *Archives General Psychiatry, 68*(9), pp. 920-928	4-5, 23-24, 26.
Moreland, R. L., & Beach, S. R. (1992). Exposure effects in the classroom: the development of affinity among students. *Journal of Experimental Social Psychology, 28,* pp. 255–276.	207, 245-247.
Mueser, K.D., Goodman, L. B., Trumbetta, S. L., Rosenberg, S.D., Osher, F.C., Vidaver, R., Auciello, P. & Foy, D.W. (1998). Trauma and post-traumatic stress disorder in severe mental illness, *Journal of Consulting and Clinical Psychology, 66* (3), pp. 493-499.	13, 68-69.

PSYCHOLOGY SORTED: KEY RESEARCH FOR STUDENTS AND TEACHERS
BOOK 2 – APPLIED PSYCHOLOGY

Name	Pages
Nicholls, D., Chater, R. & Lask, B. (November 2000). Children into DSM Don't Go: a comparison of classification systems for eating disorders in childhood and early adolescence. *International Journal of Eating Disorders,28*(3), pp. 317-324.	5, 7, 24-26, 35.
Nicholson, E. L., Bryant, R. A., & Felmingham, K. L. (2014). Interaction of noradrenaline and cortisol predicts negative intrusive memories in posttraumatic stress disorder. *Neurobiology of Learning and Memory, 112*, pp.204-211.	11, 56-57.
Otte, C., Hart, S., Neylan, T. C., Marmar, C. R., Yaffe, K., & Mohr, D. C. (2005). A meta-analysis of cortisol response to challenge in human aging: importance of gender. *Psychoneuroendocrinology, 30*(1), pp. 80-91.	162, 182-183.
Pänkäläinen, M., Kerola, T., Kampman, O., Kauppi, M., & Hintikka, J. (2016). Pessimism and risk of death from coronary heart disease among middle-aged and older Finns: an eleven-year follow-up study. *BMC Public Health, 16*(1), 1124, pp. 1-7.	159, 173-174.
Paulus, M., Licata, M., Kristen, S., Thoermer, C., Woodward, A., & Sodian, B. (2015). Social understanding and self-regulation predict pre-schoolers' sharing with friends and disliked peers: A longitudinal study. *International Journal of Behavioral Development, 39*(1), pp. 53-64.	100, 119-120.
Peskin, M., & Newell, F. N. (2004). Familiarity breeds attraction: effects of exposure on the attractiveness of typical and distinctive faces. *Perception, 33*(2), 147-157.	207, 247-248.
Piaget, J., & Cook, M. (1952). *The Origins of Intelligence in Children* (Vol. 8, No. 5). New York: International Universities Press.	99, 113-114.
Piliavin, I.M., Rodin, J.A. & Piliavin, J. (1969), Good Samaritanism: An underground phenomenon? *Journal of Personality & Social Psychology, (13)*, pp 289-299.	200, 215-217.
Quist-Paulsen, P., & Gallefoss, F. (2003). Randomised controlled trial of smoking cessation intervention after admission for coronary heart disease. *British Medical Journal, 327*(7426), p. 1254.	163, 187-188.
Regan, P. C., Lakhanpal, S., & Anguiano, C. (2012). Relationship outcomes in Indian-American love-based and arranged marriages. *Psychological Reports, 110*(3), pp. 915-924.	207, 248-249.
Repacholi, B. M., & Gopnik, A. (1997). Early reasoning about desires: evidence from 14-and 18-month-olds. *Developmental Psychology, 33*(1), pp. 12-21.	107, 152-153.
Risch, N., Herrell, R., Lehner, T., Liang, K. Y., Eaves, L., Hoh, J., ... & Merikangas, K. R. (2009). Interaction between the serotonin transporter gene (5-HTTLPR), stressful life events, and risk of depression: a meta-analysis. *Jama, 301*(23), pp. 2462-2471.	9, 40-41.

PSYCHOLOGY SORTED: KEY RESEARCH FOR STUDENTS AND TEACHERS
BOOK 2 – APPLIED PSYCHOLOGY

Name	Pages
Rosenhan, D. L. (1973). On being sane in insane places. *Science, 179* (4070), pp. 250-258.	7, 31-33.
Rosenstock, I. M. (1974). Historical origins of the health belief model. Health education monographs, 2(4), pp.328-335.	159, 170-171.
Rothbaum, B.O., Hodges, L., Alarcon, R., Ready, D…. et al. (1999). Virtual reality exposure therapy for PTSD Vietnam veterans: a case study. *Journal of Traumatic Stress, 12*(2), pp. 263-271.	17, 87-88.
Rutter, M., Andersen-Wood, L., Beckett, C. et al. (1999). Quasi-autistic patterns following severe early global privation. *The Journal of Child Psychology and Psychiatry and Allied Disciplines, 40*(4), pp.537-549.	102, 127-128.
Samuel, J. & Bryant, P. (1984). Asking only one question in the conservation experiment. *Journal of Child Psychology and Psychiatry*, 25, pp 315-18.	99, 115-116.
Schmaal, L., Veltman, D. J., van Erp, T. G., Sämann, P. G., Frodl, T., Jahanshad, N., … & Vernooij, M. W. (2016). Subcortical brain alterations in major depressive disorder: findings from the ENIGMA Major Depressive Disorder working group. *Molecular psychiatry, 21*(6), p. 806.	9, 42-43.
Schultz, E., Heilman, R., & Hart, K. J. (2014). Cyber-bullying: An exploration of bystander behavior and motivation. *Cyberpsychology: Journal of Psychosocial Research on Cyberspace, 8*(4), article 3.	200, 217-218.
Selye, H. (1936). A syndrome produced by diverse nocuous agents. *Nature, 138* (3479), p. 32.	161, 177-178.
Sherif, M., Harvey, O. J., White, B. J., Hood, W., & Sherif, C. (1961). *Intergroup conflict and cooperation: The Robbers' Cave experiment* (Vol. 10 pp. 150-198). Norman, OK: University of Oklahoma Institute of Intergroup Relations.	210, 212, 260-261, 270.
Silva, K., Shulman, E. P., Chein, J., & Steinberg, L. (2015). Peers increase late adolescents' exploratory behavior and sensitivity to positive and negative feedback. *Journal of Research on Adolescence, 26*(4), pp. 696-705.	101, 126-127.
Silva, R.R., Alpert, M., Munoz, D.M., Singh, S., Matzner, F. & Dummit, S. (2000). Stress and vulnerability to posttraumatic stress disorder in children and adolescents. *American Journal of Psychiatry, 157*(8), pp.1229–1235.	12, 61-62.

PSYCHOLOGY SORTED: KEY RESEARCH FOR STUDENTS AND TEACHERS
BOOK 2 – APPLIED PSYCHOLOGY

Name	Pages
Silverman, W.K., Lissette, M., Saavedra, M.S. & Armando, A. Pina (2001). Test-Retest Reliability of Anxiety Symptoms and Diagnoses with the Anxiety Disorders Interview Schedule for DSM-IV: Child and Parent Versions. *Journal of the American Academy of Child and Adolescent Psychiatry, 40* (8), pp. 937- 944.	8, 35-37.
Simmons, R.G.; Klein, S.D.; Simmons, R.L. (1977). *Gift of Life: the social and psychological impact of organ transplantation*. London, UK: Wiley.	201, 218-219.
Singh, D. (1993). Adaptive significance of female physical attractiveness: role of waist-to-hip ratio. *Journal of Personality and Social Psychology, 65*(2), pp. 293-307.	205, 237-238.
Singh, J. B., Fedgchin, M., Daly, E. J., De Boer, P., Cooper, K., Lim, P., ... & Kurian, B. (2016). A double-blind, randomized, placebo-controlled, dose-frequency study of intravenous ketamine in patients with treatment-resistant depression. *American Journal of Psychiatry, 173*(8), pp.816-826.	15, 76-77.
Smith, T.B. & Griner, D. (2006). Culturally adapted mental health interventions: a meta-analytic review. *Psychotherapy: Theory, Research, Practice & Training, 43*, pp. 531-548.	19, 90-91.
Sroufe, L. A., Bennett, C., Englund, M., Urban, J., & Shulman, S. (1993). The significance of gender boundaries in preadolescence: Contemporary correlates and antecedents of boundary violation and maintenance. Child Development, 64(2), pp. 455-466.	105, 147-148.
Stephan, W. G., Ybarra, O., Martinez, C. M., Schwarzwald, J., & Tur-Kaspa, M. (1998). Prejudice toward immigrants to Spain and Israel: An integrated threat theory analysis. *Journal of Cross-Cultural Psychology, 29*(4), pp. 559-576.	211, 265-266.
Tajfel, H., Billig, M. G., Bundy, R. P., & Flament, C. (1971). Social categorization and intergroup behaviour. *European Journal of Social Psychology, 1*(2), pp. 149-178.	212, 271-271.
Tannen, D. (1990). *You Just Don't Understand: Women and Men in Conversation*, USA: Harper Collins.	208, 250-251.
Tauer, John M., Harackiewicz, Judith M. (June 2004). The Effects of Cooperation and Competition on Intrinsic Motivation and Performance. *Journal of Personality and Social Psychology, Vol 86*(6), pp. 849-861.	210, 262-263.

PSYCHOLOGY SORTED: KEY RESEARCH FOR STUDENTS AND TEACHERS
BOOK 2 – APPLIED PSYCHOLOGY

Name	Pages
Taylor, L..S., Fiore, A. T., Mendelsohn, G. A., & Cheshire, C. (2011). 'Out of my league': A real-world test of the matching hypothesis. *Personality and Social Psychology Bulletin*, *37*(7), pp. 942-954.	206, 244-245.
The European Agency for Safety and Health at Work, European Communities, 2009.	162, 181-182.
Toft, U., Bloch, P., Reinbach, H. C., Winkler, L. L., Buch-Andersen, T., Aagaard-Hansen, J., ... & Glümer, C. (2018). Project SoL—A Community-Based, Multi-Component Health Promotion Intervention to Improve Eating Habits and Physical Activity among Danish Families with Young Children. Part 1: intervention development and implementation. *International journal of Environmental Research and Public Health*, *15*(6), p.1097.	164, 195-196.
Van Ijzendoorn, M. H., & Kroonenberg, P. M. (1988). Cross-cultural patterns of attachment: A meta-analysis of the strange situation. *Child Development*, pp. 147-156.	104, 139-140.
Vygotsky, L. S. (1962). *Language and Thought.* Ontario, Canada: Massachusetts Institute of Technology Press.	99, 116-117.
Wakefield, J.C. (1992). The Concept of Mental Disorder: on the boundary between biological facts and social value. *American Psychologist, 47(*3), pp.373-388.	5, 21-22.
Walster E., Aronson, V., Abrahams, D., & Rottman, L. (1966). Importance of physical attractiveness in dating behavior. Journal of Personality and Social Psychology, 4(5), pp. 508-516.	206, 241-242.
Wedekind, C., Seebeck, T., Bettens, F., & Paepke, A. J. (June, 1995). MHC-dependent mate preferences in humans. *Proceedings of the Royal Society, London: Biology, 260* (1359), pp. 245-249.	205, 238-239.
Werner, E. (2005). Resilience and recovery: Findings from the Kauai longitudinal study. *Research, Policy, and Practice in Children's Mental Health*, *19*(1), pp. 11-14.	102-103, 131-133.
Whiting, B., & Edwards, C. P. (1973). A cross-cultural analysis of sex differences in the behavior of children aged three through 11. *The Journal of Social Psychology*, *91*(2), pp. 171-188.	105, 142-143.

PSYCHOLOGY SORTED: KEY RESEARCH FOR STUDENTS AND TEACHERS
BOOK 2 – APPLIED PSYCHOLOGY

Name	Pages
Wild, J., Smith, K. V., Thompson, E., Béar, F., Lommen, M. J. J., & Ehlers, A. (2016). A prospective study of pre-trauma risk factors for post-traumatic stress disorder and depression. *Psychological Medicine*, *46*(12), pp.2571-2582.	12, 59-61.
Williamson, H. C., Nguyen, T. P., Bradbury, T. N., & Karney, B. R. (2016). Are problems that contribute to divorce present at the start of marriage, or do they emerge over time? *Journal of Social and Personal Relationships*, *33*(8), pp.1120-1134.	209, 257-258.
Witte, K., & Allen, M. (2000). A meta-analysis of fear appeals: implications for effective public health campaigns. *Health Education & Behavior*, *27*(5), pp.591-615.	164, 192-193.
World Health Organisation (2017). *Depression and Other Common Mental Disorders. Global Health Estimates.* Geneva: WHO	13-14, 66-67, 70.

Made in the USA
Middletown, DE
19 July 2019